Women as Veterans in Britain and France after the First World War

This is the story of how women in France and Britain between 1915 and 1933 appropriated the cultural identity of female war veteran in order to have greater access to public life and a voice in a political climate in which women were rarely heard on the public stage. The 'veterans' covered by this history include former nurses, charity workers, secret service agents and members of resistance networks in occupied territory, as well as members of the British auxiliary corps. What unites these women is how they attempted to present themselves as 'female veterans' in order to gain social advantages and to give themselves the right to speak about the war and its legacies. Alison S. Fell also examines the limits of the identity of war veteran for women, considering as an example the wartime and post-war experiences of the female industrial workers who led episodes of industrial action.

Alison S. Fell is Professor of French Cultural History at the University of Leeds and Director of the Leeds Arts and Humanities Research Institute. She is Co-Investigator of the Gateways to the First World War AHRC Public Engagement Centre. She regularly acts as a historical consultant and interviewee for television and radio, including the *Woman's Hour* drama *The Camel Hospital* and the BBC's *The World's War: Forgotten Soldiers of Empire*.

D1596740

Studies in the Social and Cultural History of Modern Warfare

General Editor
Jay Winter, *Yale University*

Advisory Editors
David Blight, *Yale University*
Richard Bosworth, *University of Western Australia*
Peter Fritzsche, *University of Illinois, Urbana-Champaign*
Carol Gluck, *Columbia University*
Benedict Kiernan, *Yale University*
Antoine Prost, *Université de Paris-Sorbonne*
Robert Wohl, *University of California, Los Angeles*

In recent years the field of modern history has been enriched by the exploration of two parallel histories. These are the social and cultural history of armed conflict, and the impact of military events on social and cultural history.

Studies in the Social and Cultural History of Modern Warfare presents the fruits of this growing area of research, reflecting both the colonization of military history by cultural historians and the reciprocal interest of military historians in social and cultural history, to the benefit of both. The series offers the latest scholarship in European and non-European events from the 1850s to the present day.

A full list of titles in the series can be found at:
www.cambridge.org/modernwarfare

Women as Veterans in Britain and France after the First World War

Alison S. Fell

University of Leeds

CAMBRIDGE
UNIVERSITY PRESS

CAMBRIDGE
UNIVERSITY PRESS

University Printing House, Cambridge CB2 8BS, United Kingdom

One Liberty Plaza, 20th Floor, New York, NY 10006, USA

477 Williamstown Road, Port Melbourne, VIC 3207, Australia

314-321, 3rd Floor, Plot 3, Splendor Forum, Jasola District Centre, New Delhi - 110025, India

79 Anson Road, #06-04/06, Singapore 079906

Cambridge University Press is part of the University of Cambridge.

It furthers the University's mission by disseminating knowledge in the pursuit of education, learning and research at the highest international levels of excellence.

www.cambridge.org
Information on this title: www.cambridge.org/9781108444026
DOI: 10.1017/9781108348935

First published 2018
First paperback edition 2020

A catalogue record for this publication is available from the British Library

ISBN 978-1-108-42576-6 Hardback
ISBN 978-1-108-44402-6 Paperback

Contents

Figures

Acknowledgements

This book has taken several years to write, and I have been supported, guided and helped by many colleagues, students, friends and family along the way. I owe a particular debt of gratitude to Laura Lee Downs, Susan Grayzel, Christine Hallett, Chris Millington, Lucy Noakes and Siân Reynolds, who all read parts of my manuscript and offered invaluable insights. Catherine Ambroselli de Bayser, Mark Levtich, Simon Platt, Caroline Stevens, Special Collections staff at the University of Leeds and the staff of Rawtenstall library generously helped me with illustrations. The Gateways to the First World War team at the University of Kent – Brad Beaven, Helen Brooks, Sam Carroll, Mark Connelly, Zoë Denness, Emma Hanna and Lucy Noakes – have been a pleasure to work with, and an excellent source of knowledge and suggestions. The core team of colleagues and partners at the University of Leeds who form the Legacies of War research and public engagement hub – Simon Ball, Gareth Dant, Graeme Gooday, Andrea Hetherington, Jessica Meyer, Alexia Moncrieff, Lucy Moore, Ingrid Sharp, Claudia Sternberg and Dave Stowe – have provided a stimulating and collegial environment in which to work and write, and I have learnt an enormous amount from them. In the worlds of First World War studies and women's history, I would also like to thank Carol Acton, Holger Afflerbach, Maggie Andrews, Nadia Atia, Christine Bard, Samraghni Bonnerjee, Jessamy Carlson, James Connelly, Margaret Darrow, Santanu Das, Emmanuel Debruyne, Stefan Goebel, Nancy Sloan Goldberg, Margaret Higonnet, Diana Holmes, John Horne, Martin Hurcombe, Kimberly Jensen, Jennifer Keene, Alice Kelly, Erika Kuhlman, Jenny Macleod, Andrea McKenzie, Wendy Michallat, Manon Pignot, Chris Phillips, Jane Potter, Tammy Proctor, Pierre Purseigle, June Purvis, Sophie de Schaepdrijver, Angela K. Smith, Hew Strachan, Janet Watson, Oliver Wilkinson and Jay Winter, who have all helped to deepen my knowledge and understanding. I have thoroughly enjoyed sharing and discussing some of the issues raised by the women whose voices form the core of this book with my undergraduate and postgraduate students –

particularly Philippa Read and Laura Boyd – and also with numerous public audiences during the period of the centenary of the First World War. The editorial team at Cambridge University Press, Lisa Carter, Julia Hrischeva and Sunantha Ramamoorthy, have been unfailingly patient and helpful. I would like to thank my family – my father Alan and siblings Jane, Catherine and Ben, and my husband Paul and children Rosie and Aidan – for their patience with my obsession with all things First World War, and for their love, encouragement and good humour. Finally, I would like to dedicate this book to my mother, Ann Fell, without whose research, engagement and wisdom this book would be much the poorer.

Introduction

In a veterans' congress that took place in Vichy in May 1926, former Red Cross nurse Germaine Malaterre Sellier, who had since the Armistice become an active campaigner for pacifist and feminist organisations, addressed the ex-servicemen gathered before her with the following words:

> I am one of you, not only because like you I lived through the war, and like you shed my blood for France, but also because I sense that what unites you are not only concerns for your personal interests, but for the superior interests of France, and this distinguishes you from many other citizens.[1]

Malaterre Sellier, despite her non-combatant status as a nurse, is expressing a sentiment of shared experience and a shared social identity with French veterans.[2] A similar sense of generational and experiential solidarity in relation to the war years is evident six years later in the preface to British former volunteer nurse Vera Brittain's autobiography *Testament of Youth*, in which she explains her decision to publish her memoirs:

> For nearly a decade I have wanted, with a growing sense of urgency, to write something which would show what the whole War and the post-war period . . . has

---

[1] 'Discours de Mme Mallaterre-Sellier [*sic*]', *Journal des mutilés, réformés et blessés de guerre*, 22 May 1926, p. 6. This and all future translations are my own. For a discussion of Malaterre Sellier's case, see Alison S. Fell, 'Germaine Malaterre-Sellier, la Grande Guerre et le féminisme pacifiste de l'entre-deux-guerres', in Christine Bard (ed.), *Les Féministes de la première vague* (Rennes: Presses universitaires de Rennes, 2015), pp. 207–16.

[2] 'Social identity' is of course a loaded term. The women whose lives I evoke in this book were bearers of multiple identities. They were members of an occupation, a class and a nation. They were women, sisters, wives, daughters and parents. Several had a strong political, regional or faith identity. Drawing on the work of Charles Tilly, I understand these women as social actors who publicly identified with, and constructed through their writings and speeches, the shared social identity of the 'war veteran' or 'war generation' using 'the cultural means at their disposal and drawing on collective memory, adopting or adapting available models.' Charles Tilly, *Stories, Identities and Political Change* (Oxford: Oxford University Press, 2002), p. 49.

1

meant to the men and women of my generation, the generation of those boys and girls who grew up just before the war broke out.[3]

In these declarations, the two former volunteer war nurses do not position themselves in the way that women were often positioned in relation to the war in the interwar period: as representatives of 'the civilian' and 'the home' in the oppositional pairings combatant/civilian and front/home that, at least to some extent, continued to structure popular understandings of the war and its legacies.[4] Rather, they place themselves on the other side of the dividing line, as members of what French and British societies were culturally constructing as the 'war generation'.

Women and the 'War Generation'

The concept of a 'Generation of 1914' in the post-war years, as Robert Wohl argues in his influential 1979 study, was not so much a demographic reality as a 'device by which people conceptualize[d] society and [sought] to transform it'.[5] In France, the majority of the 'males from the middle layers of society whose main activity was writing'[6] evoked by Wohl did not see women as part of this 'génération du feu'. Rather, and crucially, these male writers and commentators saw women as a group *against* which men who identified with a war generation defined themselves. Wohl's focus on elite male journalists and writers means that women like Germaine Malaterre Sellier, who had a different take on women's relationship to the war generation, are ignored. In the case of Britain, however, Wohl cites Vera Brittain's autobiography as a key text in the construction of the myth of the British version of the 'Generation of 1914', the 'Lost Generation', arguing that her memoir

---

[3] Vera Brittain, *Testament of Youth: An Autobiographical Study of the Years 1900–1925* (London: Virago, 1978 [1933]), p. 11. Brittain was a Voluntary Aid Detachment (VAD) nurse.

[4] For discussions of the complexity of the relationship of women to evolving definitions of combatant/civilian during the First World War in France and Britain, see Margaret Darrow, 'French Volunteer Nursing and the Myth of War Experience in World War 1', *The American Historical Review* 101: 1 (1996): 80–106; Susan R. Grayzel, *Women's Identities at War: Gender, Motherhood and Politics during the First World War* (Chapel Hill: University of North Carolina Press, 1999); Nicoletta Gullace, *'The Blood of Our Sons': Men, Women and the Renegotiation of British Citizenship during the Great War* (New York: Palgrave Macmillan, 2012); Trudi Tate, *Modernism, History and the First World War* (Manchester: Manchester University Press, 1998); Janet Watson, *Fighting Different Wars: Experience, Memory and the First World War in Britain* (Cambridge: Cambridge University Press, 2007).

[5] Robert Wohl, *The Generation of 1914* (Cambridge, MA: Harvard University Press, 1979), p. 5.

[6] Wohl, *The Generation of 1914*, p. 4.

'made explicit, as no other war book had, the narrative sequence within which many English survivors of the war had come to perceive their past'.[7] What is unusual about Brittain's case, of course, although Wohl does not explicitly discuss this, is that unlike the male-authored war memoirs she was using as her literary models, she was telling what was to become a culturally dominant British narrative of the First World War from the point of view of a non-combatant woman. No other woman's war memoir has had such an impact on British cultural memories of the First World War.[8] Yet Brittain's dual self-presentation in *Testament of Youth* as both a grieving female relative and an active participant in the war – as a bereaved sister and lover, but also as a female veteran who had both the right and the moral duty to speak on behalf of the dead about the war and its consequences – was by no means unique.

This book explores the different ways in which the cultural identity of the 'female veteran' was used by women in France and Britain from 1915 to 1933.[9] The First World War female veteran is a social and cultural identity that has not to date been considered in depth by other scholars.[10] In this book, I focus on women in the interwar period who either defined themselves or were defined by others primarily in relation to their war service or war work, and I use the term 'female veteran' to refer to them. The reason I have chosen to use the term 'veteran' to refer to this diverse set of French and British women is because I argue that they appropriate,

---

[7] Wohl, *The Generation of 1914*, p. 111.

[8] For more on the influence of Brittain's narrative on public perceptions of the First World War in Britain, both on its publication in 1933, and as a result of its renewed popularity in the 1970s and 1980s, see Dan Todman, *The Great War: Myth and Memory* (London: Hambledon Continuum, 2005); Watson, *Fighting Different Wars*; Alison S. Fell, 'Myth, Countermyth and the Politics of Memory: Vera Brittain and Madeleine Clemenceau Jacquemaire's Interwar Nurse Memoirs', *Synergies Royaume Uni et Irlande*, 4 (2011): 11–24.

[9] My period begins in the second year of the war as women who were invalided out of the war after having served in its early months presented themselves as 'war veterans' or as part of the 'war generation'. It ends in the year of the publication of Brittain's memoirs, a year that also marks the rise of fascism in Germany and an increasing awareness in France and Britain of the prospect of another war, a political context that marked both men's and women's war writings published in the later 1930s.

[10] See individual chapters for secondary literature on the selected case studies. For a discussion of the experience of demobilisation for British ex-servicewomen, see Lucy Noakes, 'Demobilising the Military Woman: Constructions of Class and Gender after the First World War', *Gender and History* 19 (2007): 143–72. Denise Poynter also refers to former First World War nurses and VADs as 'female veterans' in her discussion of pensions, psychological trauma and homecoming. See in particular chapter 4 in 'The Report on the Transfer Was Shell-Shock': A Study of the Psychological Disorders of Nurses and Female VADs Who Served alongside the British and Allied Expeditionary Forces during the First World War, 1914–1918', Unpublished doctoral thesis, University of Northampton, 2008. Available online at http://nectar.northampton.ac.uk/2682/1/Poynter20082682.pdf

in different ways and to different ends, certain aspects of the social and cultural identity of the male war veteran in the post-war years. And, importantly, they do so in order to have greater access to public life, to have a voice in a political climate in which women were rarely heard on the public stage. The most straightforward definition of a veteran – a former member of the armed services – does not of course apply to the majority of French and British women who carried out a form of active service during the war. While British female members of the auxiliary services of the armed forces can legitimately be labelled as veterans or ex-servicewomen, there is no French equivalent.[11] My definition of 'female veteran' is a broad one, and covers former nurses, journalists, charity workers, secret service agents and members of resistance networks in occupied territory, as well as members of the British women's auxiliary corps. However, I also consider in my final chapter the limits of the identity of female veteran, considering as an example the wartime and post-war experiences of female industrial workers who led episodes of industrial action. For these women, and particularly for French strikers, their war experiences had a more dubious status in relation to post-war claims to service and sacrifice. While women could present factory work as a form of war service, and contrasted it positively with the post-war bogeymen of shirkers and war profiteers, those who had participated in industrial action were met with widespread accusations of selfishness, defeatism and treachery. Wartime experience was therefore a narrow and fragile platform for women wishing to claim veteran status in the interwar years.

The case studies highlighted in this study demonstrate the wide range of activities, different socio-economic backgrounds and political alle-giances of women who were identified (or who self-identified) as veterans, as well as significant divergences between the two national contexts. What unites them is the concept of 'active service': all of these women were operating beyond the domestic sphere. Some of these roles, such as nurses or factory workers, were 'top-down' initiatives led by the state. Others, such as journalists or charity workers, were instigated and funded privately. Although some women combined a wartime role with working within the home, or caring for relatives or children, they therefore all engaged in activities that constituted 'war work' or 'war service'. Janet Watson has argued that British men and women's understanding of their

---

[11] For a discussion of attitudes towards the possible militarisation of French women during the war, see Margaret Darrow, *French Women and the First World War* (Oxford: Berg, 2000). For a study of the civilian women who worked for the French army during the war, see Andrew Orr, *Women and the French Army during the World Wars* (Bloomington: Indiana University Press, 2017).

wartime activities as 'work' or 'service', an understanding largely based on social class, led to divergent experiences and memories of the war.[12] In contrast, in this study I argue that, while social class remained an important factor in an individual's ability to access public life, self-identifying with a 'war generation' who had 'served' could minimise differences between individuals – such as whether war work was waged or unwaged – in favour of a collective, generational identity that brought with it a degree of visibility and social benefit. This public identification or self-identification as 'war veteran' could of course be contested, and frequently was. Many of the women whose lives I explore in my chapters encountered others – both men and women – who challenged their claims to membership of the veteran community or the 'war generation'. But what interests me in this study is women's *attempts*, particularly in their writings, speeches, diaries and letters, to present themselves as having been on a form of 'active service' during the war and therefore as 'female veterans'.

However, the pool of women from which my case studies are drawn constituted a minority in relation to the female populations of the two nations as a whole. The women who were able to appropriate their war service as a key factor in their identities in the 1920s were predominantly – although by no means exclusively – single or childless. The ages of the case studies of women whose stories and voices appear in the chapters that follow vary, but they were all born between 1865 and 1900. The significance of focusing on this particular cohort is, I argue, that an exploration of the ways they viewed and presented the war years in the 1920s gives us a new understanding of the impact of the First World War on French and British women's lives. In particular, it shows us that in this period claiming to be a 'war veteran', or to be part of a 'war generation', allowed certain groups of women to make inroads into different fields of public life in the post-war years.

So why and in what ways did women adopt the identity of veteran in the decade following the Armistice? And what was at stake – culturally, socially and politically – when they did so? Jay Winter and Bruno Cabanes, amongst others, have disproved the notion of a clear-cut 'war generation' as a demographic reality, in Britain and France, respectively.[13] Yet historians of veteran cultures in both nations tend to agree on the extent to which the *idea* of a war generation gained currency in the interwar years. Further, claiming membership of this generation

---

[12] Watson, *Fighting Different Wars*.
[13] Jay Winter, *The Great War and the British People* (London: Macmillan, 1986); Bruno Cabanes, 'Génération du Feu: aux origines d'une notion', *Revue Historique*, 641 (2007): 139–50.

could bring with it not only a shared sense of identity but equally an amount of social prestige. This relates to the broader sense in which post-war memories and cultural evocations of war have tended to prioritise and sacralise a war story in which the male combatant plays the central role. As Lucy Noakes points out: '[W]omen's memories of wartime are less likely to appear in official discourse. ... When women write, or speak about these experiences, their voices often sound less confident, and quieter, than men's.'[14] Aligning themselves to the identity of 'war veteran', then, was one way in which women could find a way for their voices, and their stories, to have greater resonance.

In relation to France, Antoine Prost and Chris Millington argue that the strength of the interwar veterans' movement in France pays testament to the widespread appeal of the equation of combatants' war service with social and moral authority. This was true on both sides of the political spectrum. As Millington summarises:

[T]he victorious Great War veteran, whether perceived as living incarnation of order, moral authority and the nation, or a hero of the working class opposed to capitalist warmongers, was said to understand better than anyone the interests of a nation for whom he had shed his blood. This 'veteran mystique' provided a convenient mobilising myth for an array of veteran and non-veteran groups. ... It made the veterans a potentially powerful political force.[15]

Although the British Legion was less of a political force than its French counterparts, the 'veteran mystique' was also evident in Britain. Niall Barr notes that social attitudes towards ex-servicemen moved after the Great War from a position of 'suspicion and hostility' to one of 'a certain amount of national respect'.[16] As in France, the British Legion espoused high-minded ideals, seeking to create a 'brighter Britain' through the collective action of ex-servicemen, and believing that as a group they had the right, founded on their war service, to be heard on the public and political stage.[17] In many cases, the rhetoric was not matched by concrete achievements in terms of the influence of veterans' associations on national and political life. Yet for the purposes of my study, the emergence of the First World War veteran as a significant social and

---

[14] Lucy Noakes, 'Gender, War and Memory: Discourse and Experience in History', *Journal of Contemporary History* 36: 4 (2001): 663–72 (p. 664). See also Miriam Cooke, *Women and the War Story* (Berkeley: University of California Press, 1998).
[15] Antoine Prost, *Les Anciens Combattants et la société française 1914–1939*, 3 vols. (Paris: Presses de la fondation nationale des sciences politiques, 1977); Chris Millington, *From Victory to Vichy: Veterans in Interwar France* (Manchester: Manchester University Press, 2012), p. 3.
[16] Niall Barr, *The Lion and the Poppy: British Veterans, Politics and Society, 1921–1939* (Westport, CT: Praeger, 2005), p. 9.
[17] Barr, *The Lion and the Poppy*, p. 192.

cultural collective identity – despite its limitations in terms of effecting real social or political change – offered a blueprint that certain women in both nations were able to adopt and adapt.

The terminology of French sociologist Pierre Bourdieu provides a useful framework for understanding the interwar attitudes towards, and social, political and cultural appropriations of, the identity of the war veteran. Bourdieu's model of social relations, which has its roots in Marxist theories of class and conflict, suggests that the goal of all groups is to gain legitimacy through the amassing of capital. Capital is extended beyond economic capital to cover any material and symbolic goods that present themselves as worthy of being sought after within a particular social formation.[18] In Bourdieu's terms, the identity of war veteran brought with it a significant degree of cultural and moral capital in both France and Britain. Male veterans referred to war service not only in order to lobby for improved pensions and other benefits but equally as a means of claiming the right to a public voice in diverse political and social debates. While an important function of veterans' groups was to provide networks of mutual support, a space in which men could find comradeship and a shared sense of belonging to a collective past, this was not their only attraction for their members.

Some French and British ex-servicemen used the cultural and moral capital with which the identity of veteran potentially endowed them to argue in favour of nationalist and right-wing political ideologies.[19] On the opposite side of the political spectrum were ex-servicemen who tried to use veterans' moral authority to militate for the causes of international demilitarisation and moral disarmament.[20] Away from the organised ex-servicemen movement, other men highlighted their veteran status in attempts to achieve a degree of social mobility, boost their chances of gaining employment, of entering public office, or, in the field of war literature, of having their writings published.[21] However, as Nicoletta

---

[18] Pierre Bourdieu, 'The Forms of Capital', in John G. Richardson (ed.), *Handbook of Theory and Research for the Sociology of Education* (New York: Greenwood Press, 1986), pp. 241–58.

[19] Influential in this respect has been George Mosse's 'brutalisation' thesis, according to which male veterans sought to extend their combatant identities by joining paramilitary, often right-wing, groupings. See George Mosse, *Fallen Soldiers: Reshaping the Memory of the World Wars* (Oxford: Oxford University Press, 1990).

[20] Julia Eichenberg and John Paul Newman (eds.), *The Great War and Veterans' Internationalism* (Basingstoke: Palgrave Macmillan, 2013). On veterans who turned to the radical left see Millington, *From Victory to Vichy*; David Englander, 'The National Union of Ex-Servicemen and the Labour Movement', *History* 76 (1991): 24–42.

[21] See for example Simon Ball, *The Guardsmen: Harold Macmillan, Three Friends, and the World They Made* (London: HarperCollins, 2004); Graham Wootton, *The Politics of Influence: British Ex-Servicemen, Cabinet Decisions and Cultural Change* (London: Routledge, 1963).

Gullace has shown in relation to Britain, the nature of the First World War allowed women as well as men to claim service and sacrifice in relation to their wartime activities. As Gullace notes, 'a host of commentators [in Britain] began to cast patriotism, rather than manhood, as the fundamental qualification for citizenship.'[22] Charles Ridel makes a similar point in his work on the powerful cultural figure of the *embusqué* (slacker or shirker) in France, which functioned as the negative 'other' to positive representations of war service and sacrifice: 'On the home front, non-mobilised men and women, as well as non-combatants, were subjected to the full force of combatant representations of the *embusqué*, which exerted enormous social pressure.'[23] This book demonstrates the ways in which appropriating the identity of war veteran in both nations allowed certain women to draw upon the positive connotations of active war service in order to attempt to intervene in public debates and participate in public life in ways that may otherwise have been closed off to them.

As I noted earlier, the war veteran was a jealously guarded and highly contested social identity in the interwar years. Many male veterans saw it as inherently incompatible with female non-combatants, however worthy their war service. In France, women were commonly classified as 'war victims', alongside orphans and other civilian casualties, and rarely as any kind of equivalent to 'combatant'. Margaret Darrow and Susan Grayzel have both concluded that this relates to a broader reluctance in France to associate women with military service because historically that had brought with it the rights and responsibilities of Republican citizenship.[24] It was front-line combat experience that was most often presented as worthy of veteran status in post-war France. As Prost concludes in his study of French veterans: 'To have the right to speak, it was necessary to have experienced the dirt, lice, rats and mud, and above all the suffering and fear, the never-ending waiting, fraternity, pity and sacrifice. It was this privileged experience that had no equivalent that gave combatants, at least according to them, the right to intervene in national life.'[25] Despite their experiences of fear and of the physical risks of being near the front as nurses or as civilians under bombardment, women could never claim to have shared in front-line combatant experience as, with a handful of exceptions, they did not bear arms.

[22] Gullace, *'The Blood of Our Sons'*, p. 4.
[23] Charles Ridel, *Les Embusqués* (Paris: Armand Colin, 2007), p. 296.
[24] Darrow, 'French Volunteer Nursing'; Susan R. Grayzel, '"The Souls of Soldiers": Civilians under Fire in First World War France', *The Journal of Modern History* 78: 3 (2006): 588–622.
[25] Prost, *Les Anciens Combattants*, 1, pp. 111–12.

Echoing Prost, Janet Watson notes that the focus on 'gruesome bloodshed' in the trenches in the post-war years meant that 'valid voices' about the war in Britain were also generally seen to belong 'only ... to those men who had shared this "experience."'[26] What is more, a concentration on the 'combatant spirit' and 'trench experience' excluded not only women but also a significant percentage of mobilised men who had not been on the front lines, and who as a result could not claim membership of what was understood as a veteran elite. In France, these tensions were played out in the 1920s veterans' press in debates over who should have the right to carry the 'carte du combattant' (combatant card), which gave veterans certain rights and privileges.[27]

Even if the use of 'ex-servicemen' rather than 'ancien combattant' does not imply the same privileging of front-line combat experience in Britain, similar notions were nonetheless at play in the British Legion's emphasis on the promotion of an ideal of male comradeship amongst ex-servicemen, which was seen to mirror and reproduce the positive aspects of wartime life. The reluctance of many members of the British Legion to allow First World War ex-servicewomen to participate in their activities is also evidence of British veterans' desire to limit membership to men who had seen active service. It had been initially decided at a conference in 1921 not to allow ex-servicewomen to join the Legion and to form a Women's Auxiliary Section, but this decision was revoked in 1922. However, the social side of Legion membership remained reserved for men, and the Women's Section was open not only to ex-servicewomen but also to female relatives of ex-servicemen, which to some extent aligned it with other women's organisations such as the Women's Institute. At a local level, prejudice often remained against ex-servicewomen in branches of the British Legion.[28] In sum, in both Britain and France, a clear hierarchy of veterans existed, at the top of which were male combatants who bore arms and who risked life.[29]

As John Horne points out, moreover, it was only ever a minority of ex-servicemen who joined ex-servicemen's organisations, even in France,

[26] Watson, *Fighting Different Wars*, p. 306.
[27] Jean-François Monte, 'L'Office National des anciens combattants et victimes de guerre: Créations et actions durant l'entre-deux-guerres', *Guerres mondiales et conflits contemporains* 205 (2002): 71–83.
[28] Barr, *The Lion and the Poppy*, pp. 48–50.
[29] In this context, Adrian Gregory's and Nicoletta Gullace's discussions of the wartime debates around 'sacrifice' and 'service' in First World War Britain continue to be relevant in a post-war context in which the question of who had borne the greater burdens of war continued to create conflict and tensions. See Adrian Gregory, *The Last Great War: British Society and the First World War* (Cambridge: Cambridge University Press, 2008); Gullace, *'The Blood of Our Sons'*.

where veterans' associations constituted the largest civic movement in the country.[30] It was therefore a self-selecting group of men who chose explicitly to foreground the identity of veteran in relation to many other identities available to them in the post-war period, and they did so for diverse social, ideological and economic reasons. The same was true for women who had been active during the war. Relatively few of these women chose to extend their wartime identities into the post-war years, with the majority of women prioritising domestic roles as wives and mothers after the Armistice. For example, only around 8 per cent of the 40,000 or so members of Queen Mary's Army Auxiliary Corps (formerly the Women's Army Auxiliary Corps) became active members of its Old Comrades' Association, attending events, forming regional branches, and contributing to its *Gazette*.[31] The case studies I have chosen to focus on in this book reveal that those women who turned to their wartime identities as a key factor in their self-presentations during the post-war years often did so because they did not fully identify with – or, in some cases, overtly rejected – other more dominant identities available to women during this period.

Gendered Identities in the 1920s

The impacts of the war on women's rights, roles and identities in the interwar period in France and Britain have been much debated by historians and cultural critics in the past fifty years.[32] In the 1960s and 1970s, the war was frequently characterised as a watershed moment in women's history, transforming gender relations and, potentially at least, 'emancipating' women from the pre-war limitations of middle-class domesticity, offering in its place new opportunities and identities. This was especially the case in Britain, where this approach was influenced in 1977 by the Imperial War Museum's exhibition, which was accompanied by the publication of Arthur Marwick's lavishly illustrated book *Women at War 1914–1918*.[33] Both were influential in educating the public about

[30] John Horne, 'Beyond Cultures of Victory and Cultures of Defeat? Inter-War Veterans' Internationalism', in Julia Eichenberg and John Paul Newman, *The Great War and Veterans' Internationalism* (Basingstoke: Palgrave Macmillan, 2013), pp. 207–22.
[31] Statistics taken from the QMAAC *Old Comrades Association Gazette*.
[32] For other useful overviews of the historiography, see Françoise Thébaud, 'Femmes et genre dans la guerre', in Stéphane Audoin-Rouzeau and Jean-Jacques Becker (eds.), *Encyclopédie de la Grande Guerre 1914–1918* (Paris: Bayard, 2004), pp. 613–25; Birgitta Bader-Zaar, 'Controversy: War-Related Changes in Gender Relations: The Issue of Women's Citizenship', in *1914–1918 Online. International Encyclopedia of the First World War*. doi: http://dx.doi.org/10.15463/id1418.10036
[33] Arthur Marwick, *Women at War 1914–1918* (London: Fontana, 1977).

women's diverse roles during the conflict, and Marwick's study attempted to include the experience of ordinary women as well as that of exceptional 'heroines', which had been the focus of David Mitchell's more celebratory 1966 study, *Women on the War Path*.[34] Focusing on the variety of women's wartime activities, *Women at War* argued that the war had opened doors for women, effectively improving their social status. Yet both the book and the exhibition reproduced the photographs compiled for the Imperial War Museum's 'Women at Work' collection in 1917–18 mainly uncritically, not analysing the extent to which Horace Nicholls' photographs had been used for the government promotion of female wartime employment.[35] The conclusions of Marwick's book were challenged in the 1980s by historians such as Gail Braybon, Deborah Thom and James McMillan, who argued that European women's progress in terms, for example, of employment rights was both limited and temporary.[36] Margaret and Patrice Higonnet expressed the point by means of the metaphor of the 'double helix' whereby 'relationships of domination and subordination are retained through discourses that systematically designate unequal gender relationships.'[37]

The interwar years saw a spate of anti-feminist novels, newspaper articles and images bemoaning an apparent erosion of the traditional dominance of the ideal of woman as wife and mother, and, along with the mass redundancies of female war workers, are used as evidence by proponents of the second key approach to post-war gender relations that directly challenges the 'emancipatory' narrative. This approach focuses on the notion of a 'backlash' against (real or perceived) wartime transformations, on the desire to reconstruct conservative models of both femininity and masculinity. In the early 1990s two influential cultural histories of the war by American historians – Mary Louise Robert's *Civilization without Sexes: Reconstructing Gender in Post-War France, 1917–27* (1994) and Susan Kent's *Making Peace: The Reconstruction of*

[34] David Mitchell, *Women on the War Path: The Story of the Women of the First World War* (London: Cape, 1966).

[35] See Gail Braybon, 'Winners or Losers: Women's Role in the War Story', in Gail Braybon (ed.), *Evidence, History and the Great War: Historians and the Impact of 1914–1918* (Oxford: Berghahn, 2003), pp. 86–113.

[36] Gail Braybon, *Women Workers in the First World War* (London: Croom Helm Ltd, 1981); James F. McMillan, *Housewife or Harlot? The Place of Women in French Society 1870–1940* (Brighton: Harvester Press, 1981). See also essays in Margaret Higonnet, Jane Jensen, Sonya Michel and Margaret Collins Weitz (eds.), *Behind the Lines: Gender and the Two World Wars* (New Haven, CT: Yale University Press, 1987) and Richard Wall and Jay Winter (eds.), *The Upheaval of War: Family, Work and Welfare in Europe, 1914–1918* (Cambridge: Cambridge University Press, 1988).

[37] Margaret and Patrice Higonnet, 'The Double Helix', in *Behind the Lines: Gender and the Two World Wars* (New Haven, CT: Yale University Press, 1987), pp. 31–47.

Gender in Interwar Britain[38] (1993) – crystallised this approach. Both analyse widespread cultural images expressing anxieties about the impact of war on gender norms in order to argue that the interwar period was characterised by the privileging of discourses that attacked women who forged identities outside of traditional models of women as wives and mothers, such as single, childless, lesbian and working women. Both authors also link the drive towards the reconstitution of pre-existing gender norms to the demise of feminism as a political force. Kent concluded that in Britain '[p]rewar feminists had vigorously attacked the notion of separate spheres and the medical and scientific discourses about gender and sexuality upon which those spheres rested. Many feminists after World War I, in contrast, pursued a program that championed rather than challenged the prevailing ideas about masculinity and femininity.'[39]

Studies such as these that present the post-war period as an inescapable return to a conservative gender order rely on top-down history, taking as primary evidence those discourses that make it their business to define and police the boundaries of women's roles. But other work, such as Adrian Bingham's study of the interwar British women's magazines, and Siân Reynolds' study of the politics of gender in interwar France, suggests that predominantly focusing on antifeminist journalists and popular novelists risks exaggerating the power and influence of a conservative 'back to the hearth' message. Bingham notes that: 'Certainly, newspapers often stereotyped and patronized women, and the women's sections they included were dominated by fashion and domestic advice. But ... rather than trying to confine women to a narrow domesticity, newspapers generally embraced modernity, encouraged women to become active citizens, and included careers advice for those unable or unwilling to achieve marriage and motherhood.'[40] Reynolds concludes in her political history that although French women remained disenfranchised, having 'responsibility without power' in the interwar years, the 'permeability of public life' for women was nevertheless fundamentally changed by the nation's experience of war, which undermined the all-male monopoly over public life.[41]

---

[38] Mary Louise Roberts, *Civilization without Sexes: Reconstructing Gender in Post-War France, 1917–27* (Chicago: University of Chicago Press, 1994); Susan Kent, *Making Peace: The Reconstruction of Gender in Interwar Britain* (Princeton, NJ: Princeton University Press, 1993).

[39] Kent, *Making Peace*, p. 6.

[40] Adrian Bingham, 'An Era of Domesticity: Histories of Women and Gender in Interwar Britain', *Cultural and Social History* 1 (2004): 225–33.

[41] Siân Reynolds, *France between the Wars: Gender and Politics* (London: Routledge, 1996), chapter 7.

The view of the post-war period as a 'reconstruction' of a 'collapsed' gender system was nuanced in the late 1990s and early 2000s by studies by, amongst others, Susan Grayzel, Nicoletta Gullace and Janet Watson. They incorporated a cultural analysis of wartime evidence to reveal the war's impulses towards both change and continuity, societies and individuals that might yearn for equal treatment while also celebrating, even elevating, gender difference.[42] From this perspective, the Higonnets' 'double helix' metaphor, which proposes fixed power relationships in which women are doomed to remain forever subordinate to men, fails to account for the subtle and gradual shifts in expectations and aspirations that can be discerned amongst many women in the interwar period. This is the case if we consider, for example, significant changes in leisure activities, reading habits and sexual behaviours, not to mention the renegotiating of the public sphere and notions of citizenship.[43] Some cultural studies of interwar domesticity such as those by Alison Light highlight the arrival of an apparently paradoxical period of 'conservative modernity'.[44] This exploration of the tension between a nostalgic drive for the past and the intermingled excitement, acceptance and tolerance of modernity and its changes in everyday life merits further attention. This can be seen in the coexistence of positive and negative stereotypes of the 'modern woman' in post-war popular culture. For some, she was a beacon of the future while for others she was a symptom of decline. Like the contradictory evidence from the war years themselves, the experiences and cultural expectations of post-war women (and men) simultaneously emphasised new opportunities, heightened anxieties and grievous losses.

In many ways, interwar France and Britain, like much of interwar Europe, was characterised by the promotion of a traditional 'breadwinner model', as evidenced by the rise of the Welfare State that positioned women primarily as wives and mothers.[45] There were several reasons for this, both economic and social. Equally, widespread cultural anxieties existed around perceived changes in female behaviour, as explored by Roberts and Kent, and these anxieties found their way into the broader

---

[42] Grayzel, *Women's Identities at War*; Watson, *Fighting Different Wars*; Gullace, 'The Blood of Our Sons'.

[43] See for example Birgitte Søland, *Becoming Modern: Young Women and the Reconstruction of Womanhood in the 1920s* (Princeton, NJ: Princeton University Press, 2000).

[44] Alison Light, *Forever England: Femininity, Literature and Conservatism between the Wars* (London: Routledge, 1991).

[45] Laura Levine Frader, *Breadwinners and Citizens: Gender in the Making of the French Social Model* (Durham, NC: Duke University Press, 2008); Susan Pederson, *Family, Dependence and the Origins of the Welfare State, Britain and France 1914–1945* (Cambridge: Cambridge University Press, 1993); Gisela Bock and Pat Thane, *Maternity and Gender Policies: Women and the Rise of European Welfare States 1880s–1950s* (London: Routledge, 1991).

cultural milieu, including many novels, images and newspapers of the period. However, while acknowledging the power of the ongoing Western gender system and the centrality of motherhood and soldiering as linked oppositional ways to define the essential national/public function of women and men, we also need to understand how the war set in motion elements of change that allowed women in particular to begin to carve out identities beyond those circumscribed by traditional models.

In this study, I analyse the ways in which certain women turned to models other than those of wife and mother in the post-war years. The women whose trajectories I highlight in the chapters that follow do not all reject out of hand the idealised model of a heterosexual stay-at-home mother. Some women, such as volunteer nurse Germaine Malaterre Sellier, with whom I began this introduction, turned to a maternalist understanding of female identity as a basis of their feminist pacifism. But they rely in different ways on their wartime activities as a means of constructing a generational model of identity, founded on that of the war veteran. The social prestige generally associated with war service in the 1920s allowed these women to attempt to assert that they had a right to be heard, and many thus demanded a right to participate in public debates in a number of different spheres: in commemorative activities, in the field of war literature and journalism, and in political movements of both the right and the left. Examining women like this reveals the limitations of an understanding of the interwar years as uniquely oppressive for women. However, my final chapter shows that whereas some women's claims to veteran status on the basis of their war service were broadly accepted, other women's war experiences did not fit the model of female war veteran in the same way. The identity of veteran as constructed by the male veteran movement created a legitimised public space in and from which female veterans could construct and assert a model of female identity that was not predicated on women's domestic roles. However, as was the case for men, not all forms of women's war service accrued cultural capital in the post-war years.

Britain and France

In a comparative study of Britain and France it is essential to consider both differences and similarities in an examination of the ways in which women evoked their war experiences in the post-war years. As two of the most important and powerful participant nations in the war, they shared some key characteristics in terms of their widespread and consistent espousal of a dominant Western gender system that emphasised the primacy of motherhood in women's relationship to the state.[46] However, my case studies reveal some dissimilarities between the contexts in which women could claim a status as 'war veteran' in the interwar period. The difference most often pointed to between Britain and France in relation to women's lives is the fact that French women remained disenfranchised until 1944, whereas in Britain the laws passed in 1918 and 1928 enfranchised women. Yet this should not lead to an oversimplified characterisation of a new era of gender equality in Britain versus gender oppression in France. Rather, both nations were grappling with the question of supporting and encouraging women in what was understood as their crucial role as 'repopulators' of the nation while dealing with the economic reality of women's waged work. Susan Pederson has shown that in the interwar period in Britain debates were dominated by a male-breadwinner logic, in which a strict division is maintained between women's waged work and motherhood, whereas in France 'parental policies [did] not assume that women are necessarily dependent, nor that men always have "families to keep". Rather they presume[d] the dependence of children alone and hence redistribute[d] income primarily across family types and not along gender lines.'[47] In both Republican and Catholic circles, the welfare of children and families tended to be understood as a public concern, which allowed some French women after the First World War to claim social protection based on their status as both mothers and workers.[48] In both nations, women (and men) who defended mothers' right to work based on gender equality grounds rather than on family welfare grounds remained a small minority, and motherhood was understood as both duty and necessity for the nation's future well-being.[49]

In this study, two key differences between Britain and France take centre stage: the relation of women to the armed services, and the nature of 1920s veteran cultures. The manpower crisis of 1917 in Britain led to the creation of the women's auxiliary services that endowed women with a military identity – even if they were clearly differentiated from male combatants, did not bear arms and were not subject to military discipline.[50] This created Britain's first cohort of

[46] Grayzel, *Women's Identities at War*.

[47] Pederson, *Family, Dependence and the Origins of the Welfare State*, p. 17.

[48] Laura Frader, 'Social Citizens without Citizenship: Working-Class Women and Social Policy in Interwar France', *Social Politics: International Studies in Gender, State and Society* (1996): 111–35.

[49] Birte Siim, *Gender and Citizenship: Politics and Agency in France, Britain and Denmark* (Cambridge: Cambridge University Press, 2000), p. 57.

[50] Lucy Noakes, *Women in the British Army: War and the Gentle Sex 1907–1948* (London: Routledge, 2006).

legitimised 'ex-servicewomen' who could claim a place side by side with servicemen in the post-war years. In France, although women were employed in a civilian capacity by the French army, the government did not militarise women, despite the same acute shortages of manpower in the latter years of the conflict. The reluctance to take this step reveals, as Margaret Darrow suggests, a more obstinate belief in France in the fundamental incompatibility of women and warfare, as well as the centrality of military service to Republican definitions of male citizenship.[51] However, it is important to add that although the lack of women's auxiliary services shored up the gendered division between combatant and non-combatant, that line was blurred to some extent by France's experience of occupation. The women who participated in resistance movements in occupied France and Belgium or who worked for the intelligence services in the First World War were often heroised as 'combatants'.[52] This was largely understood to have been a temporary role in exceptional circumstances, which of course is very different from a state-sanctioned waged role as a member of an auxiliary corps of the armed services. Nevertheless, it allowed a handful of French women to claim a form of 'combatant' war service in the post-war years.

In addition, core differences between British and French veteran cultures provide an important framework for my case studies. As I have already noted, in France the veterans' movement was larger and had more political clout than the Legion and other ex-servicemen's organisations in Britain. The hundreds of 'specialised' veteran groupings that sprang up in early 1920s France provided a ready-made model for groups of French women to follow. This was not the case in Britain, which helps to explain, for example, why ex-war nurses and war widows did not organise in the same way as was the case in France. If the concept of an 'ex-servicewoman' remained unthinkable in the interwar period years, then, the powerful veterans' movement made it more possible to forge collective identities as 'women who had served'. This was particularly the case with French ex-war nurses who, as I show in Chapter 3, grouped together in organisations affiliated to the main male veterans' associations.

[51] Darrow, *French Women*, chapter 7.
[52] Tammy Proctor, *Female Intelligence: Women and Espionage in the First World War* (New York: New York University Press, 2006); Emmanuel Debruyne and Alison S. Fell, 'Model Martyrs: Remembering First World War Resistance Heroines in Belgium and France', in Peter Tame et al. (eds.), *Mnemosyne and Mars: Artistic and Cultural Representations of Twentieth-Century Europe at War* (Newcastle: Cambridge Scholars Press, 2013), pp. 145–65.

Despite these national differences, the contexts in which women were commenting on their war roles in the interwar years remain strikingly similar in both nations. Both states can be seen as pursuing pronatalist policies in the interwar years, while simultaneously culturally constructing a generational notion of citizenship and patriotism that was based more on questions around war service and sacrifice than on gender. In the chapters that follow, I often consider British and French women side by side rather than separately, commenting on the different national contexts where they play a particularly significant role. Chapter 1 begins with women who were considered veterans by others and explores the ways in which these women were positioned as veterans in commemorative culture. It analyses the uses made of 'symbolic' women included in war memorials to the male dead, particularly the nurse, who became a symbol in both nations of patriotic female participation in war. It also considers the ways in which memorials and other commemorations of women who were killed or who died on active service in the war attempted to define female deaths as 'war deaths', thereby implying a degree of equivalence to the male war dead.

My second chapter turns to those who were designated as 'war heroines', either officially, such as Edith Cavell, or more locally, by the press, regional authorities or members of organisations. I also trace in this chapter the 'afterlives' of surviving British and French wartime heroines as they attempted to reintegrate into peacetime life after the Armistice. Where women died, their heroine status remained largely uncontested, as they were fixed forever in the public imagination as 'martyrs' of the war. For the women who survived, however, their experiences were more varied. Some women were able successfully to use their heroine status to intervene in public life in various ways, becoming public speakers, joining male veterans' associations, or publishing their stories in books and newspapers. Others, however, were less accepted once the guns had fallen silent, and found the post-war years dissatisfying. Their writings often express a degree of nostalgia for their wartime lives, a sense in which their experience as veterans was one of disappointment with the limitations of peacetime – a sentiment also found in many male veterans' writings of the period.

Chapter 3 focuses on collective expressions of female veteran identity, examining the publications and activities of two groups of female war veterans: war nurses, and British ex-members of Queen Mary's Army Auxiliary Corps.[53] These groups of women formed associations in the

---

[53] The corps was originally named the Women's Army Auxiliary Corps (WAAC) and this is generally the term that I use, as it remained the name by which they were popularly known in the interwar years.

early 1920s that were modelled on those formed by their male counterparts. As was the case for male veterans' associations, they had both private and public functions, on one hand providing networks of support and care for their members, and on the other operating as political lobby groups attempting to draw public attention to women's sacrifices and contributions to the war, and arguing for equal treatment by the state in relation to pensions and other veterans' benefits. I explore the uses former nurses and auxiliary workers made of these networks, and in particular trace the trajectories of women who continued to make use of their veteran status to allow them to access professions or roles that may otherwise have been unavailable to them.

My fourth chapter examines women who sought to enter the literary market in the 1920s. It looks at two groups of female writers who used their war experiences as the raw material for their published works with the aim of entering the male-dominated 'war literature' market: nurses and women who were part of resistance movements in occupied France and Belgium. I consider how these women adapted the genres created by male writers to present themselves as war writers. In order to do so they cast themselves as war veterans, thereby endowing their autobiographical narratives with authenticity and authority. As I show, sometimes this resulted in a degree of reinvention and fictionalisation to fit in with the generic tradition established by male combat writers. An analysis of the memoirs of female members of resistance networks, for example, reveals the importance of aligning themselves to positive models of service and self-sacrifice associated with war heroism so as to distance themselves from widespread cultural stereotypes of female spies as untrustworthy prostitutes, often embodied in the figure of Mata Hari.

Finally, in Chapter 5 I consider women who, unlike heroines, war nurses and British ex-servicewomen, did not occupy state-sanctioned roles in wartime. Rather, I focus on female industrial workers who led episodes of wartime industrial unrest, particularly the widespread factory strikes amongst women workers that took place in 1917 and 1918. Women who had led strikes on behalf of women workers were able to gain positions of influence within left-wing networks after the war because they were seen to have proven skills in the successful mobilisation of women workers. This mattered because the post-war years were a period in which unions and political parties were keen to recruit more working-class women. However, an analysis of these women's post-war rhetoric demonstrates the limits of the identity of war veteran for women – when and by whom it could be claimed, and when it was better to finesse or avoid altogether mention of one's wartime history. Although these women attempted to claim both cultural capital and solidarity with others through their evocation of the wartime sacrifices of industrial workers in relation to the immorality of profiteers or shirkers, the association of the strikes of 1917 and 1918 with social and political revolution, particularly in France, meant that they were unable to claim to have selflessly served the nation in the same way as nurses or women who had temporarily taken over farms and family businesses.

Women who were active in the war, including the women whose stories appear in the chapters that follow, often aligned themselves with the 'War Generation'. By so doing, and despite opposition and scepticism, they staked a claim for the importance and validity of their stories and perspectives. This book explores the reasons why they did so, and asks what their interwar evocations of their war experiences can tell us, not simply about the complex ways in which the war changed how these women understood their lives, roles and identities, but more importantly about how they used their war experience to construct public identities as war veterans. In doing so, they influenced public discourse about gender and women's role as citizens on both sides of the Channel.

1   Women as Veterans in the Commemorative Landscapes of Interwar Britain and France

On 26 August 1970, a small group of French women carrying a banner declaring '[t]here is someone more unknown than the Unknown Soldier: his wife' attempted to lay wreaths on the tomb of the Unknown Soldier at the Arc de Triomphe in a carefully orchestrated and highly provocative symbolic gesture. It was one of the earliest public demonstrations carried out by the post-1968 French feminist activists who were to form the core of the Mouvement de libération des femmes (Women's Liberation Movement).[1] Widely reported in the press (journalists were informed in advance), this theatrical action was designed, according to one of the participants, 'to denounce [women's] oppression in a spectacular and humorous fashion'.[2] Fifty years after the ceremonies for the Unknown Warrior had taken place in Paris and London, this new generation of feminists cast the tomb as the ultimate symbol of the hegemony of masculinist culture, as a synecdoche for the oppression, belittling and silencing of women under patriarchy. Although the context and politics were very different, a similar sense of dissatisfaction with what was understood as women's exclusion from war commemoration was evident in the campaign for the British 'Women and World War II' memorial unveiled in 2005.[3] In a press release, Betty Boothroyd, former speaker of the House of Commons who galvanised the campaign, stated how proud she was 'to finally see a memorial to the wonderful women who contributed so much to the war effort', adding that John Mills' sculpture would

---

[1] Sylvie Chaperon, *Les Années Beauvoir 1945–1970* (Paris: Fayard, 2000), p. 360; Jean Rabaut, *Histoire des féminismes* (Paris: Stock, 1978), p. 338; The 'Mouvement de libération des femmes' (MLF) was the name the French press gave to the women who laid the wreaths, thereby aligning them with the American Women's Liberation Movement (the French action coincided with the Women's Strike for Equality that took place in the United States on the same day).

[2] Anne Tristan and Annie de Pisan, *Histoires du MLF* (Paris: Calmann Lévy, 1977), p. 55.

[3] This argument builds on Frances Casey's unpublished paper 'Gender and UK War Memorials', delivered at the 'War and Gender' conference, Newcastle University, 12 March 2011.

'make a symbolic and dramatic tribute'.[4] The chosen location of the memorial in Whitehall, its design and positioning boldly mirroring those of the Cenotaph, guides the public to interpret the memorial as a corrective to the perceived absence of women from Edwin Lutyen's 1920 national war memorial. This intention is summed up in the response of Edna Storr, one of the trustees of the memorial and a former Auxiliary Territorial Service (ATS) worker: 'It's a wonderful sculpture. Best of all, it's going next to the Cenotaph. We are going to stand side by side, with the men, where we belong.'[5]

Historians have concurred that First World War memorials and other commemorative discourses constructed a male-dominated vision of gender roles that either excludes or offers a highly restricted interpretation of women's contributions and experiences during the war. John Gillis concludes for example that 'for the women who had contributed so much to the world's first total war effort, there would be no monuments.'[6] Daniel Sherman, taking a Foucauldian understanding of the oppressive and insidious nature of patriarchal power structures as a theoretical framework, argues in similar vein that French interwar war memorials and their unveiling ceremonies, planned and designed by committees dominated by men, functioned to express and to attempt to allay the anxieties of a nation threatened by the perceived erosion of traditional gender roles in wartime. Taking his lead from Mary Louise Roberts' analysis of interwar French novels, memoirs and journalism by ex-servicemen that criticise perceived changes in social mores,[7] Sherman summarises that 'commemoration served to reinscribe gender codes that World War I had disrupted in France ... [it] played out, in gendered terms, a pervasive cultural unease in which nothing less than the masculine cast of politics and of national citizenship was at stake.'[8] Sherman thus argues that both men and women were calcified into a limited number of allegorical roles that functioned to differentiate the sexes according to pre-war gender

---

[4] Heritage Lottery Fund Press Release, 'National Heritage Memorial Fund Gives Nearly £1 Million to Create UK's First National Memorial to Women of World War II', 29 April 2004.

[5] Quoted on www.mod.uk/aboutus/history/ww2/index/womensmonument.htm. Accessed via the National Archives web archive at http://webarchive.nationalarchives.gov.uk/.

[6] John R. Gillis, 'Introduction', in John R. Gillis (ed.), *Commemorations: The Politics of National Identity* (Princeton, NJ: Princeton University Press, 1994), p. 12; see also Darrow, *French Women*, p. 2; William Kidd, '"To the Lads Who Came Back": Memorial Windows and Rolls of Honour in Scotland', in William Kidd and Brian Murdoch (eds.), *Memory and Memorials: The Commemorative Century* (Aldershot: Ashgate, 2004), pp. 120–27 (p. 121).

[7] Roberts, *Civilization without Sexes*.

[8] Daniel Sherman, 'Monuments, Mourning and Masculinity in France after World War I', *Gender and History* 8 (1996): 82–107 (p. 84).

imperatives: 'Men were active, heroic, resourceful [...] women were grieving, suffering, emotional'.[9]

But did commemorative culture in the wake of the First World War operate exclusively as an oppressive force, 'sculpturally consigning post-war women to conventionally gendered roles'?[10] Clearly, the principal female function in commemorative discourse in both Britain and France was as the bereaved wives and mothers of servicemen, echoing not only their primary relation to the deaths being commemorated but equally a traditional understanding of women's role as domestic.[11] Yet, as I argue in this chapter, women's relationship to commemoration in the interwar years was more proactive, more dynamic and more varied than has frequently been suggested. The grieving widow or mother was not the only version of female identity found on war memorials and represented in unveiling ceremonies. Further, not only did thousands of women actively respond to and participate in the rites and rituals of commemoration, but women also instigated, planned, designed and sculpted memorials and ceremonies, shaping rather than being shaped by interwar commemorative culture. In so doing, women were presented as war veterans in two ways. First, some war memorials were designed to commemorate the sacrifices of whole communities to the war effort, and not only the sacrifices of the dead. In these memorials to 'total war', women were included in the evocations of those who had been on active service, and who therefore deserved the respect and recognition of their community and country. Second, memorials that commemorate women who died or who were killed in the war often presented the deaths of such women as war deaths, thereby aligning them with the deaths of servicemen. The discourse of sacrifice in the service of the nation had implications for the relationship of these women to the state, especially in France

---

[9] Sherman, 'Monuments, Mourning and Masculinity', p. 93. Sherman and Michelle Perrot comment on the tendency for female figures to be in allegorical mode, whereas male figures (the 'poilu') are more realist. Daniel Sherman, *The Construction of Memory in Interwar France* (Chicago: University of Chicago Press, 1999), pp. 203–04; Michelle Perrot, 'Préface', in Françoise Thébaud, *Les Femmes au temps de la guerre de 1914* (Paris: Stock, 1986), pp. 7–13. Although it is true that female figures in contemporary dress are rare on memorials, the 'poilu' figures serve to embody abstract qualities of heroic masculinity in the same way as the classically inspired widows and mourning mothers embody abstract qualities of femininity, so the distinction is to some extent an artificial one.

[10] William Kidd, 'The Lion, the Angel and the War Memorial: Some French Sites Revisited', in Nicholas J. Saunders (ed.), *Matters of Conflict: Material Culture, Memory and the First World War* (London: Routledge, 2004), pp. 149–65 (p. 152).

[11] This is borne out statistically. The majority of female figures in both French and British memorials relate to mourning, and most often feature women as mother figures. See Grayzel, *Women's Identities at War*.

where an inscription of 'mort pour la patrie' ('died for the fatherland') necessarily evokes the tenets of Republican citizenship.

Over the past twenty years, the historiography of First World War commemoration has sometimes constructed what is essentially a false dichotomy between the private/psychological and public/political meanings and uses of war memorials. In this chapter, I take memorials to be public and politicised sites that mediated private grief; one does not and cannot exclude the other.[12] Both Sherman's study of France and Alex King's study of Britain reveal the diverse motivations inherent in the planning and erection of war memorials, reminding us that these enterprises 'entailed assembling resources and creating a large audience, ... [offering] funds which could be put to philanthropic uses, a market for artists, a platform for politicians'.[13] Commemoration in the interwar period was mostly done by committee, and necessitated frequent negotiation and compromise between the various stakeholders involved, including ex-servicemen, local organisations and businesses, the bereaved, donors, fund-raisers, municipal and sometimes national authorities, religious leaders and urban planners and developers.[14] Jay Winter has shown how women responded privately to war memorials as mourners, the ceremonies acting as *rites de passage* on route to what Winter refers to, deploying a Freudian optic, as the 'necessary art of forgetting'.[15] What has been less discussed, however, is the extent to which women as well as men exploited the public opportunities that commemoration offered, taking up as they did so a variety of roles: as wealthy patrons influencing the aesthetics and ideological messages of memorials, as volunteers or charity workers furthering or publicising philanthropic causes, as members of a profession remembering colleagues and promoting their achievements or, occasionally, as suffragists, lending weight to arguments that sought to claim full citizenship for women.

[12] Stephen Heathorn, 'The Mnemonic Turn in the Cultural Historiography of Britain's Great War', *The Historical Journal* 48: 4 (2005): 1103–24; Jenny Macleod, '"By Scottish Hands, with Scottish Money, on Scottish Soil": The Scottish National War Memorial and National Identity', *The Journal of British Studies* 49: 1 (2010): 73–96; Stefan Goebel, 'Re-Membered and Re-Mobilized: The Sleeping Dead in Interwar Germany and Britain', *Journal of Contemporary History* 39 (2004): 487–501.

[13] Alex King, *Memorials of the Great War in Britain: The Symbolism and Politics of Remembrance* (Oxford: Berg, 1998), p. 2.

[14] For an analysis of the interaction between these various stakeholders in the erection of interwar London memorials, see Stephen Heathorn, 'The Civil Servant and Public Remembrance: Sir Lionel Earle and the Shaping of London's Commemorative Landscape, 1918–1933', *Twentieth Century British History* 19: 3 (2008): 259–87.

[15] Jay Winter, *Sites of Memory, Sites of Mourning: The Great War in European Cultural History* (Cambridge: Cambridge University Press, 1995), p. 115.

In this chapter I discuss two different aspects of women's relationship to commemoration: the meanings ascribed to female figures in memorials and ceremonies, and interventions by individual women in the planning, designing and sculpting of war memorials. These aspects are frequently interlinked, as women's interventions often resulted in the construction of alternative visions of womanhood to those that cast women as mourning mothers or as allegorical embodiments of an abstract quality or nation. These alternative visions of women as having actively served in the war necessarily evoked claims for memory and recognition that were often grounded in the political or ideological beliefs of the instigators, funders or designers of the memorial.

Women as Citizens

Despite the predominance of women cast as bereaved mothers, wives or sisters in monuments and ceremonies, women appeared in other guises in commemorative discourse in the interwar years, some of which complemented and some of which competed with their primary roles as mourners. The nurse was the most familiar and most acceptable symbol of female service and sacrifice during the war.[16] In the cultures of commemoration in the interwar period it retained its position as the dominant way in which women's contribution to the war effort was represented in both Britain and France. The nurse was set up as an idealised role model that had broad appeal, being easily subsumed into dominant conceptions of femininity while also being positioned as a female equivalent of mass male mobilisation.[17] Many evocations of the wartime nurse thus drew on traditional understandings of women's rights and roles, and offered reassuringly domesticated versions of mobilised women on active service during the war. Yet within the cultures of commemoration, representations of the wartime nurse frequently had different, even competing, objectives. While some drew on conceptions of nursing as an extension of women's maternal or domestic role in order to make their wartime service embody abstract values such as humanity, civilisation, reconciliation and healing, others positioned nurses as citizens, their work being

---

[16] For an extended discussion of representations of the nurse, see Alison S. Fell, 'Remembering the First World War Nurse', in Alison S. Fell and Christine Hallett (eds.), *First World War Nursing: New Perspectives* (New York: Routledge, 2013), pp. 173–92.

[17] Kathryn McPherson notes in this context that '[nurses'] presence in the public space, whether in their daily work or in memorials, did not fundamentally challenge prevailing perceptions of appropriate femininity.' 'Carving Out a Past: The Canadian Nurses' Association War Memorial', *Histoire sociale/Social History* 29 (1996): 417–29 (p. 419).

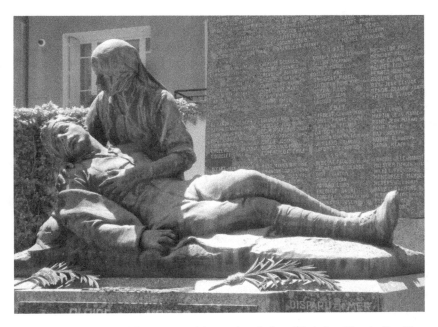

Figure 1.1 War memorial, sculpted by Christian-Henri Roullier-Levasseur, Charlieu (Loire), 1922. Photograph by Marc Lacelle.

understood in this context as an admirable example of an individual's fulfilment of civic or patriotic duty to the nation.

Certain evocations of the nurse in the interwar years effectively combine the roles of nurse and grieving woman, the nurse depicted as a *pietà* with a dead or wounded soldier presented as a Christ figure. This is particularly the case in France, where interwar commemoration was permeated, as Annette Becker notes, by the 'religious and mystical realm ... when Judeo-Christian catechisms were entwined with the secular gospels of patriotism'.[18] The war memorial in Charlieu (Loire) (Figure 1.1) is of this type. Sculpted by Christian-Henri Roullier-Levasseur and unveiled in 1922, it features a nurse wearing a First World War uniform and cradling a dead French soldier, his helmet by his side. This rare appearance of a realist sculpture of a uniformed nurse on a French memorial is perhaps explained by the fact that the Mayor of Charlieu was Jean Louis Vitaud, who had worked as a doctor in the

[18] Annette Becker, 'From Death to Memory: The National Ossuaries in France after the Great War', *History and Memory* 5 (1993): 32–49 (p. 32). See also Annette Becker, *La Guerre et la foi: De la mort à la mémoire* (Paris: Armand Colin, 1994), p. 122.

French army during the war.[19] A similar depiction of a nurse caring for a dying soldier can also be found on a plaque in the Eglise Saint-Louis des Invalides in Paris that is dedicated to French Red Cross nurses. In the foreground, a uniformed nurse is bandaging the wounds of a prostrate soldier while in the background a ruined French village burns. Despite their contemporary dress, the nurses in these memorials are recognisable as Marian figures, the ancient *Stabat Mater dolorosa*. A nurse is also central to the 1922 memorial in Saintes (Charentes-Maritime), sculpted by Emile Peyronnet, in which a bent-headed nursing sister supports a prostrate soldier. Here, the nurse embodies a maternalist vision of the French Republic, caring and grieving for its dead, as well as offering a powerful depiction of the healing power of womanhood in the wake of war.[20]

In Britain, however, nurses who appear on First World War memorials tend to be positioned in similar poses to soldiers, rather than in maternal, nurturing or grieving mode. In this way, they served to embody the sacrifices and contributions made by women to the war effort, a feminised version of masculine war service. Some of these memorials overtly positioned them as citizens who have been on active service, despite the fact that very few women were named on the list of the fallen. The war memorial in Bold Venture Park, Darwen, Lancashire, for example, sculpted by Louis Roslyn and unveiled in 1921, features a tall square pedestal with bronze reliefs on three of its sides representing a soldier, sailor and a nurse, while at the top of the pedestal stands a winged figure representing Victory.[21] The nurse is in First World War uniform, but

---

[19] Archives départementales de la Loire, article accompanying an exhibition entitled 'La Loire au service des blessés', 10–30 November 2008. Available online at www.loire.fr/jcms/c_825883/les-archives-en-ligne.

[20] I would like to thank Laura Lee Downs for alerting me to this example.

[21] Roslyn sculpted a similar memorial at Blackley, Greater Manchester, with four figures holding emblems representing the Army, Navy, Air Force and Nursing Services (since removed), that was unveiled in 1921. William Kidd discusses four memorial windows in Scottish churches that also contain nurses appearing alongside soldiers, sailors and airmen in Newlands South Church, St James's, Pollock, Glasgow, St John's Cupar and St John's, Dunoon. See Terry Wyke and Harry Cocks, *Public Sculpture of Greater Manchester* (Liverpool: Liverpool University Press, 2004), pp. 139–40; Kidd, 'To the Lads', pp. 121–22. There was also a proposal by the Mayor of Oxford for a design including 'four figures in bronze ... an infantry soldier, a gunner, a yeoman, and a nurse', *The Observer*, 2 May 1920. The Oxford War Memorial Committee, however, eventually chose the design by John Thorpe, Gilbert Gardner and Thomas Rayson. See Alex Bruce, 'The Oxford War Memorial: Thomas Rayson and the Chester Connection', *Oxoniensia* 56 (1991): 155–68. In the case of Darwen, the newspaper report notes there had been some female deaths: 'women were amongst the town's fallen, true heroines of the war', *The Darwen News*, 24 September 1921. The memorial does not list names, but Martha Emily Jenkins, a forty-two-year-old former cotton weaver who worked as a stewardess in the Mercantile Marine, was listed in the Roll of Honour in *The Darwen News*,

unlike the French examples she is not evocative of religious iconography. Her sleeves are rolled up, she is carrying the tools of her trade like the soldier carries his rifle, and she wears a medal as proof of the value of her service to the state. Her dress, pose and gaze mirror those of the war-weary men on the other reliefs. It is possible that Roslyn was influenced by George Frampton's 1920 memorial to Edith Cavell, as the word 'Humanity' is engraved below the nurse, expressing a specifically female brand of wartime sacrifice, whereas beneath the male military figures is the word 'Freedom'.

A similar conception of nursing as the feminised version of male military service, although this time understood in terms of a Catholic conception of martyrdom, is found in the stained-glass windows of the memorial chapel at the national ossuary in Douaumont in France, painted and designed by George Desvallières in 1927 (Figure 1.2).[22] All of the windows in the chapel revolve around the theme of sacrifice and redemption, with two of them devoted to a nurse and a soldier who are presented as sainted martyrs, ascending to heaven in the arms of angels. Having converted to Catholicism in 1904, in 1919, Desvallières set up the Atelier d'art sacré, with painter Maurice Denis, with the aim of revitalising religious art.[23] Male and female sacrifice embodied in the figures of soldier and nurse is also present in the frieze Desvallières painted for the private chapel of Jacques Rouché at Saint-Privat, which he completed in 1925. In 'Dieu le père' ('God the Father') (1920), Jesus holds a protecting cloak over a French soldier (modelled on Desvallières' dead son, Daniel) and nurse who kneel side by side, while the Virgin Mary welcomes them into heaven.[24] The nurse in the stained-glass window memorialises three French nurses killed when their hospital was shelled in 1917, but the nurse has a greater symbolic function.[25] As

4 January 1919. She was lost at sea on 27 March 1915 and her death is commemorated on the Tower Hill Memorial, London.

[22] For details about the genesis of the windows, see Catherine Ambroselli de Bayser, *George Desvallières et la Grande Guerre* (Paris: Somogy éditions d'art, 2013), pp. 147–57. See also Catherine Ambroselli de Bayser (dir.), *George Desvallières, Catalogue raisonné de l'œuvre complet* (Paris, Somogy éditions d'art: 2015), vol. 3, pp. 476–91.

[23] Desvallières also frequently painted the poilu as Christ in re-imaginings of the Way of the Cross, such as the murals depicting the soldier's 'way of the Cross' at the Catholic housing project in the 14th arrondissement of Paris. Becker, *La Guerre*, pp. 130–31; Winter, *Sites of Memory*, p. 53.

[24] Bayser, *George Desvallières et la Grande Guerre*, pp. 141–44. See also Bayser, *George Desvallières, Catalogue raisonné de l'œuvre complet*, vol. 3, pp. 408–21, CR 1640, pp. 414–15.

[25] Mme Vostey, Eugénie Pietrowska and Jeanne Fichot were killed on 17 August 1917 at Dugny-sur-Meuse near Verdun. The window was dedicated to their memory by their colleague Yolande de Baye, who was seriously injured in the same attack, and who was also a prominent member of the Association nationale des infirmières blessées et mutilées de guerre after the war (see Chapter 3).

Figure 1.2 George Desvallières, *Triptyque de l'Ascension, L'Infirmière,*
1927. Stained-glass window, 230 × 140 cm (CR 1856, p. 484).

Jean-Philippe Rey notes, in Desvallières' redemptive vision the idealised nurse–soldier couple becomes representative of humanity: 'The sacrifice of the soldiers becomes the remedy for sin. The communion of saints is restored, the chosen couple (poilu and nurse) intercedes on behalf of the inhabitants of the earth.'[26] Desvallières himself was explicit about the meaning of his depiction of the soldier and nurse in this respect: 'On the left and on the right, the great Angels accompany the Ascension of our Saviour, lifting in their powerful arms the two heroes of the war: the Soldier who died for his country, and the Nurse, who sacrificed herself for those who suffered and died.'[27] Thus, while the nurses who appear on Roslyn's Darwen memorial and in Desvallières' religious art are placed within different conceptions of sacrifice – civic and religious – in both cases, the sexes are not placed in a hierarchical relationship, but side by side. Men and women are understood as having been united by a collective spirit of sacrifice. The nurse's and the soldier's contributions are therefore presented as having some degree of equivalence, and as metonymically standing in for the sacrifices made by the broader community of those on active service.

Another British memorial that offers a vision of collective sacrifice in its presentation of 'total war' is located in St Mary's Church Memorial Gardens in Rawtenstall, Lancashire (Figure 1.3). This memorial, also sculpted by Louis Roslyn, features a tapered granite obelisk with bronze reliefs beneath which show various figures including soldiers, sailors, airmen, a farmer, a miner, a nurse, a woman and child, a fisherman, a medical orderly, a railwayman and a labourer. In this vision of wartime life, each member of the community offers his or her own form of service and sacrifice, propping up the four 'pillars' of the servicemen who are strategically placed at the four corners of the frieze. It was instigated by a wealthy local woman, Carrie Whitehead, who also unveiled it in 1929 (Figure 1.4).[28] There had been prolonged debate in Rawtenstall as to what form the memorial should

---

[26] Jean-Philippe Rey, 'Desvallières et la guerre de 1914–1918', *Société de l'histoire de l'art français* (1988), 197–211, quoted in Becker, *La Guerre*, p. 131.

[27] Letter from George Desvallières, 15 September 1927. Quoted in Bayser, *George Desvallières et la Grande Guerre*, p. 154.

[28] Carrie Whitehead engaged in social work for her community from the beginning of the war. A 1915 article stated that she 'had been a very good friend to a large numbers of soldiers' wives and widows in the borough, by whom she is held in great respect. She has taken a prominent part in the work connected with the various relief funds and also the fund for providing comforts for Rossendale lads serving abroad with the Army and Navy. She is President of the recently-formed Borough Girls' Guild, which has a membership of 1,000 girls and young women, who are busily engaged in knitting and sewing various articles for local and wounded soldiers who are serving abroad.' *Rossendale Free Press*, 5 November 1915. She also paid for the first British war memorial, which was unveiled in Rawtenstall cemetery in September 1915.

Figure 1.3 War memorial, sculpted by Louis Roslyn, Rawtenstall, 1929. Steven Bennett / Alamy Stock Photo.

take. Initially, a memorial swimming bath was proposed 'as a suitable and useful War Memorial'. This fell through, and local authorities received letters from both the British Legion and Carrie Whitehead proposing alternatives.[29] It is clear from the 1929 unveiling ceremony that it was Whitehead's vision that won through. Her speech underlined the ways in which the committee intended the memorial to represent the sacrifices of a whole community – including women – during the war:

The War Memorial Committee has erected this tribute of honour not only for the men who have left us but for all who took part in winning safety for our Empire. The architect who has designed it has had our desires in view. There is nothing sad in the colour of the granite, nor in the artistic shading of its bronze, the figures carved round it are full of life as they march along. . . . This tribute of honour has a threefold link. It is erected in honour of those who made the supreme sacrifice, it is erected in honour of those who fought for us and got back, some, thank God, physically fit, some halting and maimed and blinded who will suffer on for our sakes, all the days of their lives, and it is erected in honour of all who worked strenuously at home to help to win the war: to the miners, the munition workers, the land workers, the manual and textile workers, the matrons, sisters, nurses and girls who worked in our

---

[29] *The Manchester Guardian*, 1 July 1929; Rawtenstall Corporation Minutes, 1923–24, Rawtenstall Library.

Figure 1.4 Carrie Whitehead © Lafayette.

hospitals, and to the women the men left behind them to carry on in their homes . . ., the women who did their bit day and night to keep the home fires burning.[30]

In this example, it is not just the procession and audience at the unveiling that functions to represent all facets of a community, but the iconography of the memorial itself. Carrie Whitehead was elected to the town council in 1920 as Rawtenstall's first female councillor, and in the 1930s became Alderman and served on the magistrate's bench and as Mayor.[31] She was deeply involved in community life, serving on multiple committees, as did many unmarried and childless women of her class. Although she was not an active suffragist, the war memorial reflects her belief in the importance of women's contributions in wartime, and its inscription deliberately empha-sises the fact that the memorial is erected to honour the sacrifices of male and female civilians as well as those of servicemen: 'A tribute of honour to the men who made the supreme sacrifice/ to the men who came back/ and to those who worked at home/ to win safety for the Empire'.

---

[30] *Rossendale Free Press*, 6 July 1929.   [31] *Rossendale Free Press*, 29 September 1945.

It is apparent from her speech that Whitehead was aware that the committee's decision might be controversial, and she defended the memorial from accusations of disrespect for the dead. Other commentators, while not rejecting its meanings completely, were quick to emphasise elements that shore up more traditional understandings of gendered roles in wartime. The newspaper report published a letter from the local vicar that placed the emphasis back upon the widow and child as embodiments of bereavement:

If the artist's idea was to remind future generations ... of four years of close and solid cooperative effort, when class distinctions were well-nigh swept away in face of a common danger and for the sake of a common cause ... then indeed the artist has admirably achieved his purpose. ... I am particularly glad that the mother and child are represented, for it was my lot to witness their long anxiety and lonely grief, and the noble part they played.[32]

The journalist reporting on the ceremony was careful to stress the superiority of the dead serviceman's sacrifice, 'the gallant dead who are the most alive of all [Rawtenstall's] citizens', while commenting that 'the most poignant group were the widows and children of the fallen.' As the discussions of the Rawtenstall memorial show, evocations of women's sacrifice in wartime could relate both to their bereavement and to their efforts as paid or unpaid war workers. Memorials that emphasise collective struggle and sacrifice tend to pay attention to both of these aspects, offering as they do so a broad definition of service that encompasses a wide variety of wartime activities, including those carried out by women and other non-combatants.

An emphasis on active service and communal sacrifice in wartime, this time on a national scale, is also central to the Scottish National War Memorial in Edinburgh Castle, which was finally unveiled in 1927 after being first mooted as a possibility during the war, and to the enormous painting of more than 5,000 French and Allied figures entitled the 'Panthéon de la guerre' ('Pantheon of the War'), begun in Paris in 1914 and first exhibited two weeks before the Armistice. Both are interesting examples of patriotic and militarist memorials that sought to carve out a space for women's contributions – albeit within carefully designated and controlled parameters – within their commemorative discourse. The Scottish National War Memorial was the brainchild of the Duke of Atholl, who dominated the committee, and largely reflects his nationalist-Unionist and Presbyterian beliefs.[33] Its genesis lay initially in Atholl's

[32] *Rossendale Free Press*, 6 July 1929.
[33] See Macleod, 'By Scottish Hands'; Angus Calder, 'The Scottish National War Memorial', in William Kidd and Bryan Murdoch (eds.), *Memory and Memorials: The Commemorative Century* (Aldershot: Ashgate, 2004), pp. 61–74.

anger at an announcement made in 1917 by Commissioner for Works Sir Alfred Mond that the National War Memorial in London would be a site 'in which he was sure that Highland Regiments would be proud to put their trophies and be memorialised'.[34] The memorial aims to be comprehensively inclusive, embracing Scottish contributions to the war effort made by all Scots both at home and abroad. This was partly for financial reasons: the memorial cost more than £100,000, and propaganda and fund-raising efforts 'played on the shared sense of Scottishness throughout the diaspora'.[35] But its inclusivity also serves to emphasise a shared sense of the losses borne and service rendered by a whole nation.

The theme of collective sacrifice resonates throughout the iconography of the memorial, with bays in the Hall of Heroes dedicated not only to the twelve Scottish regiments and to Scots who were killed serving in other regiments, but also to non-combatants and to various auxiliary services, including women's services. In the bay dedicated to non-combatants, the viewer is even asked to '[r]emember also the humble beasts that served and died', with an accompanying panel depicting canaries and mice, and a frieze featuring the heads of various transport animals, both by sculptor Phyllis Bone.[36] At the heart of the memorial is an octagonal shrine with a bronze frieze sculpted by Alice Meredith-Williams, who also sculpted the bronze panels to the Women's Services and Nursing Services in the south-west bay of the Hall of Heroes. This detailed frieze is reminiscent of Roslyn's Rawtenstall memorial, in that it reproduces a series of figures performing different war-related tasks, incarnating the collective efforts necessitated by total war. The Scottish example, however, containing seventy-four figures, includes a greater variety of combatant, auxiliary and non-combatant roles, from members of the Russian Expeditionary Force wearing snowshoes and of the Imperial Camel Corps in shorts and sun helmet, to chaplains, munitions workers, signallers, drivers, pipers and air mechanics, all carrying symbolic tools of their trades. The female figures include nurses and members of the main auxiliary services, the WAAC, Voluntary Aid Detachment (VAD), Women's Royal Naval Service (WRNS) and Women's Royal Air Force (WRAF). The women may come last in the procession, but their realist uniforms, poses and positioning mirror those of the men they stand alongside. The inscription

---

[34] Letter from Atholl dated 18 August 1919. Papers of the Duke and Duchess of Atholl concerning the Scottish War Memorial. Box 1, Scottish National War Memorial Committee. Reports and correspondence, National Library of Scotland.

[35] Macleod, 'By Scottish Hands', p. 82.

[36] For a detailed description of the Scottish National War Memorial, see Ian Hay, *Their Name Liveth: The Book of the Scottish National War Memorial* (London: Bodley Head, 1931).

in the shrine – 'The souls of the righteous are in the hands of God. There shall no evil happen to them. They are in peace.' – strongly suggests to the viewer that this is a procession of the glorious dead, resuscitated by the remembrance of the living. Angus Calder argues that the procession 'moves like a herd of doomed creatures', equating them to Wilfred Owen's 'those who die as cattle'.[37] Yet the theme of redemption and resurrection is omnipresent in the Scottish National War Memorial, suggested in particular by Charles d'Orville Pilkington Jackson's statue entitled 'Réveillé' over the doorway of the Hall of Honour, which represents purification through sacrifice. The prominence of this statue serves to distance Meredith-Williams' frieze from Owen's bleaker vision.[38] If the theme of redemption through sacrifice is familiar to interwar commemoration, the inclusion of male and female non-combatants in the frieze, and the fact that in the memorial more generally evocations of combatants are accompanied not only by those of male and female auxiliaries but also by scenes from the home front such as factory work and air raids, troubles a simple hierarchy in which grateful civilians pay homage to sacrificial servicemen. Combatants and non-combatants, men and women, are included in the procession of the 'glorious dead' by virtue of their efforts in wartime; all are situated as deserving of national gratitude and commemoration.[39] This desire for inclusion was repeated in the unveiling ceremony, in which the Duchess of Atholl wore her VAD uniform and presented the women's Roll of Honour, followed by uniformed representatives of different women's services.[40]

There are interesting parallels between the frieze in the Scottish National War Memorial and the 'Panthéon de la guerre' memorial

---

[37] Calder, 'The Scottish National War Memorial', p. 71.

[38] Hay decodes the statue 'Réveillé' in the following terms: 'The figure represents the Spirit of Man purified by the flames of Sacrifice. The flames still play about the feet: the left hand grasps a broken sword blade, symbol of the End of War, while the right holds the hilt aloft – the Cross Triumphant. The eyes gaze into the Shrine; indeed they seem to penetrate beyond, as if beholding a new Heaven and a new Earth.' Hay, *Their Name Liveth*, p. 86.

[39] The inclusion of non-combatant scenes is rare in First World War commemoration, although St Mary's Church, Swaffham Prior, Cambridgeshire, includes amongst the interesting 1919 set of memorial windows designed by Thomas Figgins Curtis scenes of male orderlies and female nurses, female munitions workers, a military chaplain and a YMCA hut. See Imperial War Museum, War Memorials Register, 3573.

[40] While the iconography of the war memorial is inclusive, there was some debate as to which areas of women's war work should be represented during the unveiling ceremony. The Duke of Atholl commented in this regard that 'I do not see why the Women's Land Army, which was not an Army or anything more to do with the War than munition[s] workers, should be represented,' and favoured nurses and the women's auxiliary services. Letter from Atholl to Scottish Command, 29 June 1927, Box 23, Opening of the Scottish National War Memorial 1927, National Library of Scotland.

painting, which was produced by twenty artists under the leadership of Pierre Carrier-Belleuse and Auguste-François Gorguet. Billed as the 'world's largest painting', the 'Panthéon' was an enormous cyclorama of the war featuring about 5,000 individual full-length portraits of men and women from the Allied nations. It was unveiled to great public acclaim by President Raymond Poincaré on 19 October 1918 in a special building constructed near the Hôtel des Invalides.[41] The largest section of the painting featured a 'Temple of Glory' devoted to France's heroes. René Bazin's preface to the catalogue when the work was first exhibited describes the scene in terms of a 'Sacred Union' of French men and women rising up in unison to defeat an old enemy: 'For four years, a magnificent multitude has risen up from our towns and countryside, a mass of young people, relatives and friends, who have suffered and struggled to such an extent that the enemy, who had been preparing for war for a long time, did not succeed in their aim to bring the Fatherland to its knees.'[42] The portraits of the French heroes were placed on an enormous staircase and organised according to rank, with generals and other civilian leaders occupying the base (Figure 1.5). While the majority were servicemen, several women were included in their number. The roll call of French heroines included the usual suspects of nurses, resistant nuns and brave employees of the French postal service who defied the enemy advance. Names lauded by the press and decorated by the state, such as Emilienne Moreau, Edith Cavell, Louise de Bettignies, Soeur Julie and Jeanne Macherez, all featured.[43] The Pantheon painters did not stray far from propagandists in their choices of which women deserved recognition as war heroines.[44]

Directly facing the Staircase of Heroes was a war memorial, on the top of which was a cenotaph held aloft by four French infantry soldiers in bronze. At the base of the memorial, and dwarfed by its size and scale, knelt a weeping widow cloaked in black, head bowed, grieving and paying tribute. Here, then, was woman as the embodiment of a nation in mourning for all its dead heroes, whether officially recognised as such or not, her

[41] Mark Levitch, *Panthéon de la Guerre: Reconfiguring a Panorama of the Great War* (Columbia: University of Missouri Press, 2006), pp. 7–8. It was visited not only by Parisians but equally by Allied servicemen, servicewomen and nurses while on leave. See for example Liddle Collection, Brotherton Library, University of Leeds, GA/CEM/9.

[42] René Bazin, Preface to exhibition catalogue, *Le Panthéon de la guerre*, 1918, Bibliothèque Nationale Française.

[43] See Chapter 2 for a discussion of these war heroines.

[44] As Levitch notes, this was also the case for the other Allied nations represented: 'Most national sections included – albeit rarely prominently – a handful of female figures. Most often, these consisted of some combination of nurses, charity workers, civilian women who had suffered under or resisted the Germans, royalty, and generic female types (such as refugees), often in national costume.' Levitch, *Panthéon*, p. 54.

Figure 1.5 'Panthéon de la guerre', Staircase of Heroes, 1918.

wreath bearing the inscription 'Aux héros ignorés' ('To the unknown heroes'). Yet it remains significant that she was not the only female figure in the painting. Opposite her were scores of women whom the painters designated as exceptional, and who took their place on the staircase deserving of civilian praise and gratitude like the servicemen (many of whom had been killed in action) that they stood beside.

The 'Panthéon de la guerre' should be understood as a 'home-front-based view of the war', which 'lost credibility as combatants started narrating their own trench experiences'.[45] Unlike the Scottish National War Memorial, it was begun in the early days of the war, and its aesthetic and ideological messages became less palatable in the interwar years. But like Roslyn's memorial in Rawtenstall and Meredith Williams' frieze in

[45] Mark Levitch, 'The Great War Re-Remembered: The Fragmentation of the World's Largest Painting', in Nicholas J. Saunders (ed.), *Matters of Conflict: Material Culture, Memory and the First World War* (London: Routledge, 2004), pp. 90–109 (p. 97).

Edinburgh, the 'Panthéon de la Guerre' depicted women as actively involved in the war effort in order to construct an 'imagined community' of citizens who had suffered and sacrificed together, and who were subsequently united in mourning for their dead. This vision was summed up in the text written by Charlotte Carrier-Belleuse, daughter of the painter and secretary of the 'Panthéon', which was produced to accompany a coloured slide show that toured the country in 1919. Her narrative guided the audience to perceive all French citizens as unified in their sacrifices and glories. As the first slide was shown, for example, the narrator would read the following words, as if addressing the painted subjects being described:

Here is the imposing crowd: generals and soldiers with your decorated chests, civilians, victims of your devotion, eminent prelates . . ., women, young girls, valiant nurses who cared for your wounded on the very battlefields; all of you, the heroes of France, enter this Temple of Glory triumphantly, Victory is smiling proudly and opening her golden arms to you. For her, you have selflessly spilled your generous blood, here she is, superb, shining down, lighting up your foreheads with her dazzling splendour and scattering laurel leaves at your feet.[46]

Members of the audience were invited not only to pay their respects to their heroic countrymen and women but were equally interpellated themselves as French citizens who may have also served or sacrificed family members during the war, and who deserved a place in the Victory parade. Of course, this vision of unity was far removed from the schisms and discord that were often a feature of interwar debates not only about the meanings and hierarchies of 'war sacrifice', but also about the ways in which the war should be remembered and commemorated. It also failed to address the fact that the continued disenfranchisement of the 'heroines of France' necessarily set them apart from their male counterparts. In terms of the gendered meanings of war commemoration, however, all of the examples discussed in this section carved out a space not only for women as mourners, grieving and paying tribute to the war dead but equally for women's active contributions to the war effort. This use of female figures in commemorative discourse extended women's role beyond that of civilians bereaved, and placed them firmly in the realm of a community of active citizens who had also served.

Women as Veterans

The memorials that constructed a vision of a community united in collective sacrifice still distinguished, though, between the kinds of service

---

[46] Charlotte Carrier-Belleuse, *Le Panthéon de la guerre* (Paris: Georges Michau, 1919), p. 2.

carried out and sacrifices offered by men and by women. Nurses were praised for the way in which they extended their 'devotion' and 'humanity' beyond the home front to the front itself. They were presented as having acted out to the full a specifically female brand of service to their nation, supporting, nurturing and healing the servicemen who were often designated symbolically as their sons or brothers. Other First World War memorials, however, and particularly those that commemorated the relatively few women who were killed on active service during the war, presented women not as feminised citizens but as female veterans, as more direct equivalents of dead servicemen.[47]

Women who were killed in the war proved valuable commodities in forms of political communication designed to tarnish the enemy, as the examples of martyr-heroines Edith Cavell and Louise de Bettignies that I discuss in Chapter 2 demonstrate. Helen Gwynne-Vaughan, Chief Controller in France of the WAAC, makes this point in her memoirs when describing the media response after nine members of the corps were killed during a bombing raid in 1918: 'When I got back to my headquarters I found a group of journalists in the mess all wanting a story and prepared to execrate the enemy for killing women.'[48] During the war, women's deaths were also reported widely in the press, emphasising in the reports a community united in its shared sacrifices. In Britain, nurses and mercantile marine stewardesses had a high profile; in France, 'invasion heroines' dominated the early years, before being replaced with nurses and prisoners of war in the later war years as the press' favoured female victims.

Many women who died, especially nurses or those who worked for the British auxiliary services, were given full military funerals. In Britain, there was a debate in late 1917 between the Army Council and the War Office as to whether members of the WAAC were entitled to a government-funded military funeral, but despite some resistance from the War Office it was agreed that WAACs should have the right to funded funerals.[49] After the war, however, the commemoration of women who

---

[47] Not all women (and not all men) who died while on war service qualified as official 'war deaths'. Deaths in munitions factories, for example, were excluded from government commemoration and pension schemes in both countries. Conversely, some deaths that qualified for pensions purposes as 'war deaths' were not necessarily caused by injuries or illnesses contracted while on active duty. Many deaths in 1918 were due to influenza, for example, the contraction of which may or may not have been the direct result of war service. See Anne-Marie Hughes, 'Death, Service and Citizenship in Britain in the First World War', unpublished PhD thesis, University of Manchester, 2009.

[48] Helen Gwynne-Vaughan, *Service with the Army* (London: Hutchinson, 1942), p. 57.

[49] There was also discussion as to whether the relatives of female members of the auxiliary services who died should be given the same benefits as those of servicemen killed in the war. TNA WO 162/50 'Gratuity for Deceased Officials'.

had died on war service took different forms and served different purposes. While to some extent, like all commemorations, interwar memorials and ceremonies functioned as a focus for private grief, those
exclusively devoted to female deaths were equally, and in some cases
primarily, vehicles for public messages about women and their contribution to the war. Some used women's deaths as a means of flagging up the
sacrifices and importance of certain professions or voluntary groups who
had served in the war, while others used the possibilities offered by the
'ultimate sacrifice', the 'blood tax' paid by a few women, in order to
proclaim publicly the validity of all women's claims to full citizenship.

While nurses sometimes featured in national commemorations of the
dead, there were also memorials instigated by nursing organisations
themselves, both volunteer and professional, commemorating the deaths
of their members. The commemorative discourse in these memorials
combined private mourning with public affirmation of the women's
deaths as honourable war deaths, underlining the organisations' sacrifices
and devotion to the nation, and thereby implicitly demanding public
recognition and gratitude. A French example of this kind of memorial
to nurses was unveiled in 1923 after having been commissioned by one of
the three organisations that made up the French Red Cross, the Union
des Femmes de France (UFF) (Union of Women of France).
The sculptor was Berthe Girardet, who had herself nursed for the UFF
during the war, and who produced several commemorative pieces in the
interwar years.[50] It was unveiled in the headquarters of the UFF in Paris,
and comprised a bas-relief featuring a group of nurses, with two plaques
listing forty-eight UFF members who had died during the war. UFF
president Mme Henri Galli described the bas-relief in the following
terms during the commemoration ceremony: 'With profound artistry
fed by superior intelligence, and with religious sensibility, [Mme
Girardet] has been able to reproduce the solemn dignity and the intense
interior life exuded by these faces … which, as if they had haloes, have the
character of religious icons.'[51] These Red Cross nurses thus embraced, at
least to some extent, dominant conceptions of nurses as transhistorical
incarnations of saintly womanhood. The 1923 ceremony, however, which

[50] Berthe Girardet was a Swiss-born sculptor and wife of the engraver Paul Girardet whose
son, Jean-Paul Girardet, an architect turned pilot, was killed in a flying accident in 1917.
Like Desvallières, Girardet produced sculptures that interpreted the losses of the war
within a Catholic framework of suffering, sacrifice and redemption. Her works included
'A l'hôpital pendant la Grande Guerre' (1919) and 'Aux héros inconnus' featuring
a mourning female figure that was exhibited in the ossuary at Douaumont in 1923.
Placed on a classical pedestal and wreathed in victory laurels, a veiled Virgin holds her
fingers to her lips, suggesting the need for respect, silence and resignation.
[51] *Bulletin mensuel de l'Union des Femmes de France*, 1 January 1923, p. 9.

took place during a monthly meeting of the UFF nurse–veterans' association, functioned equally to shore up the identity of the Red Cross nurses
as veterans. The president's speech directly aligned the nurses' deaths
with the 'supreme sacrifice' made by soldiers:

The emotions that bring us together today are sorrow and grief, but also pride,
and we reverently pay homage to the memory of these valiant women who paid
with their life for the fervent sense of altruism, heroic devotion and superior and
patriotic virtues that they possessed. ... Let the memory of the generosity of the
nurses' lives that you grieve for ..., of the good that they did, ... and finally the
memory that they too served France as her heroic defenders, that they carried out
the noblest of missions, let these poignant memories relieve your suffering.[52]

The discourse here is familiar from unveiling ceremonies for war memorials that took place in every town and village in France and Britain in the
years following the Armistice, in which the grieving audience was 'urged
to convert its grief to pride', except that the subjects of grief, gratitude and
glorification were women rather than male combatants.[53]

It is a discourse that was repeated in other commemorative activities for
First World War nurses that took place after the Armistice. The 1919
report by board member Colonel de Witt-Guizot on the activities of the
Société de Secours aux Blessés militaires (SSBM) (Society to Aid
Wounded Soldiers) used overtly military language and nationalist ima-
gery when evoking the wartime deaths of the Society's nurses:

If I could I would invite you to stand, shout 'Attention' and call for the playing of
the Last Post. ... To honour their memory I want the General Secretary to
establish a 'Roll of Honour' which, when read in schools and in family homes,
will remind our children that French women spilled blood for them on the sacred
ground of their homeland ... and future generations will pass on their names,
wreathed in glory.[54]

Similarly, the newspaper article recounting the unveiling ceremony of the
Irish Nurses' Memorial, in Arbour Hill Garrison Chapel, Dublin, in 1921,
was entitled 'What Sacrifice May Teach', and the Rev C. A. Peacocke's
sermon, while praising the Irish nurses for 'showing the highest qualities of
womanhood', equally asked the congregation to 'go away strengthened,
helped and lifted up' after seeing in the memorial 'a wonderful record of

---

[52] *Bulletin mensuel*, p. 7.
[53] Catherine Moriarty, 'Private Grief and Public Remembrance: British First World War
Memorials', in Martin Evans and Ken Lunn (eds.), *War and Memory in the Twentieth
Century* (Oxford: Berg, 1997), pp. 125–42 (p. 135).
[54] Croix Rouge Française, *Assemblée générale du 23 nov 1919 de la Société de Secours aux
Blessés Militaires: Rapport du Colonel de Witt-Guizot* (Paris: Au siège de la Société,
1920), p. 9.

service, of character, of fortitude, of the highest and best gifts that God gave to man and woman'.[55]

Many commemorations of female nurses who died on war service contained in this way a blend of traditional images of nurses as icons of womanhood with a discourse that set up their deaths as quasi-military sacrifices for the defence of the nation, or of civilisation itself. During the service held for the unveiling of the Scottish Nurses' War Memorial at St Giles' Cathedral in Edinburgh in 1921, for example, General Sir Francis Davis simultaneously praised the 'sympathy and magic touch' of the nurses as 'ministering angels', while stating that the memorial should serve as an example to future generations, asserting: 'These ladies did not earn their crown in the day of battle. They earned it in the patient discharge of their duty, some killed by enemy action, victims of the malice of our foes'.[56] In France, the report of the unveiling of the 'Monument à la memoire des infirmières' ('Monument to the Memory of Nurses') in Berck-sur-Mer (Pas de Calais), unveiled in 1924, recognised the 'sublime role' and 'unceasing devotion' of the nurses while emphasising that they had 'fallen on the field of honour', and noting that the ceremony ended with 'the tricolor, the flag of glory and gratitude, that covered the monument being slowly raised'.[57] The equation of nurses killed in the war with the male war dead is equally discernible in a statue designed by Maxime Réal del Sarte, a prolific nationalist sculptor of war memorials and Joan of Arc devotee, for the 'Monument national aux infirmières françaises tuées à l'ennemi' ('National Monument to French Nurses Killed in Action') in Pierrefonds (Oise).[58] This 1933 statue featured an androgynous *pietà* figure with outstretched arms supporting the body of a dead nurse, whose arms are also outstretched and who is dressed in medieval clothing reminiscent of Joan of Arc. Its design reverses in gender terms many *pietàs* that feature on French war memorials, including some examples by Réal del Sarte

---

[55] *Irish Times*, 7 November 1921.   [56] *Glasgow Herald*, 4 November 1921.

[57] *L'Echo de Paris*, 24 November 1924.

[58] The text on the 1933 fundraising leaflet for this memorial also combined traditional images of nurses as 'animated by altruism and reminding poilus, by their gentleness and their self-abnegation, of a mother, wife or sister', with a direct alignment to dead soldiers: 'France has shown that she knows how to remember her dead: since the war her soil has been covered in memorials erected to the memory of those who died for their country. But a cruel omission must be noted: in this vast, pious homage to combatants killed in action no memorials remember the heroic sacrifice of our nurses.' Leaflet, 'Monument national aux infirmières françaises tuées à l'ennemi', 1933, Bibliothèque Marguerite Durand. The memorial was eventually erected on the spot where one Red Cross nurse, Jeanne Elisabeth Jalaguier, was killed aged twenty-seven in an air raid on 20 August 1918, and included an inscription of her citation for bravery.

himself, in which the body of a Christ-like French infantryman is supported in the protective embrace of a Mary or Joan of Arc figure.[59]

While military authorities and veterans tended to prioritise transcendent feminine virtues in memorials to nurses killed in the war, nursing organisations themselves tended to place the emphasis more on the risks to life and health of wartime nursing in a bid to underscore the value of their service to the state. In 1922, the British Military Nurses Memorial Committee, chaired by Matron-in-Chief Sarah Oram, commissioned a statue for St Paul's cathedral by sculptor Benjamin Clemens entitled 'Bombed' (that was ultimately not accepted by the cathedral authorities due to lack of space), a commission that suggests a desire for a representation of nursing work that emphasised front-line risk.[60] The sculpted figures on the Scottish nurses' memorial in St Giles' Cathedral in Edinburgh are also interesting in terms of the meanings with which they are charged. The stylised female figure on the left is kneeling, her head bowed, carrying a wreath, while the warrior-like female figure on the right holds her head upright and carries a dagger in her hand. Above the statues are a list of the Scottish members of the Queen Alexandra's Imperial Military Nursing Service (QAIMNS) and Queen Alexandra's Imperial Military Nursing Service Reserve (QAIMNSR) killed in the war. The iconography of this memorial pointed to the dual role of the nurses, both as mourners paying tribute to their lost colleagues and the men they nursed, and as active participants who risked death.

In sum, although it is true, as Sherman notes, that in the majority of commemorative activities 'unlike dead soldiers women . . . could serve as models only as remembering subjects paying tribute to men', the ceremonies that commemorated women who had been killed in the war challenged, whether directly or indirectly, an understanding of war service and sacrifice based exclusively on gender.[61] In raising the dead nurses to the level of lost combatants, the nursing organisations were, on one hand, attempting to comfort bereaved families, and, on the other, making public, political gestures. Judith Butler argued in relation to the commemoration of the 9/11 terrorist attacks in New York that 'the obituary functions as the instrument by which grievability is publicly distributed.

---

[59] See for example Réal del Sarte's *pietà* on the Monument du 106e regiment, Les Eparges. Reproduced in Martin Hurcombe, 'Raising the Dead: Visual Representations of the Combatant's Body in Interwar France', *Journal of War and Culture Studies* 1: 2 (2008): 159–74 (p. 169).

[60] Minutes of the Military Nurses Memorial Committee, 23 June 1922, TNA WO 222/2135. Benjamin Clemens sculpted the realist bronze pieces 'St John's Ambulance Bearers' in 1919 and 'VAD Worker' in 1920 that no doubt had been seen by the committee.

[61] Sherman, *The Construction of Memory*, p. 305.

It is the means by which a life becomes, or fails to become, a publicly grievable life, an icon for national self-recognition, the means by which a life becomes noteworthy.'[62] This insight is relevant to the interwar context in which certain individuals and organisations were claiming lost female lives as 'publicly grievable' sacrifices for the nation.

The impulse to recognise the deaths of women war workers as equivalent in status and meaning to those of combatants was particularly evident in national monuments to women killed in the war that were erected in France and Britain. The 'Monument à la gloire des infirmières française et alliées victimes de leur dévouement' ('Monument to the Glory of French and Allied Nurses, Victims of Their Devotion') was unveiled in Rheims in 1924. Its committee was presided over by eighty-eight-year-old Juliette Adam, well-known feminist and *femme du monde* who had converted to Catholicism in the early 1900s.[63] The iconography of Denys Puech's sculpture clearly drew on the familiar, Catholic-inspired French vision of nurses as grieving *pietàs* over the dead Christ/poilu (Figure 1.6). If the figures placed the nurse in a familiar position of idealised maternal devotion, however, the memorial's inscription aligned the work of nurses with that of soldiers: 'On land and sea, they shared the soldier's dangers. They braved, in shelled and torpedoed hospitals, enemy fire, contagion and exhaustion. In relieving suffering, they aided victory. Let us honour them. They will forever live in the memory of their proud and grateful nations.' The design and inscription were undoubtedly influenced by the sentiments of the committee's chair, Juliette Adam, reflecting her religious faith and her fervent patriotism as well as her continued support for women's rights, including the right to vote. The genesis of the Rheims nurses' memorial was not sparked by private grief but by the committee's, and particularly Adam's, desire to express publicly a combination of religious, nationalist and feminist beliefs.

A strident Germanophobe, Adam wrote in a letter at the outbreak of the war that '[c]ertain words are ringing in my head: France, Fatherland, Alsace-Lorraine', and her speech at the unveiling ceremony reiterated her *revanchiste* sentiments, expressing the wish that the monument should be

[62] Judith Butler, *Precarious Life: The Power of Mourning and Violence* (London: Verso, 2004), p. 34.
[63] Juliette Adam published an early feminist text, *Les Idées antiproudhoniennes*, in 1858, and remained an active suffragist all her life. She published *Chrétienne* in 1913 (after having published *Païenne* in 1883), publicly announcing her conversion to Catholicism. Throughout the war she devoted herself to the war effort, helping to fundraise for charities aimed at helping soldiers, and founding *Le Journal des Poilus*. She continued to write articles attacking Germany as she had done since the Franco–Prussian War, but also published in 1919 *La Vie des âmes*, expressing her horror at the loss of life. See Anne Hogenhuis-Seliverstoff, *Juliette Adam* (Paris: L'Harmattan, 2001).

Figure 1.6 'Monument à la gloire des infirmières françaises et alliées victimes de leur dévouement', Rheims, sculpted by Denis Puech, 1924. Photograph by Ludovic Péron.

a 'call to arms for future nurses' as she felt that the hopes of pacifists were illusory given her experiences in two wars against the same enemy.[64]

---

[64] Letter from Juliette Adam to Queen Amélie, 5 August 1914. ANF Fonds de la famille d'Orléans; *Bulletin mensuel de l'Union des Femmes de France*, 1 February 1925, p. 29.

If one of her aims was to celebrate France's victory against the 'old enemy' and warn against future attacks, another was to promote feminist causes, particularly female suffrage, through the glorification of women's war work and war deaths. Like the majority of French feminists, and particularly in her later years, Adam espoused moderate Republican reformist feminism, adhering to the rhetoric and ideology of 'separate spheres' in order to argue for the need to recognise women's particular contribution to the state.[65] Her speech, like the monument's inscription, draws on traditional understandings of nurses' 'feminine' virtues, describing the 'courageous devotion' of the 'heroic victims', while at the same time underlining the equivalence of their sacrifice to that of male combatants. One way in which the latter is done is through the compilation of a 'Livre d'or' ('Roll of Honour') listing 979 names of Allied nurses who died in France, with an accompanying inscription on the monument stating that '[t]he town of Rheims will faithfully keep in its archives the Roll of Honour of these noble women who fell on the field of honour.'[66]

Thomas Laqueur argues that the extensive naming of the dead of the First World War, particularly significant for the hundreds of thousands of cases of missing bodies, was 'an enormous and unprecedented part of . . . the memorials of the war'. Naming a soldier (and especially a common soldier who might normally have expected to be buried anonymously in a common grave) was to individualise, to commemorate and to dignify him without necessarily limiting the meaning of his death to a specific 'cause', to resort 'to a sort of commemorative hyper-nominalism'.[67] Recording, inscribing and sacralising the names of women who had died as a result of war service was thus a way of integrating their deaths within the mainstream of First World War commemoration. In the case of the Rheims monument, other officials followed Adam's lead and embraced her categorisation of the nurses as 'mort[es] pour la France'. Sub-Prefect of Rheims M. Mennecier, for example, declared 'on behalf of the government' in his speech that:

Today, perhaps for the first time, but forever more, we will proclaim together in front of this monument, illuminated like other monuments by the glory of sacrifice, that it is right and necessary to unite in our gratitude, as they have already been united in immortality, the names of soldiers killed in action with

---

[65] See Christine Bard, *Les Filles de Marianne: Histoire des féminismes* (Paris: Fayard, 1995).

[66] These were originally deposited in the Red Cross archives in Rheims, but were transferred to the Rheims municipal archives in 2005.

[67] Thomas Laqueur, 'Memory and Naming in the Great War', in John Gillis (ed.), *Memory and Commemoration* (Princeton, NJ: Princeton University Press, 1993), pp. 150–67 (pp. 164, 160).

the names of these admirable nurses who also, and in their thousands, responded to the call to arms, risked life and limb in order to carry out their duties.[68]

Thus, while the iconography of the Rheims memorial to Allied nurses positioned them as 'ministering angels', the 'livre d'or' and other inscriptions placed their deaths squarely within the framework of military commemoration.

A similar desire to construct women as veterans deserving of gratitude and recognition can be seen in a British memorial to women killed in the Great War that was unveiled in York Minster in 1925. The memorial consisted of the restoration of the 'Five Sisters' Window' and the erection of an oak screen with a Roll of Honour naming 1,513 women from Britain and the Dominions who died as a result of war service.[69] The fund-raising for the memorial was carried out by two women, Helen Little, a colonel's wife who was involved in nursing work in Egypt during the war, and Almyra Gray, a suffragist, former president of the National Council for Women Workers (which became the National Council of Women) (NCWW), local magistrate and social reformist.[70] The memorial was in part agreed to by the Chapter and Dean of York Minster because of the desperate need for funds to restore the stained glass windows, which had been removed and buried because of the threat of bombing in 1916.[71] The women carried out the fundraising independently, and raised the £3,500 needed in nine weeks.[72] The publicity material, as for many memorials, emphasised the extent to which the memorial could be a unifying force for women from different social classes, highlighting donations from Princess Mary at one end of the spectrum, and 'an aged woman pensioner [who] gave a week's pension' at the other.[73] Through Almyra Gray's international connections, forged through her work with the NCWW, the memorial committee also organised ceremonies to be carried out simultaneously in Canada, South Africa and Australia,

---

[68] *Bulletin mensuel*, p. 30.

[69] I would like to thank John Anderson for providing an accurate figure for the women named on the memorial.

[70] Helen Little went to Egypt with her husband, Charles Blakeway Little, a retired colonel of the Somerset Light Infantry. Almyra Gray served on the York Board of Guardians and became a recognised authority on women's health and citizenship. She founded the York Women's Citizens' Association and the York Health and Housing Reform Association and was senior stewardess of the York Female Friendly Society. *Yorkshire Gazette*, 10 November 1933; *York Herald*, 10 November 1939.

[71] 'Report of the Inaugural Meeting Held on 9 November 1920, Chapter House, York Minster', York Minster Window Preservation Fund, York Minster Archives.

[72] Minutes of the Window Preservation Fund, 1 June 1923, York Minster Archives.

[73] Helen D. Little, *The Restoration of the Five Sisters' Window, York Minster* (York: Yorkshire Herald Newspapers, 1925), York Minster Archives.

thereby emphasising the contributions of what Gray referred to as the 'Imperial sisterhood'.[74]

Like Adam, Little and Gray were motivated by a combination of religious, patriotic and feminist beliefs in their desire to erect a memorial to women who died in the war. In a letter to *The Times* published at her request after her death in 1933, Helen Little narrated a vision that she claimed lay behind the memorial project:

On November 30, 1922, I had the following vision: I was going into Evensong and entered by the South Transept door as usual. Just as I reached the choir door in the dim light I saw two little figures in white standing hand in hand in the middle of the North Transept: one beckoning to me, the other pointing upwards to the window. I moved towards them, and then recognised my two little sisters, both of whom had died as children. As I followed the little pointing finger I saw the window move slowly backwards as if on hinges, revealing the most exquisite garden . . . a number of girls and women . . . came gliding up the garden in misty grey-blue garments. They came nearer and nearer . . . I looked down and saw that both my little sisters were pointing upwards to the window. I had risen in my sleep, and was standing when I woke, and cried out, my words being heard by my husband – 'The Sisters' Window for the Sisters'.[75]

Little's mystical vision is redolent of the rise in popularity of spiritualism, and the many cultural representations of the 'return of the dead' that were produced during the interwar period. Such representations functioned, as Martin Hurcombe notes, 'not . . . to reassure the living but to unsettle and to challenge them', embodying a 'metaphor of redemptive sacrifice that suggests the debt owed to the war dead and, by association, to . . . veterans'.[76] Little's dead sisters in the vision functioned to remind her (and by extension the memorial's viewers) of the sacrifices made by, and the debt owed to, the ghostly 'girls and women' who died in the war. She stressed the duty of living women to remember these dead 'sisters', a duty that was effectively fulfilled via the inscription on the painted Roll of Honour: 'This screen records the names of women of the Empire who gave their lives in the war 1914–1918 to whose memory the Five Sisters' Window was restored by women.'

At the same time, as Hurcombe argues, representations of the returning war dead implied by extension a debt of gratitude to all veterans, in this case specifically to female veterans. This was a vital function of both the Rheims and York memorials, whose erection was about the debts society

---

[74] Little, *Restoration*.

[75] *The Times*, 30 November 1933. Helen Little was born Helen Drage Beckwith and was the daughter of clergyman Ambrose Beckwith. Her sister Mary Margaret E. Beckwith died aged two in 1872, and a second sister, Edith Julia Beckwith, died aged four in 1878.

[76] Hurcombe, 'Raising the Dead', pp. 159–60. See also Winter, *Sites of Memory*.

owed to the living as well as to the dead women war workers. The Five Sisters' Memorial in particular flagged up the dual roles of women, as mourners carrying out acts of remembrance, and as active participants, united in Little's vision in a kind of mystical universal sisterhood. The public aims of the York memorial were openly acknowledged by the memorial committee. In the same letter, for example, Little stated:

During the early part of the war I was present when the first trainloads of wounded arrived at Cairo from Gallipoli, and was witness to the untiring devotion under great difficulties of the nurses and other women who gave themselves up, entirely regardless of their own health, in some cases with fatal results, to alleviate the suffering of the men. After the war was over, when memorials on all sides were being erected to our brothers, I often thought that our sisters who also made the same sacrifice appeared to have been forgotten.

Here, she expressed the desire to endow female sacrifices with the same status as male sacrifices, implying that war commemoration in the 1920s had been hitherto inadequate in its acknowledgement of the part played by women.

The glorification of female war work was no doubt one of the reasons the scheme appealed so readily to suffragist and social activist Almyra Gray, who mobilised 'mayoresses, teachers, nurses, the Branches of the National Council of Women, members of Women's Institutes, organized Units and many others' to great effect.[77] The two women also went to great lengths to compile as full a list as possible of the dead, corresponding with numerous government departments in Britain and in the Dominions.[78] The unveiling ceremony on 26 June 1925 was designed to highlight similarities between male and female service and sacrifice. While the Duke of York unveiled the York municipal war memorial erected to the 1,162 men of York killed in the war, the Duchess of York did the same for the Five Sisters' Window memorial in the Minster. The Duke of York inspected troops and addressed veterans; the Duchess of York inspected guards of honour composed of seventy female VADs of the North Riding of York British Red Cross Society and fifty Girl Guides.[79] The address by Cosmo Lang, Archbishop of York, underscored this message in his address, making a direct reference to the 1918 Representation of the People Act as another 'great memorial' to women's war service: 'Through [the window's] pure and delicate colours there now shines and will ever shine the light of service and self-sacrifice

[77] Little, *Restoration*.
[78] Note that cross-referencing with the Commonwealth War Graves Commission database shows the list in York to be incomplete, and there are several spelling errors.
[79] Souvenir and Form of Service, The Unveiling of the Five Sisters' Window and the War Memorial, 24 June 1925, York Minster archives.

which ennobled the women of our land and Empire in the dark days of the Great War. ... Their loyalty, efficiency and devotion have already won a great memorial in the gift to women of full citizenship of the Empire.'[80]

Conclusion

Hundreds of thousands of women actively participated in the rites and rituals of commemoration. For some, memorials to both men and women were focuses of private mourning for friends and relatives. The York Minster archives, for example, contain letters from relatives of the named women, expressing their pride and gratitude for the public commemoration of their loved ones.[81] For others, memorialisation constituted an opportunity to make a bold public statement about women's value to the state as volunteers or workers during a period of crisis, and to demand the recognition and rewards this deserved. The latter role was generally confined to a small majority of socially and politically elite women, and thus reflected their political and class interests as well as their religious or ideological beliefs. Juliette Adam, Helen Little and Almyra Gray were all elite women whose roles on war memorial committees were motivated at least in part by a drive to include women in the ranks of the 'glorious dead', and thereby stake a claim for the importance of women's sacrifices for the nation during the war.

As the examples in this chapter demonstrate, moreover, it was not only committed suffragists or feminist activists who manifested a desire to construct women as honourable citizens or as veterans deserving of civilian gratitude, equating their war activities with those of the millions of male combatants who died. Indeed, the Duchess of Atholl, who was intimately involved along with her husband in the decision to commemorate women's services as part of the Scottish National War Memorial, was a noted anti-suffragist before the war and opposed equal suffrage in 1924.[82] It is true that in both nations feminists regularly turned to women's war service as possible leverage in their women's rights campaigns. Yet the rhetoric in the unveiling ceremonies of memorials to dead

---

[80] *York Herald*, 26 June 1925.
[81] See for example letter from Catherine Whittell, sister of QAIMNS nurse Annie Gledhill, 1 October 1926, York Minster Archives. Gledhill died of dysentery while nursing in Palestine in 1918, TNA WO 399/3147. There are also letters in the Imperial War Museum from relatives of the women whose names were included in the Roll of Honour organised by Agnes Conway for the Imperial War Museum Women's Work Collection, expressing similar sentiments of pride at their relatives' deaths being recognised as war deaths. Women's Work Sub-Committee War Shrine Correspondence, IWM, EN1/3/DEA/20.
[82] Gullace, *'The Blood of Our Sons'*, p. 188.

nurses, including that of French Republican politicians, church and army
officials, many of whom were anti-feminist, also aligned these women to
male combatants and demanded the gratitude and respect of viewers and
attendees. In both nations, women's deaths, like those of militarised men,
were frequently placed within a patriotic, Christian-inflected understanding of sacrifice. The women were presented as having died, Christ-like, to
save not only their nation, but civilisation itself.[83] It is important to
acknowledge that for all the rhetoric of women's quasi-military sacrifice
there was clearly no equivalent risk in women's war work – not only were
the numbers killed a fraction of those of male combatants, but the relative
risk to life (the 'blood tax') was also low.[84] However, female service and
sacrifice was not absent from interwar commemoration. Women in the
interwar period often enacted a living image of female service, by parading
in uniforms at unveiling ceremonies.[85] Memorials were erected to women
who had died on active service, thereby raising their deaths to the level of
'supreme sacrifice'. In so doing, they implicitly elevated the activities of
surviving women workers, particularly nurses who could claim an ele-
ment of risk and who fell within pre-existing understandings of women's
sphere of influence, to the level of patriotic service for the nation, thereby
aligning them with veterans.

First World War memorials were multilayered sites in which notions of
women's sacrifice intersected with other social, political and religious
discourses – imperialism, Christianity, patriotism and feminism – that
inflected the versions of female service and citizenship that the memorials
attempted to express.[86] The existence of competing and sometimes contradictory messages in memorials is inherent in their nature.
The conversion of individuals into abstract generalisations meant that it
was possible to interpret the figure of a nurse, for example, in a number of
different ways: as martyr, as embodiment of a nation, as *pietà*, as essence
of womanhood, as a health professional or as a female combatant.
The extent to which the memorial to women in York Minster was acceptable to a wide range of ideological and political positions is shown by the
guest list to its unveiling, which reads like a 'Who's Who' of British
women's war service. Alongside Quaker pacifist Ruth Fry were those
fighting for improvements in women's professional lives, such as nurse

[83] Philippe Contamine, 'Mourir pour la patrie', in Pierre Nora (ed.), *Lieux de mémoire*, vol. 2
(Paris: Gallimard, 1986), pp. 11–43; Gregory, *The Last Great War*, p. 112.
[84] Watson, *Fighting Different Wars*, p. 289.   [85] King, *Memorials*, p. 199.
[86] Antoine Prost demonstrated that within the French context, civic, Republican–patriotic,
conservative–patriotic and religious discourses contested the terrain of collective memory. 'Les Monuments aux morts', in Pierre Nora (ed.), *Lieux de mémoire*, vol. 1 (Paris:
Gallimard, 1984), pp. 195–225.

leaders and female doctors, as well as the leaders of the women's auxiliary services and other organisations that had been prominent in the war. Yet church leaders and male members of the military and political establishment were also present at the service.[87] Although their individual reactions are not recorded, the very presence of such a diverse congregation supports the proposition that the rhetoric of female sacrifice and service could be recast to suit the ideological and political positions of a wide range of men and women in the interwar years.

[87] Little, *Restoration*.

2   The Afterlives of First World War Heroines

This chapter considers some of the most acclaimed and high-profile female veterans in the interwar period: war heroines.[1] Although few are remembered today, the First World War produced scores of heroines who became household names in their respective nations.[2] From 1914 onwards, British and French journalists, artists and writers sought out women who could be constructed as heroic and lauded them in the press, in posters and in popular fiction. First World War heroines tended to have a double function: firstly, although cast as exceptional, they were equally set up as gendered embodiments of the finest qualities of a 'race' or a national identity, as role models to bolster morale and mobilise the nation for the war effort. Secondly, their gender was used to underscore the 'barbarous' and 'uncivilised' nature of the enemy. If they had died, their deaths were presented as 'murders' or 'assassinations' that served above all to condemn the enemy. It was usually activities on the front line that marked women out for heroine status. This proximity to the front, along with the patriotic and heroic qualities of courage, devotion, self-lessness, tenacity and sang-froid with which they were endowed, meant that heroines were often discussed in terms normally reserved for male combatants. However, it is equally notable that in propagandistic and

---

[1] An earlier version of this chapter appeared in Alison S. Fell, 'Remembering French and British First World War Heroines', in Christa Hämmerle, Oswald Uberegger and Birgitta Bader Zaar (eds.), *Gender and the First World War* (Basingstoke: Palgrave, 2014), pp. 108–26.

[2] While in this chapter I concentrate on specific case studies, it is important to note that the First World War saw the emergence of new or reconfigured heroine 'types', which served as a vital backdrop to the way in which individual heroines were constructed by journalists, artists and writers. On the British female munitions worker as heroine see Deborah Thom, *Nice Girls and Rude Girls: Women Workers in World War I* (London: I. B. Tauris, 1998); Angela Woollacott, *On Her Their Lives Depend: Munitions Workers in the Great War* (Berkeley: University of California Press, 1994). On French nurse-heroines and Resistance heroines see Darrow, *French Women*. On the influence of both Joan of Arc and Franco–Prussian models of female heroism in fin-de-siècle France see Margaret Darrow, 'In the Land of Joan of Arc: The Civic Education of Girls and the Prospect of War in France, 1871–1914', *French Historical Studies* 31 (2008): 263–91.

cultural representations of war heroines produced both during and after the conflict, there were clear attempts to redraw the dividing lines between front and rear, and between male and female versions of heroism in wartime. At the same time as heroines' (temporary) transgressions of gender stereotypes were celebrated, in other words, efforts were made in the popular press and in other cultural sources to define their activities within a more traditional understanding of men's and women's roles.

For instance, in 1914 and 1915 in France and Belgium a group of women was singled out as 'invasion heroines': plucky peasants, nuns and postal workers who defied invading soldiers in order to preserve life or foil attempts to take their territory. Yet in order for these women to function as embodiments of the finer qualities of their nations, journalists consistently emphasised their 'feminine' qualities such as self-sacrifice, frailty, piety, grace and maternal solicitude. As Margaret Darrow notes:

[T]he ideal heroine was small, young, pretty and, if possible, orphaned. . . . If the heroine could not be young and little, she could be simple and above all, feminine. . . . The central moment in most of the stories was the confrontation of the frail French woman and the brutal German officer. In tale after tale, French civilization, embodied in French femininity, cowed and conquered German brutality by its nobility, courage and moral rectitude.[3]

It was for this reason that nursing work of some form featured in many female heroism stories. Nursing allowed women to be close to the front while remaining firmly situated within traditional understandings of the feminised domestic sphere. In popular representations of female heroism, nurses at the front were not becoming 'honorary soldiers', they were extending their 'feminine' influence, bringing the home/ domestic front to the soldiers, the reason why in many popular accounts the nurse functioned as a synecdoche for the lost/absent home. This desire to '(re-)feminise' women who were active at or near to the front explains why the French resistance heroines I discuss in this chapter, Louise de Bettignies and Emilienne Moreau, were frequently referred to as nurses in wartime and post-war journalistic accounts of their activities even though neither of them worked in either a voluntary or professional capacity as nurses.

After the war, the public perception of war heroines who had survived depended largely upon the extent to which their wartime activities were understood as transgressive in gender terms.[4] While in some cases

---

[3] Darrow, *French Women*, pp. 109–10.
[4] I concur with Tammy Proctor in this context that broadly speaking, '[i]n a climate where "back to normalcy" was the fervent hope of many people in Europe, honorable she-soldiers and daring women spies had no place.' Proctor, *Female Intelligence*, p. 121.

wartime heroism enabled women to access public political or cultural life in a way they may not have been able to do otherwise, in other cases their heroic activities were less acclaimed, or even denigrated, in post-war society. The case studies I have chosen include women who were active in different spheres of action: nursing, aviation, resistance and combat. They also came from diverse sociocultural backgrounds. While during the war their actions allowed them, at least to some extent, to transcend these differences, in the interwar period it proved more difficult to cross class and cultural boundaries. What unites the surviving heroines that I discuss, however, is their use of the war as the key reference point around which their post-war identities were constructed. They presented themselves as veterans whose perspectives and experiences deserved respect and recognition.

Louise de Bettignies

Women who died on active service during the war, including those women engaged in resistance activities in occupied France and Belgium, were a valuable commodity for propagandists. Tammy Proctor has shown that while in wartime these women's activities necessarily blurred the line between (male) combatant and (female) civilian, with men and women performing similar functions in the intelligence networks in which they operated, death 'refeminised them', transforming them into innocent martyrs, 'violated by the bullets that pierced their chests'.[5] The most famous 'martyr-heroine' of this type was undoubtedly Edith Cavell. In addition, Louise de Bettignies and Gabrielle Petit also achieved iconic status in their respective nations.[6] In the commemorations to these women that took place in the interwar years, they were represented in ways that interpreted their deaths as emblematic of broader national or transnational qualities or sentiments. It might seem

---

However, this chapter argues that some of these women nevertheless succeeded in recasting their wartime heroism in ways that enabled them to access public acclaim in the interwar years.

[5] Proctor, *Female Intelligence*, p. 99.

[6] Belgian Gabrielle Petit was executed by firing squad after being found guilty of espionage in April 1916. A memorial to her was unveiled in Brussels in 1919, and several hagiographic accounts of her life and death were published. See Laurence van Ypersele and Emmanuel Debruyne, *De la guerre de l'ombre aux ombres de la guerre: L'espionnage en Belgique durant la guerre 1914–1918* (Editions Labor: Bruxelles, 2004); Sophie de Schaepdrijver, *Gabrielle Petit: The Death and Life of a Female Spy in the First World War* (London: Bloomsbury, 2015). Tammy Proctor reminds us that while women such as Bettignies and Petit became national heroines 'hundreds of other women quietly pursued their work as agents until the [A]rmistice' and remained anonymous in the interwar years. Proctor, *Female Intelligence*, p. 5.

at first glance that these memorials and other commemorations subverted or at least challenged dominant gender representations, featuring women as the active heroines of war rather than its passive victims. But in effect they drew on a long tradition of women as exceptional and transcendent innocent martyrs, especially in France where the cult of Joan of Arc provided a ready vocabulary. However, as for all memorials, the meanings with which these women were charged were not fixed, but were debated and contested in the interwar period, revealing the extent to which martyr-heroines could be appropriated as 'one of their own' by several different interest groups. Ultimately, the discourse of sacrifice that was central to all First World War memorialisation proved highly malleable and could be deployed by both men and women to support different political and ideological positions.

Louise de Bettignies was a wealthy, independent and well-travelled thirty-five-year-old single woman from Lille with an aptitude for languages that had made her a good candidate for her role in intelligence gathering. After undergoing a short training course in Folkestone, she ran an escape network for Allied soldiers, and gathered intelligence for both the British and French authorities.[7] She played a key role within a network of informants in Lille, and had contacts within both the Belgian and French secret services.[8] Although a Belgian report suggests that she was 'too chatty' and 'not prudent enough', her work was clearly appreciated by the British Intelligence Service, a 1918 report stating that her services 'were simply invaluable'.[9] Captured in October 1915, she was condemned to death but had her sentence commuted to life imprisonment and hard labour after the intercession of the Spanish. She died after an operation to remove a tumour while imprisoned in Germany in 1918, probably of pneumonia. After the war, she was reclaimed as a war heroine, especially in the north of France, and her body was repatriated in 1920. She was awarded medals by both the French and British governments and given a large and lavish funeral.[10] She was nicknamed the 'Joan of Arc of the North' and in hagiographic wartime propaganda it was her

---

[7] Chantal Antier, *Louise de Bettignies* (Paris: Tallandier, 2013); Jean-Marc Binot, *Héroïnes de la Grande Guerre* (Paris: Fayard, 2008), pp. 231–46; Helen McPhail, *The Long Silence: Civilian Life under the German Occupation of Northern France 1914–1918* (London: I. B. Tauris, 2001), chapter 5; Chantal Antier, Marianne Walle and Olivier Lahaie, *Les Espionnes dans la Grande Guerre* (Rennes: Editions Ouest-France, 2008), pp. 138–43.

[8] Report by Laure Tandel, 3 June 1922, Commission Archives des Services patriotiques établis en territoire occupé du Front Ouest, 1918, Brussels. Cited in Antier, Walle and Lahaie, *Les Espionnes*, p. 141.

[9] Report by Laure Tandel; Report, 23 October 1918, TNA WO 32/5406.

[10] *Le Figaro*, 5 March 1920; Hélène d'Argoeuves, *Louise de Bettignies* (Paris: La Colombe, 1956), pp. 266–72; McPhail, *The Long Silence*, pp. 152–53. The British government sidestepped the usual regulations in order to award Louise de Bettignies with the OBE,

exceptionality, youth and feminine piety that were emphasised while her spying activities were underplayed or reimagined as a quasi-religious vocation, mysterious 'voices' having called her to work as a secret service agent.[11] The comparison with Joan of Arc was taken up again in the immediate aftermath of her death, with Bishop Charost's eulogy at her 1920 funeral declaring that both heroines shared 'the same love of the fatherland ... the same solicitude for the wounded, whether friend or foe, the same invincible will to repel threats and accept martyrdom, the same supernatural serenity in the face of death'.[12] It is notable here that Charost highlights her 'solicitude for the wounded', associating her with nursing rather than with intelligence work.

In France in the 1920s it was the nationalist right who responded most readily to Bettignies' story, casting her as an icon of French national identity, the combination of Catholic piety, selfless bravery and 'instinctive', mystical patriotism that were read into her personal history and death being easily mapped onto their version of Joan of Arc. Significantly, Bettignies' story was popularised during this period by a 1924 publication, *La Guerre des femmes* (translated into English as *The Story of Louise de Bettignies*), written by journalist and ex-serviceman Antoine Redier with the help of his wife, Marie-Léonie Vanhoutte, who was part of the same network as Bettignies during the war.[13] Redier founded a short-lived nationalist right-wing veteran group called the Légion in 1924 in response to the electoral success of the Cartel des Gauches. Cheryl Koos and Daniella Sarnoff argue that Redier's vision of the ideal woman as constructed in his political writings was 'to stay at home and raise strong sons who would be the true men of the future ... to function in their "natural" roles as mothers and carers'.[14] Yet for Redier, as for many on the far right, war heroines constituted a class of women for whom the usual gender imperatives did not apply in the same way. They were not condemned as were other women for being single and/or childless, for their wartime activities outside the home elevated them not only above other women but also above the majority of men. Redier began *La Guerre des femmes* with a dedication to Bettignies:

and the King wrote a letter of condolence to her mother expressing the nation's gratitude for her daughter's services. See TNA WO 32/5406.

[11] Darrow, *French Women*, p. 284.   [12] d'Argoeuves, *Louise de Bettignies*, pp. 270–71.

[13] Antoine Redier, *La Guerre des femmes: Histoire de Louise de Bettignies et de ses compagnes* (Paris: Les Editions de la Vraie France, 1924); Antoine Redier, *The Story of Louise de Bettignies*, translated by Olive Hall (London: Hutchinson, n.d.).

[14] Cheryl Koos and Daniella Sarnoff, 'France', in Kevin Passmore (ed.), *Women, Gender and Fascism in Europe, 1919–45* (Manchester: Manchester University Press, 2003), pp. 168–89 (p. 172).

I dedicate this book to the memory of one of the noblest women who has ever honoured the French name. Louise de Bettignies is little known. . . . My ambition is to help, by means of my testimony, to rectify men's injustice in this regard, which has dimmed not only the glory of a heroic and charming young woman, but also of the French crown, which should not be deprived of any of its jewels.

In this way, Redier made Bettignies the embodiment of French national glory, of the 'true' values of France, rather than presenting her merely as an exceptional individual. It is not only the martyr-heroine Bettignies who was praised in his account, however. Redier was equally keen to promote the virtues of other heroines who survived the war, and criticised the fact that their sacrifices and heroism had not been adequately rewarded in the post-war world:

We pinned one ribbon, two ribbons onto their chest, and that was it. They pass by, and the men and women who roam the streets, chasing gold or pleasure, don't turn to look at them. . . . These women have heavy hearts and magnificent memories, and those who they wanted to save at the cost of their own lives treat them with disdain.[15]

Here, Redier aligned these idealised female heroines with honourable veterans, the 'true men' whom he believed would restore France to glory, and who were set up as elite role models in stark contrast to the selfish, hedonistic and materialistic masses.[16] Redier's understanding of gender was highly conservative in terms of his opposition to female suffrage, promotion of women's domestic role and patriarchal conception of both the family and broader social structures. Yet, as is seen with the case of veterans' attitudes towards both the nurse veterans' groups that I discuss in Chapter 3, and the resistance heroine Louise Thuliez whose memoirs I examine in Chapter 4, right-wing nationalist thinkers like Redier turned to the example of patriotic war heroines such as Bettignies as a means of underscoring the dichotomy they wished to create between 'true' and 'false' French citizens. For Redier, this was ultimately because his dichotomy was more dependent on war service and on his version of patriotism than it was on normative gender stereotypes. In Redier's vision for future French society, in other words, it was immeasurably better to have served patriotically as a 'militarised' war heroine than to have been a 'defeatist' French socialist or 'effeminate' Republican man.[17] Redier's use of women's war service and patriotism

---

[15] Redier, *La Guerre*, 'Dédicace', pp. 9–10.
[16] Cheryl A. Koos, 'Fascism, Fatherhood and the Family in Interwar France: The Case of Antoine Redier and the Légion', *Journal of Family History* 24 (1999): 317–29.
[17] Redier attacks bourgeois Republican men as 'old grandmothers' in his 1919 memoir *Les Méditations dans la tranchée*. Quoted in Koos and Sarnoff, 'France', p. 171.

may have transformed independent and adventurous young women like Bettignies into naïvely innocent martyr-heroines, but it was a version of femininity that was rooted far more in a Joan of Arc–inspired combination of piety and patriotic bravery than in the more dominant pronatalist model of the stay-at-home mother.

It is clear, therefore, that the drive to memorialise Bettignies was largely motivated by nationalist political aims, and indeed her memorial was taken up as a place of pilgrimage for right-wing nationalists in the later 1920s and the 1930s.[18] Initially, the idea of a memorial to Bettignies was instigated by the French army, with the wives of Marshal Foch and General Weyrand acting as co-chairs of the memorial committee.[19] The monument to Bettignies was unveiled in Lille in 1927 by Foch to a certain amount of national acclaim, having been sculpted by the Catholic nationalist Maxime Réal del Sarte, a prolific sculptor of French war memorials. It features a soldier kneeling in front of Bettignies, kissing her hand in gratitude (Figure 2.1). She gazes serenely towards the horizon, indicating not only her bravery in the face of the enemy but also her elevated status as a heroine set apart from the crowd, existing on a higher plane. The 1927 Lille monument compares in interesting ways to the 'Monument à Jeanne d'Arc' sculpted by Réal del Sarte two years later. Del Sarte's Joan of Arc is portrayed as a massive Mother of Mercy, dwarfing the grieving widow and baby and wounded French soldier that she encompasses in a powerful and protective embrace. Like his statue of Bettignies, del Sarte's Joan gazes impassively towards the horizon while the soldier gazes up at her in admiration.[20] Del Sarte was well known for his devotion to Joan of Arc as a nationalist and monarchist icon of French identity, and Bettignies' pose and posture resemble those of the sculptor's 1929 Joan of Arc, equating her with the same eternal and transcendental French values.[21]

---

[18] For a reference to the Duchesse de Guise and the Comtesse de Paris making a pilgrimage to pay their respects to the Bettignies memorial in the mid-1930s, see *Almanach de l'Action française* (Paris: Action française, 1936), p. 200. Louise de Bettignies was also used as a model of female heroism in schools during the Vichy regime. See Eric Jennings, 'Reinventing Jeanne: The Iconology of Joan of Arc in Vichy Schoolbooks, 1940–44', *Journal of Contemporary History* 29: 4 (1994): 711–34.

[19] Bulletin d'inscription, Comité Louise de Bettignies, BNF.

[20] This statue is reproduced in Marina Warner, *Joan of Arc: The Image of Female Heroism* (Berkeley: University of California Press, 1981), illustration no. 42.

[21] Del Sarte also produced the illustrations for nationalist writer and activist Charles Maurras' *Méditation sur la politique de Jeanne d'Arc* in 1931. See Martha Hanna, 'Iconology and Ideology: Images of Joan of Arc in the Idiom of the Action Française, 1908–1931', *French Historical Studies* 14: 2 (1985): 215–39.

Figure 2.1 Memorial to Louise de Bettignies, sculpted by Maxime Réal del Sarte, Lille, 1927.

Edith Cavell

Despite the attempts to popularise Bettignies' story, which included a 1935 play by Pierre Dumaine and Marcel Dubois and a 1937 film based on Redier's account entitled *Soeurs d'armes*, and despite official recognition of her heroism by military figureheads such as Foch, Bettignies did not have long-term appeal amongst the wider French public.[22] In a biography produced by Bettignies' niece Hélène d'Argoeuves, the Lille memorial is said to symbolise the sacrifices made by 'all war heroines, like [the tomb of the Unknown Soldier] under the Arc de Triomphe'. And indeed its inscription dedicates the memorial to 'Louise de Bettignies and all heroic women in the invaded countries'. But this claim exaggerates Bettignies' significance in popular memories of the First World War, and her fame was limited to the northern region, and, in the interwar years, to the nationalist Catholic right.[23] The same cannot be said for the martyr-heroine depicted in one of two bas-reliefs beneath Bettignies' statue, Edith Cavell.

More statues, busts and plaques commemorated Edith Cavell than any other woman in this period of history. Cavell was by far the most famous woman killed on a form of active service in the First World War, and, like Bettignies, she was set up as exceptional *because* rather than *despite* the fact that she was a woman.[24] She was executed on 12 October 1915 after having confessed to her role in organising an escape network for Allied soldiers while working as the matron of the Berkendael Medical Institute in Brussels, the first Belgian training school for nurses.[25] In cultural representations produced in France and Britain during and after the war she was made to embody two central (and frequently interlinked) concepts: the brutality of the enemy and the humanity and self-sacrifice of womanhood. These were concepts that many different sections of the

---

[22] Darrow, *French Women*, p. 284; Thébaud, *La Femme au temps de la guerre*, p. 68. The film *Soeurs d'armes* was directed by Léon Poirier and starred Jeanne Sully as Louise de Bettignies and Josette Day as Léonie Vanhoutte. Once again, the heroines of the film are set up as embodiments of eternal French values: 'When the vagaries of time and the mediocrity of everyday life tempts French men and women to forget who they are, they only have to turn the pages of their History to find in the greatness of their heroes' souls a reason to believe in the value of their race.' 'Préambule', in Léon Poirier, *Soeurs d'armes. Photographies du film* (Paris: Mame, 1937), p. 6.

[23] d'Argoeuves, *Louise de Bettignies*, pp. 274–75.

[24] Katie Pickles, *Transnational Outrage: The Death and Commemoration of Edith Cavell* (Basingstoke: Palgrave, 2007), p. 111. Anne-Marie Hughes has noted that Cavell's gender helps to explain why her commemoration was on a much larger scale than that of Captain Fry, who was also executed for espionage in Belgium, in 1916. See Anne-Marie Hughes, 'War, Gender and Mourning: The Significance of the Death and Commemoration of Edith Cavell in Britain', *European Review of History* 12: 3 (2005): 425–44.

[25] For biographical information, see Diana Souhami, *Edith Cavell* (London: Quercus, 2010).

national and international community could buy into. The former – that of an innocent nurse mercilessly gunned down by brutal Germans – dominated commemoration during the war, and was instrumentalised by anti-German and, in Britain and the United States, recruitment propagandists who reimagined her as a young, virginal and feeble war victim of a merciless oppressor that needed avenging, acting as a proxy for other vulnerable female civilians. Whereas Cavell was a forty-nine-year-old experienced professional nurse who appeared at her trial in civilian clothing, wartime newspaper articles, popular publications and propaganda images often depict a much younger Cavell wearing a Red Cross uniform, or with a Union Jack pinned to her breast.[26] A common myth suggested that she had fainted at her execution and, when the firing squad refused to shoot, a Prussian officer shot her with his handgun.[27] This version of her death allowed Allied propaganda to present Cavell as a feminised victim in a manner reminiscent of atrocity imagery and Germany as guilty of war crimes, literally holding a smoking gun. The use of Cavell as a means of execrating the enemy was evident in the 1920 Paris memorial to Cavell sculpted by Gabriel Pech for the Jardin des Tuileries. Initiated by the newspaper *Le Matin*, which launched a competition for a Cavell memorial in 1916, and with a committee dominated by male Republican politicians, the invitation to submit proposals sent to various French artists was clear about the messages the memorial was to convey: 'By means of the pure and tender effigy of the English nurse, isn't it humanity itself, a victim of barbarism and demanding revenge, that deserves to be glorified?'[28] In Pech's winning interpretation, Cavell was depicted after her execution, prostrate amongst war-torn ruins while a German helmet symbolising the barbarism of the enemy lies on top of her body. Placed squarely within the Catholic framework of martyrdom, a female allegorical figure floated above her, holding

[26] See the photograph of Cavell in civilian clothing at her trial, IWM, Edith Cavell Collection, EC 4, C4677, reproduced in Pickles, *Transnational Outrage*, p. 31.
[27] Darrow, *French Women*, pp. 278–79; Pickles, *Transnational Outrage*, pp. 44–45. As Pickles notes, contemporary accounts of Cavell's death reveal this version to have been false.
[28] 1 February 1916, quoted in Geneviève Bresc-Bautier and Anne Pingeot, *Sculptures des jardins du Louvre, du Carrousel et des Tuileries*, vol. 2 (Paris: Editions de la Réunion des musées nationaux, 1986), p. 360. The committee was presided over by Minister of Education Paul Painlevé, who had written a panegyric to Cavell in 1915. See Paul Painlevé, 'Introduction', in Anon, *La Vie et la mort de Miss Edith Cavell* (Paris: Fontemoing et cie., 1915), pp. x–xi. The models of other entries show similar interpretations, although interestingly the design that placed second, sculpted by André Vermare, had a classically draped Cavell standing defiantly, gazing towards the horizon with a much smaller French soldier and nurse seated on either side of her, a version of Cavell that resembles the London memorial. See *Le Pays de France*, 9 November 1916.

a martyr's palm in one hand and scattering flowers on the victim with the other. Cavell's martyrdom was underlined in the unveiling ceremony, with Minister of Pensions André Maginot comparing Cavell, 'the nurse-martyr', to Joan of Arc in his speech.[29] Its location, which was chosen unanimously by the committee, connotes Cavell's perceived importance via its prestige, and was given additional resonance by its proximity to James Pradier's statue of Strasbourg in the place de la Concorde, the symbol *par excellence* of anti-German sentiment in nineteenth-century France. The *revanchisme* evident in the French Cavell memorial helps to explain why German soldiers destroyed it on their entry into Paris in 1940.[30]

The most well-known British memorial to Edith Cavell, sculpted by George Frampton and situated in St Martin's Place in central London, has a similar genesis to its Parisian equivalent (Figure 2.2). It was also funded by public subscription initiated in the immediate aftermath of her death by a newspaper, the *Daily Telegraph*, and was unveiled on 17 March 1920. However, Frampton's interpretation depicted her at the moment of her execution, and presented her as an older, dignified and serene figure, bravely facing her executors and gazing towards the horizon. In her analysis, art historian Sue Malvern comments that the bearing and clothing of the Cavell figure 'repress the signs of femininity', and Katie Pickles agrees that in some senses Cavell is represented as an 'honorary man'.[31] It is true that she was represented as dying for, rather than symbolising, innocent female victims (the vulnerable mother and child that top the monument are generally assumed to represent Belgium and Serbia), but Frampton drew above all upon the tradition of the martyr-heroine, a tradition in which a particular brand of femininity (as transcendent, devout, patriotic and brave) played a central role. The intentions of the sculptor and committee for the London memorial were made manifest by the fact that the viewer was given a great deal of textual guidance. The inscription referred to the manner of her death by recording the time, 'Dawn', as well as the date and place of execution. In addition, 'For King and Country' was engraved above the statue and the words 'Humanity, Devotion, Fortitude and Sacrifice' on each of the four sides in large letters. These textual clues guided the viewer to

[29] *Le Figaro*, 13 June 1920.
[30] Christel Sniter, 'La gloire des femmes célèbres: Métamorphoses et disparité de la statuaire publique parisienne de 1870 à nos jours', *Sociétés et Représentations* 26 (2008): 153–70.
[31] Sue Malvern, '"For King and Country": Frampton's Edith Cavell (1915–1920) and the Writing of Gender in Memorials to the Great War', in David Getsy (ed.), *Sculpture and the Pursuit of a Modern Ideal in Britain, 1880–1930* (Aldershot: Ashgate, 2004), pp. 219–84 (p. 221); Pickles, *Transnational Outrage*, p. 120.

Figure 2.2 Memorial to Edith Cavell, sculpted by George Frampton, London, 1920.

prioritise Cavell's martyrdom, her embodiment of humanity and civilisation versus barbarism, in his/her interpretation of the monument.

However, despite the intention of the memorial committees, both the Paris and London Cavell monuments came to embody different messages for different audiences. Trained nurses played a prominent role in the official commemoration of Cavell in both Britain and France despite the fact that her war service, and her death, were only indirectly related to her nursing work. As early as November 1915, Anna Hamilton, pioneer of the professionalisation and secularisation of nursing in France, wrote an article in *La Petite Gironde* in 1915 backing the Comtesse d'Haussonville's request for nurses to send donations to an appeal for the erection of a memorial to Cavell.[32] At the unveiling ceremony of the Paris memorial, French nurses, wearing medals to bear witness to their war service, laid the first wreath.[33] British nurses formed a guard of honour at Cavell's state funeral after her body was repatriated in 1919, and a year later the Frampton monument was jointly unveiled by Queen Alexandra, Beatrice Monk, matron of London Hospital, and Ann Beadsmore Smith, matron-in-chief of the Queen Alexandra's Imperial Military Nursing Service (QAIMNS).[34] The memorials to Cavell may have emphasised her martyrdom and the timeless, transcendent feminine qualities she embodied rather than her status as a professional working woman, but nurses and nursing organisations responded to her commemoration actively and, on the whole, positively, attending official memorial services in large numbers. Both the Paris and London memorials were described as 'beautiful' in the *British Journal of Nursing*, and as suitable places for nurses to pay their respects to a lost colleague, although there was criticism about the inadequate representation of women on the London memorial committee and at the French ceremony.[35] Nurses also instigated Cavell memorial projects of their own, including training hospitals in Paris and Brussels and homes for nurses in London and Norwich.[36] Reading the nursing press it is clear that while some nurses responded to Cavell's death as individuals, writing articles about their memories of working with her, others seized the opportunity offered to them by the enormous international interest in her death to advance their struggle for the professionalisation of nursing, ongoing in both countries since the nineteenth century.[37] Suffragist and nurse leader Ethel Bedford Fenwick, editor of the *British Journal of Nursing*, commented in relation to Belgium in 1924, for example, that '[t]he almost canonization of Edith Cavell ... has done for the Belgian modern nursing movement

[32] *British Journal of Nursing*, 20 November 1915.
[33] *British Journal of Nursing*, 19 June 1920.
[34] *British Journal of Nursing*, 27 March 1920.
[35] See *British Journal of Nursing*, 19 June and 27 March 1920.
[36] The Hôpital-Ecole d'infirmières professionnelles françaises in Paris was inaugurated by Mme Poincaré in 1916. In 1920, the 'Institut Edith Cavell et Marie Depage' was inaugurated in Brussels. See Pickles, *Transnational Outrage*, pp. 139–55.
[37] For letters from nurses with personal reminiscences about Cavell, see for example *British Journal of Nursing*, 6 November 1916.

what the Crimea and Florence Nightingale did for the English one.'[38] In their enthusiastic embrace of the commemoration of Cavell, nursing organisations were aware of the possible advantages her high profile could bring to their profession.

It was not just nurses, moreover, who were involved in instigating and fund-raising for the hundreds of Cavell memorial projects, but large numbers of elite women with skills, spare time and experience in philanthropic activities.[39] These women included suffragists and anti-suffragists, pacifists, imperialists and jingoistic patriots amongst their ranks, yet the kinds of memorials created tend not to stray very far from the central ingredients of the Paris and London examples. One of the reasons that Cavell appealed to diverse constituencies both across the British empire and, to a lesser extent, in France during and after the war was that, with slight shifts of emphasis, she could be made to represent different ideological positions. In the early 1920s, a campaign began to persuade the authorities to add to the London monument Cavell's ambiguous reported words 'Standing as I do in view of God and Eternity I realise that patriotism is not enough. I must have no hatred or bitterness towards anyone,' and in 1924 the addition of this version (there had been some dispute as to the exact wording) was approved by the Labour government after consultation with Cavell's family.[40] The campaign was carried out in the pages of the press and in letters to public bodies, and involved well-known figures such as George Bernard Shaw. Many of those campaigning were motivated by pacifist or religious beliefs, and many were women. Despite the use of Cavell by recruiters and propagandists, pacifists did not ignore or dismiss her, but attempted to claim her as their own, as a feminist pacifist whose message had been distorted by the authorities. Indeed, as early as 1915 Helena Swanwick, suffragist and chair of the Women's International League, wrote to *The Manchester Guardian* demanding that a Cavell memorial should be based around the beliefs incarnated in her reported words. A similar sentiment was evident in a 1924 letter to the same newspaper from Marguerite Louis, press secretary of the youth section of the No More War Movement, who wrote that Cavell's example should be used amongst young girls 'to develop a spirit of comradeship with all their sisters'.[41]

---

[38] *British Journal of Nursing*, May 1924.   [39] Pickles, *Transnational Outrage*, p. 139.

[40] A nurse, Mary E. H. Ward, wrote to the Ministry of Works in 1924 enclosing a letter from the Rev Stirling Gahan, who had attended Cavell before her execution, that has a different version of her words, but the Ministry decided to use the version supplied by her family. TNA WORK 20/128.

[41] *The Manchester Guardian*, 3 November 1915, 26 May 1924.

Jane Marcus thereby maintains that the Cavell statue has a 'double voice . . . its feminist pacifism overlaid by the patriarchal state's jingoistic "For King and Country"'.[42] But it was not only politicised women, already committed to the pacifist cause and latching on to the popularity of Cavell, who intervened in the debate, which undermines the argument that the meanings of the memorial can be straightforwardly separated into two opposing camps, feminist and patriarchal, pacifist and nationalist. Heading up the campaign to add Cavell's final words was not the pacifist wing of the suffragist movement, but the female leadership of the moderate philanthropic organisation the National Council of Women (NCW), who wrote a letter to the Office of Works in 1922. The NCW membership was largely made up of women drawn from the wealthy middle and upper classes, who held a variety of ideological and political positions, both suffragist and anti-suffragist, pacifist and militarist, yet they managed to reach a consensus over their intervention in the commemoration, voting for a resolution that 'no memorial to Nurse Cavell could be complete that did not perpetuate her own self-dedication or emphasize the fact that she died not only for her country but for humanity.'[43] This statement is (no doubt deliberately) vague in its political and ideological allegiances, and could be used to uphold patriotic or anti-militarist interpretations of Cavell's death. The contested memorialisation of Edith Cavell thus reveals to us the extent to which men and women of different ideological, political and religious persuasions in the interwar period were able to find common ground around the notion of female 'service' and 'sacrifice' embodied in heroine figures who had died, without necessarily doing so for the same reasons.

While the activities of heroines during the First World War have been the focus of a number of popular and scholarly studies, there has been considerably less work on the ways in which those who survived the war extended, adapted or exploited their wartime roles in subsequent decades. Heroines who survived the war, however exceptional their war service, did not have the same widespread appeal as 'martyr-heroines' like Bettignies and Cavell. Whereas many surviving war heroines presented themselves in their post-war speeches and writings as 'female veterans' who had served alongside mobilised men, this identity was not widely accepted in the interwar years.

[42] Jane Marcus, 'The Asylums of Antaeus: Women, War and Madness. Is There a Feminist Fetishism?', in Elizabeth Meese and Alice Parker (eds.), *The Difference Within* (Amsterdam: John Benjamins, 1989), pp. 49–83 (p. 53).
[43] Letter dated 13 December 1922 from the London Branch of the NCW, TNA WORK 20/128.

Germaine Sellier: The 'Angel of Soissons'

In 1914, Germaine Malaterre Sellier was a wealthy, young, middle-class Catholic woman who, like many elite French women, had attended pre-war Red Cross training courses, and had become one of the 21,500 trained French Red Cross nurses.[44] Sellier had opted for courses run by the Association des Dames Françaises (Association of French Ladies) (ADF), and was no doubt attracted by the society's rhetoric that specifically targeted young bourgeois women, arguing that non-combatant patriotic participation would be vital for the nation's survival should a war break out. She was mobilised early in the war as an 'ambulancière major' (staff nurse) and was sent to Soissons, close to the front. There, she worked under the leadership of Jeanne Macherez, the widow of a senator and president of the ADF regional committee (Figure 2.3). A mature and experienced administrator and social activist, Macherez had in 1910 been responsible for overseeing relief efforts in the Aisne for the victims of the Paris floods.[45] When war broke out, Macherez was given charge of two auxiliary hospitals in Soissons and helped to set up and raise funds for eleven smaller temporary hospitals in the region.[46]

Soissons was at the heart of the Battle of Aisne, and was occupied by the Germans in August 1914 before being retaken by the French and British in September 1914. During the occupation and mass evacuation of Soissons, Macherez briefly represented the town in negotiations with the German officers who were requisitioning supplies.[47] When the town was retaken by the French it became like Verdun a 'ville-martyr' visited by numerous VIPs. These included politicians such as Albert Sarraut, writers such as Pierre Loti and Rudyard Kipling[48] and journalists including Gustave Babin from L'Illustration, Paul Ginisty from La Vie littéraire and Le Petit Parisien, as well as from Britain and the United States.[49] These

[44] See Fell, 'Germaine Malaterre Sellier'; Rachel Chrastil, 'The French Red Cross, War Readiness and Civil Society 1866–1914', French Historical Studies 31 (2008): 445–76.

[45] 'Rapport de Jeanne Macherez, Présidente, Soissons', in Association des Dames Françaises, Secours donnés aux victimes des inondations de Paris et des Départements (Janvier et Février 1910): Rapport Général du Comité Central (Amiens: A. Grau, 1910), p. 130. In 1909 she founded the Soissons branch of the organisation 'La Goutte de lait' that aimed to improve infant health. See Binot, Héroïnes, p. 43.

[46] Albert de Bertier de Sauvigny, Pages d'histoire locale, 1914–1919 (Soissons: Association Soissonnais 14–18, 1934).

[47] Léon Abensour, Les Vaillantes: Héroïnes, martyres et remplaçantes (Paris: Librairie Chapelot, 1917), p. 179.

[48] See Kipling's letters in Thomas Pinney (ed.), The Letters of Rudyard Kipling, 1911–1919, vol. 4 (London: Macmillan, 1999).

[49] See for example 'L'hommage des femmes françaises à Mme Macherez, maire de Soissons', Le Petit Echo de la mode, 10 October 1914; 'A Woman's Brave Rebuke to the Enemy', The Times, 16 September 1914.

Figure 2.3 Germaine Sellier and Jeanne Macherez wearing gas masks and their Croix de guerre, Soissons, 1916. SOTK2011 / Alamy Stock Photo.

individuals chronicled in their various publications the daily life of a town at the front, looking for examples and stories that suited the nationalist and patriotic ideologies they wished to propagate. In their writings, the two Red Cross nurses were transformed into idealised war heroines; while

Macherez became 'la Mairesse de Soissons' ('The Mayoress of Soissons'), Sellier was nicknamed 'La Dame Blanche de Soissons' ('The White Lady of Soissons'). Like other heroines, they were set up as symbols of the soul of France itself, defying enemy 'brutality'. Thanks in part to this publicity, Macherez and Sellier were recognised by the state for their services to the nation, even if other accounts suggest that the press articles exaggerated their role and the scope of their actions. George Muzart, for example, the man who became Mayor of Soissons later in the war, was obviously annoyed about the publicity that surrounded the two nurses. He stated in his memoirs that it had been necessary to exaggerate or even invent an injury in order that Sellier receive the Croix de guerre, and he refused to support the successful nomination of Macherez and Sellier for the prix Audiffred in 1916.[50]

After the death of her fiancé at the front, Sellier married an officer she met in Soissons, Henri Malaterre, in 1917. Proud of her decorations, she attached her Croix de guerre not only to her nursing uniform, but also to her wedding dress.[51] The marriage was covered in the press, and she was evidently happy to participate in her construction as romantic wartime heroine. After the Armistice she devoted her energies to reformist feminism and to pacifism, especially the pacifism influenced by progressive Catholic thinker Marc Sangnier and his organisation Jeune République (Young Republic). In 1920 she was elected to the committee of the Parisian section of the organisation, and became vice president in 1929. She was equally committed to feminist and suffragist organisations; she was one of the women at the head of the Union féminine pour la Société des Nations (Women's Union for the League of Nations), which was affiliated to French suffrage and feminist groupings, and led the 'Peace' section of the Conseil National des Femmes Françaises (National Council of French Women), the largest feminist organisation in France.[52] In the interwar years, she travelled around France giving talks and lectures, trying to persuade her fellow citizens of the justice of her two causes. In these talks she often referred to her wartime experiences, overtly adopting the identity of 'war veteran', not only because these

---

[50] Georges Muzart, *Soissons pendant la guerre* (Amiens: Association Soissonnais 14–18, 1998).

[51] Photograph reproduced in Sandrine Wierbicki, 'Germaine Malaterre-Sellier: Un destin aux croisées du féminisme et du pacifisme (1889–1967)', Unpublished mémoire de maîtrise, Université de Paris 1, 2001, p. 239. See also p. 46.

[52] Christine Bard comments that this organisation was led by 'feminists who had manifested their patriotism during the war' amongst whom Malaterre Sellier 'put herself forward as the great specialist of international subjects ... she passionately defended the European cause, following the example of her friends in the Jeune République'. Bard, *Les Filles de Marianne*, p. 135.

experiences had undoubtedly marked her for life but equally for strategic and political reasons.

Malaterre Sellier's talks were usually preceded by an introduction that mentioned her heroic war service. In 1932, a newspaper report of a talk she gave on pacifism noted her decorations and war service before commenting that '[s]ince 1920 Mme Malaterre-Sellier has served Peace with all the strength that she so generously devoted to her war service.'[53] Two years later, when she gave a lecture on female suffrage in Algeria, the president of the local veteran association set her up specifically as an ex-combatant: 'We could hardly understand that such a woman could consider herself as inferior to men. ... She is a committed and convincing feminist. What shirker-voter or what frontline soldier could reproach her for it? Like all combatants, Mme Malaterre Sellier has rights over us: The right to vote is one of them.'[54] He was obviously in favour of female suffrage, but it is interesting nonetheless that he gave Malaterre Sellier the status of a veteran by making reference to Clemenceau's famous statement in the Chamber of Deputies in November 1917: 'These Frenchmen that we have been forced to throw into battle, they have rights over us. ... We owe them everything, with no reserve.' In her own speeches, Malaterre Sellier was equally quick to align herself with the veteran community. As I noted in my introduction, she addressed a veteran congress in Vichy in 1926 with the words 'I am one of you, not only because like you I lived through the war, and like you shed my blood for France.'[55] In another lecture on female suffrage given in 1922, Sellier declared: 'Talk to nurses who saw thousands and thousands of our soldiers die, they will tell you that, at the last, when the sacrifice was too great, when they had to help them make their final "great journey", it was not enough to talk to them about their mothers or their wives, they had to say to them "You are dying so that your children do not have to fight like you have fought!"'[56] This time she was giving herself the right to speak on behalf of the dead. The reference in this way to the 'glorious dead' as the ultimate arbiters of interwar morality was a key element of veteran discourse in interwar France.

In interviews Germaine Malaterre Sellier said that her traumatic experiences of war guided her lifelong commitment to pacifism and social justice.[57] She is equally, moreover, an example of a woman who successfully made use

[53] *La Gazette de Mostaganem*, 13 March 1932.
[54] M. Bounine, President of the 'Amicale des Mutilés et Anciens Combattants', Bougie, Algeria. *Echo de Bougie, Organe d'union républicaine démocratique et sociale*, 4 March 1934.
[55] 'Discours de Mme Mallaterre-Sellier [sic]'.
[56] *Bulletin de l'Ordre de l'Etoile d'Orient* 7 (July 1922): 29.
[57] Interview with Etienne Constant, 'Nous voulons la paix organisée', *Femmes*, 1936. BMD, Dossier 'Malaterre Sellier'.

of her wartime notoriety, as well as the positive connotations enjoyed by elite women who worked as voluntary Red Cross nurses during the war, in order to enter public life in the 1920s and 1930s. Despite the existence of better-qualified rivals, she was the first French woman to be nominated as a technical adviser to the United Nations in 1932. Her Catholicism, feminism and pacifism made her a consensus candidate in 1930s France, but equally her war service continued to allow her to present herself not only as a brave patriot but also as somebody who could speak with authenticity and authority about the causes and consequences of international conflict.

Emilienne Moreau: The 'Heroine of Loos'

In 1914 Emilienne Moreau was the seventeen-year-old daughter of a coalminer turned shopkeeper in Loos-en-Gohelle, near Lens (Pas de Calais). She helped her father in the shop while working to pass her 'brevet' qualification in order to train to be a schoolteacher.[58] When the Germans invaded, she warned advancing French troops of the positioning of German artillery. The French troops were forced to retreat, however, and the civilian population lived under siege conditions. In December 1914 her father died as a result, according to Moreau's later autobiography, of the 'privations and anguish' of the occupation, having been imprisoned for breaking the curfew.[59] The majority of the population having fled, Moreau set herself up as a temporary teacher when the school closed. In September 1915 British troops attacked to try and retake the town. Again Moreau warned the kilt-wearing Highlanders of the 9th Black Watch of the positioning of German defences. During the battle for the village, Moreau helped a Dr Burns to care for wounded soldiers and, when attempting to move one of them to safety, was fired at by German soldiers. In response, she picked up a gun left by one of the British male nurses and shot back, allegedly killing at least two Germans. Moreau's sister was wounded by shrapnel during the fighting, and when the family took her for hospital treatment in nearby Béthune, they learned that Henri Moreau, Emilienne's brother, had been killed in action in May 1915.

Moreau was awarded medals by both the French and British governments,[60] General de Sailly commenting when awarding her the

---

[58] Binot, *Héroïnes*, pp. 107–26. For a selection of press articles on Moreau, see BMD, 'Dossier Emilienne Moreau'.

[59] Emilienne Moreau, *La Guerre buissonnière* (Paris: Solar Editeur, 1970), p. 33.

[60] In November 1915, Moreau was awarded the French Croix de guerre and the 'Croix du combattant'. In 1916, Moreau was presented with the British Military Medal and the Cross of St John of Jerusalem by Lord Bertie, the British ambassador in Paris. *British Journal of Nursing*, 5 August 1916.

Croix de guerre in 1917: 'You honour the women of France. For them you are a magnificent and reassuring example.'[61] Moreau's story had all the ingredients the press was looking for, and *Le Petit Parisien*, a powerful newspaper, quickly offered her 5,000 francs for an exclusive. Moreau was staggered by the amount: '[W]e were living in a precarious financial situation, with a military allowance of 3.50 francs per day and 1.50 to help with the children.'[62] The newspaper put her and her mother up in a luxurious château in La Maye in Versailles, bought her new clothes, got her photograph taken, and serialised her 'Memoirs' of 1914 and 1915, alongside a patriotic popular novel by Jules Mary, *L'Amour dans les ruines* (*Love in the Ruins*).[63] Her photograph was widely distributed to soldiers, and her portrait was added to the 'Staircase of Heroes' in the commemorative painting the 'Pantheon of the War' (Figures 2.4 and 2.5).[64] Her story was also made into a propagandistic Australian film in 1916, *The Joan of Arc of Loos*, directed by George Willoughby. A veritable publicity machine thus promoted the image of Moreau as a heroine, and she was used by the state for fund-raising and as a symbol of Franco–British *entente*. As she ironically recalled in her memoirs:

[W]e weren't [in the château] for pleasure. I had to work. Every day, I would fill the pages of a notebook that one of the newspaper's editors would come and pick up. My mother and I were not permitted to leave the château, as I had become an 'exclusive' for *Le Petit Parisien* and it wasn't willing to share me with its competitors. Later, the newspaper printed enormous posters of one of my photos which decorated the walls of the metro, and then the walls of every town in France. . . . As money was needed to help care for the wounded, it had been decided to appeal to the 'well-known faces' of the war: Fonck, Nungesser, Guynemer[65] . . . and me. Our role was to collect money from wherever it could be found, that is to say, from the rich. So they made me a pretty dress (I wanted a black one because I was still wearing mourning for my father and brother) and, with Guynemer, I was sent to high-society social occasions.[66]

---

[61] 'L'héroïne de Loos reçoit la Croix de guerre', *Le Petit Parisien*, 28 November 1915.
[62] Moreau, *La Guerre buissonnière*, p. 48.   [63] Moreau, *La Guerre buissonnière*, p. 49.
[64] See Chapter 1.
[65] René Fonck (1894–1953), Charles Nungesser (1892–1927) and Georges Guynemer (1894–1917) were all heroised as First World War fighter pilots. In a static war of attrition with fewer opportunities for significant individual enterprise, it is unsurprising that pilots, with their 'score sheets' of enemy hits, were amongst the most well known of First World War male military heroes. See for example the inscription on the 1923 memorial to Georges Guynemer, Poelkapellein, Belgium, in which he is described as a '[l]egendary hero who fell in glory from the sky after three years of ardent struggle. He will remain the purest symbol of the qualities of his race: indomitable tenacity, wild energy, sublime courage, animated by the most unshakable faith in victory.'
[66] Moreau, *La Guerre buissonnière*, p. 49.

Figure 2.4 Study painting of Emilienne Moreau as 'The Heroine of Loos' by Auguste-François Gorguet, 1916.

Several factors help to explain the success of Moreau's heroisation. The years 1914 and 1915 were extremely costly for the Allies on the Western Front in terms of both losses of territory and casualty rates. The Battle of Loos, for example, saw the 9th Battalion of the Black Watch suffer 700

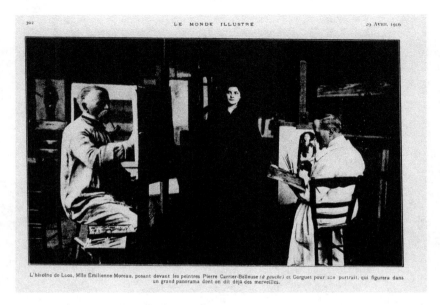

L'héroïne de Loos, Mlle Émilienne Moreau, posant devant les peintres Pierre Carrier-Belleuse *(à gauche)* et Gorguet pour son portrait, qui figurera dans un grand panorama dont on dit déjà des merveilles.

Figure 2.5 Emilienne Moreau posing for Gorguet and Carrier-Belleuse, *Le Monde Illustré*, 29 April 1916.

casualties. It was not easy for journalists to find inspiring and morale-boosting tales of heroism amid such losses. For the French, Emilienne Moreau, poignantly young in her mourning clothes, simultaneously represented stoicism in relation to heavy losses of life and territory, the bravery, resistance and sacrifices made by patriotic civilians and Allied cooperation under fire. In addition, any young woman fighting for her country against apparently hopeless odds raised the ever-present spectre of Joan of Arc, the ultimate French heroine. Moreau's gender was thus a vital factor in the communication of the different levels of meaning with which her image was charged. While journalists and popular writers focused on quasi-military qualities of courage and coolness under fire, her underlying 'feminine' vulnerability and maternal instincts were equally emphasised. Writers were swift to justify, moreover, her taking up of arms as a defence of the innocent in the face of a 'barbaric' enemy who preyed on civilians or wounded soldiers. Take the following two examples: the first is from a popular published account of the war by Scottish journalist Donald A. Mackenzie:

She seemed a born nurse, and her gentle words and sweet smile were like a tonic to the stricken soldiers. ... Through a shattered window in Emilienne's home she had seen a German soldier bayoneting a wounded Highlander in the street. 'They are killing the wounded,' she cried. ... Emilienne remained fearless and composed. For her own safety she took no thought. Her sole concern was for the wounded men under her care.[67]

The second example comes from the French journal *L'Illustration*:

There was blood everywhere. At her feet, the wounded were moaning. She could see from their striking outfits that they were the famous Highlanders that the Germans so feared. One by one, she picked them up. She wasn't strong, but her will fortified her muscles. She helped some to have a drink and bandaged others. She put them to bed as best she could, and the English surgeons found her leaning over the brave men, many of whose lives she had saved. At the entrance of the village, a song could be heard, sung out by thousands of lungs. It was 'God Save the King'. Mlle Moreau waited. When the national anthem was finished, she sang the Marseillaise at the top of her voice![68]

These two instances reveal differences between British and French accounts of Moreau's actions. While in Mackenzie's narrative a traditional version of femininity was foregrounded, featuring her as a self-abnegating nurse in the face of German barbarity, in *L'Illustration* it was her patriotism that took centre stage, endowing her with superhuman strength and willpower, and thereby suggesting that both mobilised and civilian French citizens were admirable friends in arms to Britain in the Allied defence of French territory. However, the contradictions apparent in the construction of a heroine who combined innocent civilian war victim with brave patriotic 'soldier' were not lost on the German press. The German magazine *Des deutschen Volkes Kriegstagebuch* reproduced the French press photograph of Moreau with the caption 'The so-called "Heroine of Loos" who is being celebrated in the English and French press because she murdered five German soldiers in the Battle of Loos' strategically placed next to an article stressing the German nation's desire for peace.[69] Just as Edith Cavell's guilt was emphasised by the German press, so Moreau was presented as an example of a *franc-tireur* breaking the rules of warfare rather than a brave defender of humanity in the face of barbarism. Indeed, Moreau referred in her memoirs to German hostility in relation to Allied celebrations of her actions, stating that her Croix de guerre ceremony was supposed to take place in the Place des Invalides in Paris, but 'the Germans, who had put a price on my head, had made it known via the King of Spain, Alphonse XIII, ...

---

[67] Donald A. Mackenzie, *From All the Fronts* (Glasgow: Blackie, 1917), pp. 69–71.
[68] *L'Illustration*, 20 November 1915.
[69] *Des deutschen Volkes Kriegstagebuch*, 1915, p. 2009. I would like to thank Paul Cooke for the translation of this article.

that if I was decorated in the Invalides, any civilian captured by their troops would be considered to be a franc-tireur and shot. They couldn't stand the fact that military honours were being given, not only to a civilian, but to a woman who had shot German soldiers.'[70]

Writing about her experiences many years later, Moreau distanced herself as an adult narrator from her former self, whom she presented as a naïve young girl, and emphasised a lack of agency not only in her acts of heroism but also in the construction of her public persona by the French and British authorities and media. But she also noted that she gained new experiences and a new perspective from her unexpected notoriety:

I lived at that time in a kind of whirlwind. Imagine a young girl from the Pas-de-Calais, having always lived quietly, in a peaceful little village, suddenly exposed to everyone's gaze, received and congratulated by bemedalled officials wearing cocked hats, in public squares and golden salons. . . . Think, too, that for hours, for whole days, I had to curtsey, smile, answer questions, thank people, make speeches, and congratulate other combatants who were just as intimidated as I was. So, the young girl improvised, tried to always remain calm and simple, opened her eyes and ears in order to learn from the behaviour of others in such a new world. . . . Slowly, I got used to my role, for I had a role to play. I didn't think for a minute of fleeing, because I knew that my example served to raise soldiers' morale.[71]

Although she presented her past self as overwhelmed by her sudden celebrity, in her later life it was clear that Moreau made use of her prestigious status for both personal and political reasons. Her heroism continued to be celebrated in the interwar years; she appeared as a character, for example, in a 1928 play designed to give young French Catholic girls role models to follow in later life.[72] In later life, Moreau herself turned to her prestigious status as 'female veteran' in a number of ways. Firstly, her wartime role boosted her economic as well as her cultural capital: 'The money from the *Petit Parisien* allowed us to survive. The newspaper also paid for my lessons in an institution in the boulevard Saint-Germain. I did well in my elementary and then advanced qualifications. My dream had finally been realized: I was going to be a teacher!'[73] In addition to financial gains that brought about a degree of social mobility, the resonance of her First World War role came particularly into play when the Second World War broke out. Although she had settled into civilian life after 1918, she seems to have been more than willing to take up her symbolic role once again when circumstances changed. For instance, a newspaper report reveals that in March 1940 she attended a football match between British soldiers

[70] Moreau, *La Guerre buissonnière*, p. 45.   [71] Moreau, *La Guerre buissonnière*, p. 46.
[72] *La Vie au patronage: Organe catholique des œuvres de jeunesse* (May 1928): v.
[73] Moreau, *La Guerre buissonnière*, p. 50.

and a local team from Lens as guest of honour, proudly wearing 'the French and British decorations conferred on her during the last war', and thus revivifying her role as symbol of Franco–British entente.[74] Having married socialist activist Just Evrard in 1932, Moreau saw her whole family become involved in Resistance work during the Occupation, and in 1941 Evrard was arrested and imprisoned. Moreau related in her autobiography that when German soldiers searched her house in 1942, they demanded to see her war medals, and when she produced them, 'the officer examined them in a serious manner and then shouted an order to his soldiers "Present arms". I would have willingly gone without this kind of display, but, after all, it was a fine gesture.'[75] She therefore used her past quasi-military status in order to elevate herself above other civilians, implying that the German soldiers treated her with respect because they recognised her as a war heroine. She went on to make further use of her First World War role to help her in her quest to make political gains for the Second World War Resistance movement. In particular, she hoped that her heroine status would add weight to her role as the representative of one of the Resistance networks when she escaped to England in 1944 to seek further support from the British government, and in preparation went to a French police station to get a document certifying the validity of her medals. A 1944 *Times* article reporting her arrival in England overtly linked her First and Second World War roles, using the former to bolster her claims to authenticity and authority in her testimony of conditions in occupied France. The article reminded readers that '[d]uring the battle of Loos in September 1915, Mme Moreau saved the lives of many English soldiers. ... She is now a delegate of the Resistance movement to the French collective assembly.' It then quoted her as stating, '[t]he Germans are no different from what they were in 1914', while reporting that they had carried out summary executions of members of the Resistance movement.[76] More generally, her autobiographical descriptions of the Occupation openly recalled her First World War experiences, and she adopted the same persona of instinctively patriotic, simple, adaptable and selfless heroine. Thus Moreau maintained and, at least to some extent, exploited her notoriety in her later life. Moreau's entry into political life was aided not only by her marriage to Just Evrard but equally by her ability to draw on her status as both First and Second World War heroine. She became the general secretary of the Women's Section of the Socialist Party in the Pas de Calais region in 1934, was one of only six women to be made a Compagnon de la Libération in 1945, and was a member of the

[74] *The Times*, 5 March 1940.   [75] Moreau, *La Guerre buissonnière*, pp. 73–74.
[76] *The Times*, 15 August 1944.

Steering Committee of the Socialist Party from 1945 to 1963, as well as being president of a powerful regional veterans' association.

In France, women's resistance activities in the First World War were overshadowed by the higher-profile activities of Second World War Resisters. In the 1960s and 1970s, the era in which Moreau published her family memoir, proof of Resistance heroism in 1940–44 was an entry ticket into public acclaim and, potentially, political power. It is therefore unsurprising that the cover of her autobiography describes her as 'Emilienne Moreau, Compagnon de la Libération' and features a photograph of her meeting General de Gaulle. But the cover also features the famous First World War photograph of her as a seventeen-year-old wearing mourning clothes that *Le Petit Parisien* had distributed, suggesting that her contribution as a Resistant had not completely effaced her previous identity. Ultimately, it is clear that for many French people she remained a living symbol of resistance in relation to both world wars.

What both of these case studies show is that wartime heroism could be an entry ticket into a public career for French women in the interwar years because it allowed them to position themselves as having served their country, as veterans whose voices deserved to be heard in the post-war years. However, other factors, and in particular social class, also played an important role. Germaine Sellier, whose wealthy husband was supportive of her political career, and who did not have children, was able to carve out for herself a reputation as a campaigner and spokeswoman for the causes of both feminism and pacifism in the post-war years. She was very well connected in a range of influential networks, including Catholic social activists, pacifist politicians, feminist activists and wealthy philanthropists. For this reason she was frequently elected into (largely unwaged) positions of authority in feminist and pacifist organisations. Her popularity and high profile were not appreciated by all of her fellow feminist activists. Louise Weiss described her in her memoirs as one of the 'précieuses du Lac' ('affected women in Geneva'), and Marguerite Thibert wrote in a letter in 1929 that she had 'too much eloquence and glamour and not enough technical competence'.[77] A more openly hostile letter from Marie-Louise Puech argued in derogatory terms that 'she was a politician, a social climber: she is a talented public speaker and has used this to fulfil her

---

[77] Louise Weiss, *Mémoires d'une Européenne: Vol 3, Combats pour les femmes* (Paris: Editions Albin Michel, 1980), p. 19; Letter from M. Thibert to M-L Puech, 21 May et 3 July 1929. Quoted in Michel Marbeau, 'Les Femmes et la Société des Nations (1919–1945): Genève, la clé de l'égalité?', in Yves Denéchère and Jean-Marc Delaunay (eds.), *Femmes et relations internationales au xxe siècle* (Paris: Presses Sorbonne Nouvelle, 2007), pp. 163–76 (p. 164).

personal ambition.'[78] This letter was written in an unsuccessful attempt to block her nomination to the League of Nations in 1932; it is evident, however, that her First World War decorations and experience, which were constantly mentioned when she was introduced and discussed in public meetings, enabled her to appeal to a broad constituency in interwar France. It was not until the Second World War, however, that Emilienne Moreau was able to fully capitalise on her First World War reputation and experience. As was the case for many women, her public identity as a war veteran was overshadowed by her private one as wife and mother once she married. Although alongside her husband she was active in socialist organisations in the interwar years, it was her cemented reputation as a resistance heroine of both wars that gave her new access to public life, and in the years following the Second World War she gained positions of responsibility and influence in both political and veteran organisations.

Elsie Knocker and Mairi Chisholm: The 'Heroines of Pervyse'

Another woman who attempted, although less successfully, to instrumentalise her heroine and veteran status by publishing her memoirs in the wake of the Second World War was British woman Elsie Knocker, who, along with Mairi Chisholm, was celebrated in 1914–18 as the 'Heroine of Pervyse' (Figure 2.6). Their story is relatively well known, having been rediscovered by the British press at the time of a well-attended 1977 'Women at War 1914–18' exhibition at the London Imperial War Museum.[79] In addition, more recently they have been the subjects of a well-researched biography, Diane Atkinson's *Elsie & Mairi Go to War*, that was adapted for a performance at the 2010 Edinburgh Fringe festival, a historical novel by Jean-Pierre Isbouts, *Angels in Flanders*.[80] After a fund-raising campaign instigated by Diane Atkinson, a statue was erected to both women in the garden of the Hotel Ariane in Ypres in 2014, sculpted by Josiane Vanhoutte.

In 1914, having met previously because of their shared interest in motorcycling, twenty-nine-year-old divorcee Knocker and eighteen-year-

[78] Private letter to M. Massigli, 25 July 1929, Relations avec les associations – représentation féminine – 229, Ministère des affaires étrangères. Quoted in Christian Birebent, 'Militantes pro-SDN en France et au Royaume-Uni dans les années 1920: quelle influence?', in Yves Denéchère and Jean-Marc Delaunay, *Femmes et relations internationales au* xxe *siècle*, pp. 255–66 (p. 265).
[79] See Marwick, *Women at War*.
[80] See http://edinburghfestival.list.co.uk/event/10004151-elsie-and-mairi-go-towar/; Jean-Pierre Isbouts, *Angels in Flanders: A Novel of World War I* (Santa Monica, CA: Pantheon Press, 2010).

Figure 2.6 Elsie Knocker and Marie Chisholm. Glasshouse Images / Alamy Stock Photo.

old Chisholm went to the front in Belgium as members of Dr Hector Munro's Flying Ambulance Corps. Munro was a suffragist who was keen to recruit women to prove their worth in a situation of war, although he had little official support and, according to a later interview with Chisholm, was 'looked upon as a total crank' in Belgium.[81] With the permission of the Belgian authorities they set up, funded and ran a first-aid post (Knocker was a trained nurse) near to the front lines. Like Moreau, they were awarded medals in a high-profile public ceremony, and only left Belgium after being gassed in 1918. From the very beginning, their exploits were highly publicised in the French and British press – Chisholm's diary mentions meeting two journalists and a photographer as early as September and October 1914 – who constructed them as heroines.[82] Ellis Ashmead-Bartlett, one of the journalists referenced in Chisholm's diary, who was reporting for the *Daily Telegraph*, wrote in October 1914 that '[t]heir names . . . should certainly enjoy an immortality associated with the greatest heroines of history' and

[81] Mairi Chisholm, Recorded interview, 1977, Liddle Collection, Brotherton Library, University of Leeds, WO 015.
[82] IWM, Miss M. M. Chisholm, Diary 1914, 11600 01/42/.

argued that Dr Munro's Flying Ambulance Corps was 'the most remark-able and useful organization I have ever seen in any campaign'.[83] Their quasi-military virtues of bravery and risk-taking were noted, especially in the British press with headlines such as 'Thrilling Adventures with the Belgium Army', but reporters were quick to situate them in relation to more traditional understandings of feminine virtue.[84] They were labelled, for example, 'ministering angels' and 'the Madonnas of Pervyse' by British and French newspapers, respectively.[85] More than Emilienne Moreau, though, Elsie Knocker and Mairi Chisholm exploited and to some extent controlled the mediatisation of their heroism during the war. They constantly needed funds to keep their first-aid post and ambulances going, and interrupted their nursing work to go on fund-raising lecture tours in Britain. Chisholm commented on the importance of the press coverage in their fund-raising efforts:

We were tremendously publicized over here you know. You know yourself what the press is. If they get hold of something which they think is very unusual they go to town on it and of course, this was wonderful. Then we both appeared at the Alhambra theatre, which was a very big theatre in Leicester Square, and all the most famous actors and actresses of the day gave their services for us and we had a terrific reception there. It was packed from floor to ceiling and we raised two thousand pounds that afternoon.[86]

In these public appearances, Knocker and Chisholm tended to be intro-duced and praised according to pre-existing cultural models of female heroism. One report of a public lecture given in Nairn Public Hall (near to Chisholm's family home in Scotland) on 2 May 1916 described them as 'veritable heroines', suggesting that while Florence Nightingale 'would ever be remembered by the name of the "Lady of the Lamp"', the heroines of Pervyse would 'hereafter be known as the "Ladies of the Ambulance" [applause]'.[87] In contrast, in later writings and interviews, both women were swift to emphasise their lack of conformity to tradi-tional models of femininity. While Mairi Chisholm commented that she felt she was 'a disappointment to my Mother because I wasn't in the least interested in clothes or anything like that. Mechanics interested me enormously', Elsie Knocker scorned those who doubted their ability as women to work close to the front line, recalling the following episode in her memoirs:

---

[83] *Daily Telegraph*, 26 October 1914.   [84] *The War Budget*, 4 January 1917.
[85] 'Les deux madones de Pervyse', *Le Matin*, 17 August 1917.
[86] Chisholm, Recorded interview.
[87] IWM, Baroness de T'Serclaes, Folder of Press Cuttings, 9029–2 P404.

The Red Cross driver ... flatly refused to take me, adding that it would be bad enough without any women around, since all women panicked at a crisis. Three years later I ran into that driver in Boulogne. He came up to me and said 'I want to apologize, Sister. I have been in comparative safety for the last three years, while you have been up in the front-line trenches.'[88]

However, during the war both Chisholm and Knocker were happy to exploit the feminised 'Florence Nightingale' image for fund-raising purposes, posing for example for photographs in this mode. As was the case for Moreau, a romanticised account of their adventures that they collaborated on, entitled *The Cellar House at Pervyse* (1916), was sold to publicise their cause. The introductory note by author Geraldine Mitton stated:

Of all the things told of the Great War surely this is the most uncommon, that two women should have been at the front with the Belgian Army almost from the beginning. That they should have lived as the soldiers lived, caring for them, tending them, taking cocoa and soup into the trenches and even to the outposts. And this is what has been done by the two British ladies whose names are on the title-page.[89]

The royalties from the book bought a new motorbike ambulance and, more than this, set them up as two of the most high-profile heroines of the war, combining the roles of maternal nurses, mothering 'poor little Belgium', and plucky British lady-soldiers in the public imagination. Their diaries attest to the fact, however, that there was stiff competition for the status of war heroine, even amongst their close colleagues and collaborators. There are hurt and angry entries concerning the jealousy amongst some of the other women they were working alongside when they were awarded medals by the King of Belgium. In addition, they were both furious when American journalist Arthur Gleason's popular account of the Flying Ambulance Corps, *Young Hilda at the Wars* (1915), set up his wife, Helen, an original member of the Corps, in a leading role rather than Knocker and Chisholm. In Gleason's account 'Hilda' (Helen) took all the risks, and was responsible for setting up the dressing station at Pervyse, whereas 'Mrs Bracher' (Knocker) was presented as reluctant: '"Pervyse?", cried Mrs Bracher. "Why, my dear girl, Pervyse is nothing but a rubbish heap. They've shot it to pieces. There's no one at Pervyse." "The soldiers are there," replied Hilda.'[90] Chisholm angrily wrote in her diary after reading Gleason's version:

[88] Chisholm, Recorded interview; Elsie de T'Serclaes, *Flanders and Other Fields* (London: Harrap, 1964), p. 50.
[89] Geraldine Mitton, *The Cellar House at Pervyse: A Tale of Uncommon Things* (Milton Keynes: Oakpast, 2011 [1916]), p. 9.
[90] Arthur Gleason, *Young Hilda* (New York: Frederick A. Stokes: 1915), pp. 7–11.

I can't understand what he can possibly have been thinking when he wrote it. If only he hadn't mentioned Pervyse by name, & put in Helen's portrait the thing would have been alright. . . . It is the most astounding bit of brazen cheek that has been published for many a long day. . . . Helen, knowing how hurt Gipsy [Knocker] was when Dorothie [Lady Dorothie Feilding] was given the Kudos of Pervyse & how hurt she was re our decorations ought to have been just double careful that nothing further should happen which might aggravate the old wound.[91]

Despite Mitton's declaration in the Cellar House of Pervyse that 'the Two had always hated publicity', then, both Knocker and Chisholm jealously guarded their public personae, keenly aware of the potential economic, social and cultural capital afforded by their mediatisation as heroines.[92] Knocker, in particular, was keen to differentiate her work from that of other wealthy civilians who had travelled to the front, describing the latter in her diary as the 'elderly sightseers on our ambulance column . . . They are a nuisance & I am not surprised Kitchener gets fed up with women at the front'.[93] After the war, Elsie Knocker, abandoned by her Belgian aristocratic husband after he discovered she was divorced, struggled to carve out a place for herself in the post-war world: 'The "Heroine of Pervyse" the Press called me, but ten years later it was a different story.'[94] Like many male-authored war memoirs, her autobiography is full of nostalgia for 'the sense of sharing, of comradeship and identification, the hatred of the muddle and waste of war, and then, hard on its heels, the sharp gratitude for being there in the middle of it all to make a tiny corner of sanity . . . Pervyse stood, and stands, for all that is best and most satisfying in my life'.[95] She briefly worked for the newly formed Women's Royal Air Force in 1918 'while the dew of my Pervyse fame was still fresh upon me', but this was soon disbanded.[96] She then embarked on a series of failed projects all involved with helping war veterans, thereby not only exploiting her wartime notoriety but also responding to a psychological need to reaffirm her own sense of her identity as a veteran. Her first successful opportunity to reprise her wartime role came during another national crisis, the 1926 General Strike, when she set up another first-aid post, flying the same Red Cross flag that she had flown at Pervyse, in the working-class Poplar

---

[91] IWM, Miss M. M. Chisholm, Diary, 1914, 11600 01/42/1.
[92] Mitton, *The Cellar House at Pervyse*, p. 11.
[93] IWM, Baroness de T'Serclaes, Diary, 9029–2 P404.
[94] T'Serclaes, *Flanders and Other Fields*, p. 17. Baron T'Serclaes was a Nazi collaborator during the Second World War. See Diane Atkinson, *Elsie & Mairi Go to War: Two Extraordinary Women on the Western Front* (London: Random House, 2009).
[95] T'Serclaes, *Flanders and Other Fields*, pp. 68 and 81.
[96] T'Serclaes, *Flanders and Other Fields*, p. 10.

district of London.[97] Like Moreau in her descriptions of the Second World War, in her account Knocker deliberately recreated her First World War identity, emphasising her adaptability and skills in a crisis, and effectively recreating Pervyse in London's East End:

> I went to the British Red Cross and told Eden Paget that work was badly needed in the East End. . . . I was given a very dirty, old butchers shop, in Poplar High Street, and settled down to scrub and clean. The crowd were not friendly at all, and big Armoured cars and tanks passed the shop. . . . I flatly refused to move, I said that I had come to do a definite job, and I would do it. [I asked] to bring down two men whom I had known in World War I, and would stay the course.[98]

In the late 1920s, Knocker's veteran status did bring her some economic rewards. The Red Cross offered her a small cottage on the Earl Haig estate in Ashtead, Surrey, which had been created for ex-servicemen. She named it 'Pervyse' and remained there until the final years of her life. She worked for the 'Lest We Forget' organisation in the interwar years, giving talks about her war years and helping to fund-raise. The Second World War offered her a brief opportunity to shine, and she enjoyed her time as an officer of the WAAF. But she was sometimes treated with suspicion by the younger women, and admitted to anxieties that she 'might be considered suspect as an old fogey who lived in a First World War past'.[99] In an interview given in 1977, she remained bitter about the gap between her heroine status during the war and her social status afterwards, claiming that Alexander of Teck, whom she had known during the war, 'would have a fit if he knew the circumstances I am living in now poor darling . . . I can't be a lady in this'.[100] In contrast, Mairi Chisholm, who came from a more stable and wealthy family, set up a successful business venture as a poultry breeder. She did not publish war memoirs, but in the 1970s she produced a written account in response to what she described as Knocker's 'racy account of our work in the 1914–1918 War' in order to 'stress the actual facts'. In her description of her war experience, she stressed the bravery and comradeship of the Belgian soldiers: 'Three and a half years of packed incidents; of being privileged to work in danger alongside brave men, and to recognize their immense decency to women in exceptional circumstances'. In this sense, she depicted herself as a war veteran. Yet she also differentiated herself from Knocker, stating that

---

[97] IWM, Baroness de T'Serclaes, 9029–2 P404; T'Serclaes, *Flanders and Other Fields*, pp. 115–30.

[98] IWM, Baroness de T'Serclaes, Undated account of the 1926 General Strike, 9029–2 P404.

[99] T'Serclaes, *Flanders and Other Fields*, p. 145.

[100] Baroness de T'Serclaes, Recorded interview, Liddle Collection, 1977, Brotherton Library, University of Leeds, WO 123.

'unlike [the Baroness] I have found much happiness and sense of purpose in peace time. I have been blessed with friendships of both men and women, and although my health has not always been good it has never justified self pity.'[101] Chisholm recognised in her former companion the lack of 'happiness and sense of purpose' in peacetime, suggesting that only in wartime had Knocker been able to find a private and public identity that satisfied her desire both to serve and to gain public gratitude and recognition for her service.

Marie Marvingt and Female Combatants

Like Elsie Knocker, French female aviator Marie Marvingt, a pilot and sportswoman who nursed and had brief combat roles in the war, struggled in her bid to find a post-war role, which in her case meant in the services or in the civilian air industry. Marvingt differs from my other case studies in that her construction by the French media as a heroine preceded the outbreak of the war. She was an accomplished athlete and excelled in swimming, cycling, skiing and mountain climbing. She clearly thrived on challenge and competition, becoming the third woman ever to gain her pilot's licence in 1910, and attempting numerous sporting and flying records. In magazine and newspaper articles Marvingt was presented as a courageous and glamorous modern young woman, and was nicknamed 'la fiancée du danger' ('the fiancée of danger'). In the *belle époque* she was one of the darlings of the French press. As Sîan Reynolds notes: 'Although women fliers were always a tiny minority, they were paid disproportionate attention ... [they] were role models for schoolgirls, symbols of success in a modern technological world.'[102] Newspaper articles concentrated on women pilots' appearance as much as they did on their skill, and to some extent they 'reinforced images of femininity more than they challenged them'.[103] However, Marvingt was a willing participant in her media construction as sporting and flying heroine – she had no independent wealth (her father had worked for the French postal service), and any publicity helped her to fund her exploits. In 1921, for example, when applying to the Royal Geographic Society to join an Everest expedition, she introduced herself very much in the same mode as one of the many press articles that sang her praises: 'I am Mademoiselle Marvingt, aviatrix, sportswoman, having held 17 world championship titles in all sports, and having crossed the North sea and the Channel in

[101] IWM, Miss M. M. Chisholm (1975), Typescript, 11600 01/42/1.
[102] Reynolds, *France between the Wars*, p. 65.
[103] Reynolds, *France between the Wars*, p. 78.

a balloon.'[104] In March 1914 Marvingt had obtained her pilot's license, and on the outbreak of war was initially hopeful that she would be able to fly, immediately asking the authorities if she could join as a volunteer pilot.[105] In response, the French government not only said no, but requisitioned her plane.[106] She was unwilling to give up her dream of war service as an aviator, and was one of several female pilots who formed the Union patriotique des aviatrices françaises in April 1915, who managed to get some sympathetic journalists to plead their cause in the French press. All this was to no avail. She was forced to enrol as a nurse instead, but when the opportunity presented itself apparently succeeded in persuading a camp commander to allow her to fly a reconnaissance mission when a pilot was injured. Like much of Marvingt's life, it is difficult to separate myth and anecdote from reality, but her flying in the war is mentioned in her Croix de guerre citation that she received in 1918, and in her subsequent 1933 Légion d'honneur citation.

Her other foray into combatant experience was to pose as a poilu named Beaulieu. In an interview in 1965 she claimed she was able to do this thanks to the intervention of Foch, who became a friend after the war, as well as with the help of another lieutenant. It is likely that Marvingt did serve for a brief time, perhaps three weeks, with the 42nd Battalion of the Chasseurs à Pied. She also helped the 3rd BCA evacuate troops and take provisions in the Dolomites; a photograph exists of her wearing the full uniform of the *chasseurs alpins*.[107] Unlike some women who travelled to the front with a lot of enthusiasm but no real skills, Marvingt would have undoubtedly been an asset to the army battalions she served with thanks to her extensive experience in mountaineering, skiing and shooting (she had won a military shooting competition in 1907, competing against men). Following her brief combat experience, Marvingt wrote articles as a war correspondent from the Italian front. This was the beginning of a post-war career. Writing and lecturing about her experiences, as well as nursing, would be the ways she earned money throughout her life.

The positive press coverage of her sporting and flying exploits that she enjoyed during the *belle époque* was not repeated during the war. The response of Marvingt's local *préfet* to her application for a passport to go to the Italian front in 1916 reveals the limits of acceptability of French women's wartime activities:

---

[104] Letter from Marie Marvingt dated 13 January 1921, Royal Geographic Society archives.
[105] Letter to her cousin Marthe, quoted in Marcel Cordier and Rosalie Maggio, *Marie Marvingt: La Femme d'un siècle* (Sarreguemines: Pierron, 1991), p. 91.
[106] Darrow, *French Women*, p. 240.
[107] See also Cordier and Maggio, *Marie Marvingt*, p. 96.

Mlle Marvingt is very well known in sporting circles in our region, in which she has accomplished a certain number of sporting achievements. ... Masculine in appearance, Mlle Marvingt has very free morals, and although no precise facts have been established, her behaviour in her private life leaves much to be desired. Despite this her patriotism cannot be doubted.[108]

The suspicions voiced about her private life are indicative of the extent to which her wartime activities were viewed as transgressive. This helps to explain Marvingt's failure to fully exploit her wartime service in her interwar attempts to further her career opportunities and have a voice in debates about women's contribution to both aviation and the army. In 1912 she had attempted to get a prototype of an air ambulance developed with the engineer Béchereau at the Deperdussin aeroplane factory, but the business went bust a year later and her design was never produced (Figure 2.7).[109] After the war she toured the country lecturing about the possibilities of *l'aviation sanitaire* (air ambulances). Marvingt was unstinting in her praise for the French army, and attempted in the post-war years to extend her wartime adoption of a quasi-'militarised' identity, travelling to North Africa as a 'medical assistant and war correspondent' after cashing in favours with her contacts in the French army, particularly General Hubert Lyautey. There, she flew planes and wrote and acted in a Red Cross–funded film publicising air ambulances entitled *Les Ailes qui sauvent* (*The Wings That Save*). North Africa not only further convinced Marvingt of the potential of air ambulances in the practice of both civil and military medicine, but equally the military, ex-pat community of North Africa tolerated her self-presentation as a militarised woman. It was not as easy to sell this identity in France. Throughout the 1930s Marvingt continued to promote aeromedical evacuation as a concept, and collaborated with several male doctors in the organisation Les Amis de l'Aviation Sanitaire (Friends of Air Ambulances). Despite her experience and long-term commitment, however, Marvingt was never given a leadership role in this organisation. It was not until the mid-1930s, when civil defence was becoming a greater priority for the government with the prospect of another war looming, that a flying nursing corps was established. In 1934 the Infirmières Pilotes Secouristes de l'Air (Air Ambulance Nurse-Pilots) coincided with other national defence initiatives, with the primary aim of evacuating civilians in bombing raids. Marvingt was named the first *infirmière pilote secouriste de l'air*

---

[108] Cited in Cordier and Maggio, *Marie Marvingt*, p. 98.
[109] David M. Lam, 'Marie Marvingt and the Development of Aeromedical Evacuation', *Aviation, Space and Environmental Medicine* 74: 8 (2003): 863–68.

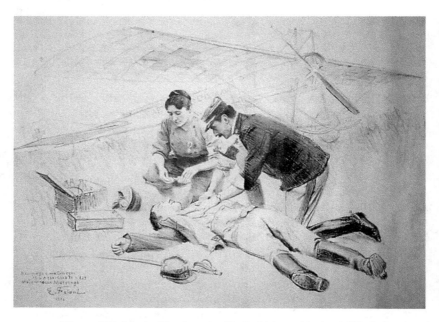

Figure 2.7 Marie Marvingt by Emile Friant, 1914. ART Collection /
Alamy Stock Photo.

(IPSA) in recognition of her championing of the cause, but by this
stage in her life (she was nearly sixty) it was an honourable title rather
than a financial coup or a career option. Unlike Germaine Sellier and
Emilienne Moreau, Marvingt was not rewarded for her war service with
a leadership or publicly funded role, and was not able to fly after the
war. In this sense, she was less successful than others in her attempts to
accrue political, economic and cultural capital by claiming veteran
status. It is notable for example that in her post-war writings and
speeches she does not refer to her wartime medals as frequently as
Moreau and Sellier, keeping to the safer ground of her sporting
achievements. Moreau's case reveals the extent to which fully fledged
combat roles, such as flying or trench warfare, were not a route for
women to interwar membership of a broader veteran community,
especially in the French context where a widespread reluctance
remained to associate women with military service.[110]

---

[110] This was despite the fact that women were employed in a civilian capacity by the French
army both during and after the war. These women were often relatives of combatants,

Conclusion

While the prestige of the heroine-martyrs who had died during the war was assured, and could remain untarnished, it was more difficult for the heroines who survived to maintain their public image in the post-war years. The personal writings of women who had been active during the conflict share many of the characteristics of those of ex-servicemen, but not all war heroines, even those who had enjoyed high public profiles during the conflict, were able to use their veteran status as a platform from which to enter public life in the interwar years. If during the war women on the front line played a vital role in the propaganda the belligerent nations wished to communicate, after the war, in a pronatalist climate that encouraged women to return to the domestic sphere, their status as war veterans was generally less welcome.

In contrast to Germaine Sellier, Emilienne Moreau and Mairi Chisholm, Marie Marvingt and Elsie Knocker did not enjoy either public acclaim or personal satisfaction in the aftermath of the First World War. Knocker's memoirs expressed a sense of yearning for the war years, despite their hardships. She implied that this was partly for reasons of social class: 'It is always such a pleasure and a privilege when one is shoved through or under or over the class barrier. It's so miserable and anti-climactic when one has to creep back to one's own "station" in life.'[111] Yet what had really changed, and what differentiated Britain and France, was that the greater professionalisation and centralisation of British women's war work in the Second World War, unlike the informal clandestine Resistance networks that developed in France, allowed less space for individual heroics by women like Elsie Knocker. Women had become accepted as a vital part of the war effort, but this very acceptance meant that the exceptionality that defined the heroines of the Great War was no longer possible. While the high status of French Resistance heroines at the end of the Second World War meant that Emilienne Moreau's social capital only increased, Knocker continued to find peacetime existence an economic struggle and psychologically unsatisfying. She constructed her autobiography around her First World War activities, nostalgic for a time in which women could join 'schemes, some official, but many, in those far-off untotalitarian days, splendidly freelance'.[112]

This was also the case for female aviators who had been active before and during the war. As Reynolds points out, women were structurally

and although paid less were largely accepted into the 'military family'. See Orr, *Women and the French Army.*
[111] T'Serclaes, *Flanders and Other Fields*, p. 130.
[112] T'Serclaes, *Flanders and Other Fields*, p. 36.

excluded from aviation in the interwar years. Marie Marvingt was unable to train in civil aviation, and was of course unable to join the French air force, which was largely staffed by First World War veterans. Of the male aviators used for fund-raising purposes in 1914 that Emilienne Moreau mentioned in her memoirs, Georges Guynemer was killed in 1917, but Charles Nungesser was able to continue his career as an adventurer, becoming the main rival to Charles Lindbergh before his aircraft *L'Oiseau blanc* was lost in 1927 during his attempt at a transatlantic crossing. René Fonck 'l'as des as' ('the Ace of Aces') survived and continued to fly in the 1920s, as well as writing his memoirs and publishing a book about his views on the role of the air force in national security. He returned to military aviation in the 1930s to become an inspector of French fighter forces.

Marvingt's fate mirrors that of other First World War female combatants. The most famous 'she-soldier', Russian Maria Bochkareva, left for America after the 1917 Russian Revolution and published her memoirs after the war to some acclaim, but was executed by the Bolshevik regime when she returned to Russia in 1920.[113] British woman Flora Sandes, who enjoyed fame and support during the war working as a volunteer for the First Aid Nursing Yeomanry (FANY) and then fighting for the Serbian army, faced some hostility and criticism on her return.[114] The women who were most able to exploit their veteran status to gain entry into public life were the ones who had not strayed too far from 'feminine' respectability, or whose social class and wealth gave them further advantages in terms of forging a career in the aftermath of the war. As the next chapter illustrates, for the women who were able to align themselves to the veteran community in this way, by presenting themselves as 'comrades in arms' while maintaining a degree of 'feminine' difference, the rewards in terms of cultural capital were potentially high.

[113] Maria Bochkareva, *Yashka: My Life as Peasant, Exile, and Soldier* (New York: Frederick A. Stokes, 1919).
[114] Alan Burgess, *The Lovely Sergeant* (London: Heinemann, 1963).

3 'That Glorious Comradeship'
Female Veteran Groups in the 1920s

As my discussion in Chapter 2 of the varied fates of war heroines in the interwar years demonstrates, women who had been active during the war were faced with both positive and negative stereotypical media constructions of their characters, behaviour and patriotism against which they were obliged to define themselves. What united both laudatory and critical early reviews of women's contribution to the war effort was a tendency to offer over-schematised versions of women war workers founded on available vocabularies of class and gender. In this chapter I explore some of the ways in which female war workers themselves conceptualised and narrated their wartime identities in the 1920s. I do so by means of a consideration of female veteran groups. The case studies that I focus on demonstrate the importance of the identity of 'female veteran' to women who not only performed different tasks during the war but who also came from diverse social backgrounds. My case studies reveal that both ex-war nurses and British ex-servicewomen were actively involved in promoting and underscoring their identities as veterans, by taking part in campaigns, representing their wartime roles in commemorative activities, writing letters to their associations' magazines and participating in social activities. In so doing, they were helping to promote a model of female identity that was not based upon the dominant domestic and maternal ideal, but that was instead based on notions of public service and sacrifice in the war years, and which differentiated them from other civilians, both men and women.

Further, the ways in which the war and their former identities as servicewomen or war nurses were evoked by members of female veteran groups also reveals a degree of nostalgia for the war years, and a sense of dissatisfaction with peacetime. To some extent, this aligned them to ex-servicemen. Communications and jointly run activities between French ex-nurses and ex-servicemen, for example, as reported in the veteran press, suggests a bond could be established between men and women who shared an identity of having being part of the 'war generation' and who expressed similar sentiments about the respect and recognition that those who had served felt they were due, and about what were perceived as some of the failings of peacetime. However, as my discussion shows, there were limits to this shared identity: whereas French nurses were able to play on their reputations as women who had served but who had not usurped a male role or transgressed gender norms, and who as a result were broadly accepted by French veteran organisations, British ex-servicewomen's status was more ambiguous, and they were not always made welcome by ex-servicemen's organisations.

The existence of groups of women who understood themselves to be female veterans of the war, even if they represented a relatively small percentage of women who were on some kind of active service, changes what some historians have concluded about gender and power relations in interwar Britain and France. Male veterans, it has been argued, were broadly misogynist in both Britain and France, and were critical of changes that they perceived women to have undergone during the war.[1] Women were seen as the antipathy of the 'veteran spirit' and were attacked for having been callous, indifferent, frivolous or sexually promiscuous during the war. This was true; but it was not true of all women. Veterans distinguished between women who had served and women who had not served, as they did in relation to men. On the right and on the left, both British and French veterans singled some women or groups of women out for praise in relation to their war work or war service and granted them membership of the 'war generation', even if it was a kind of 'honorary' membership. This complicates our understanding of interwar society, and forces us to consider the extent to which 'generation' and 'service' as well as gender set the boundaries for who was considered part of the 'war generation'.

Public and Private Functions of Female Veteran Organisations

Interwar veterans are usually understood as a new social group from which women were necessarily excluded. However, the female veteran groups that I discuss largely followed the models created by the hundreds of male veteran associations that came into existence in the immediate post-war years, and at least to some extent they considered themselves part of the broader movement. Female veteran organisations, like all interwar veteran groups, had what can be termed 'public' and 'private' functions. Like their male counterparts, in other words, these organisations served, on one hand, as pressure groups that lobbied governments

---

[1] Roberts, *Civilization without Sexes*; Kent, *Making Peace*.

for improved rights and increased recognition of women war workers and, on the other, as hubs for the construction or maintenance of the identity of 'female veteran'. Indeed, many of the women's organisations functioned primarily as social networks, as mutually supportive communities to and through which women of different social backgrounds were able to articulate a common identity predicated on their war service.

In a consideration of the functions of female veteran groups, Antoine Prost's pivotal work on French male veteran organisations provides a useful framework.[2] Prost comments that despite the apparently unifying factor of war service, the French interwar veteran movement was notable for its diversity. A central division in France and elsewhere was between wounded and disabled veterans demobilised during the war, and able-bodied veterans demobilised at the end of the war. For the former, the largest group was the centre left Union Fédérale (UF) (Federated Union of Veterans), which campaigned in particular for improved employment and pension rights. Importantly, it did not limit membership to those who had seen active service. Many groups of able-bodied ex-servicemen, on the other hand, were affiliated to the other large veteran organisation, the Union Nationale de Combattants (UNC) (National Union of Combatants). This was largely a politically conservative organisation, although it did include a number of socialist and communist members in its ranks. Through the pages of its journal, *La Voix du Combattant*, it constructed a collective veteran identity based on the ideals of camaraderie, solidarity and a sense of duty and patriotism.[3] In addition to these two main groups, Prost notes the existence of a series of smaller individualised groups that sprang up in the period 1920–24. These included professional associations, which functioned largely as political pressure groups. Following widespread dissatisfaction with the pension rates stipulated by the law of 31 March 1919, many veteran groups, including the UF and UNC, were united by their struggle over pension claims. This came to a head during the 'great pensions battle' of November and December 1924, which resulted in the Chamber of Deputies voting to raise the level of pensions.[4]

Prost focuses in the second volume of his study on the social functions of veteran groups. He defines local veteran organisations as a form of modern, secular brotherhood, whose collective identity was cemented by attendance at civic events, members' funerals and, most importantly, at commemorative events for the war dead. Regular meetings, dinners and

---

[2] Prost, *Les Anciens Combattants*.   [3] Millington, *From Victory to Vichy*, pp. 3–5.
[4] Prost, *Les Anciens Combattants*, 1, p. 97. The UF and UNC also combined forces to demand changes in government policy in the 1930s. Millington, *From Victory to Vichy*, pp. 5–6.

reunions served as both 'support and justification' for this collective identity. In addition, the organisations served as important networks of mutual support, offering advice, assisting with pension claims and financially aiding individual members in relation to the difficulties they faced in the aftermath of the war, often by means of funds collected via subscriptions. Prost argues, furthermore, that one of the important functions of local or regional groups was to act as a conduit between the local and national veteran community, allowing isolated individual members to situate themselves within a broader national framework. Indeed, Prost makes clear that the two functions I have discussed – veteran associations as protest or pressure groups on one hand, and as identity-defining social networks on the other – were always interrelated: 'The protest function ... cannot be dissociated from the function of mutual assistance and social insurance. ... [Veteran associations] are at the same time mutual aid committees and defence leagues.'[5] The national lobby movements gained their strength from the strong social networks that developed on a local level, and both combined to maintain individual and collective veteran identities based on notions of service, patriotism and a certain moral superiority in relation to non-veterans. The women's groups that I concentrate on here shared these dual public and private functions. Like the men's groups, they organised regular social meetings, as well as running trips to memorials and battlefields and parading at commemorative events, laying wreaths for men and women who had died in the war. They offered both financial and emotional support, advising women of employment opportunities, offering hardship grants, creating (in the case of the French nurses) mutual insurance schemes and encouraging the setting up of local branches of the organisations.

The public and private functions of veteran organisations inevitably evolved during the interwar period. Prost and Millington note that in France, veterans' groups in the 1930s began to reflect more closely the political affiliations and agendas of their leaders. Individual bonds between members were also weakened by time. It is notable that the female veteran groups I examine both saw the falling off of numbers in the early 1930s, before undergoing a revival of interest later in the decade when women's role in wartime was once again becoming a topic of national interest as another war became imminent.[6] In my exploration of the relationship between women's war experience and post-war self-presentations in female veteran associations, I concentrate predominantly

[5] Prost, *Les Anciens Combattants*, 2, p. 215.
[6] See Noakes, *Women in the British Army*, pp. 94–102, for a study of female veterans in the 1930s.

on the period between 1918 and 1930, the crucial period of transition for both men and women after their demobilisation from war service.

Nurse Veteran Organisations

In France, nurse veteran organisations that formed in the early 1920s fall into Prost's subcategory of smaller individualised professional associations, and were supported by both the UF and the UNC. In many ways, French war nurse veteran organisations mirrored these other specialised associations. Like them, they were initially organised to further demands for improved state benefits for their members. In France, 71,192 nurses were mobilised for the three societies that made up the French Red Cross, of whom approximately 600 died and 3,000 were wounded or medically discharged. Many nurses were awarded French medals for their war service: 375 received the Légion d'honneur, 950 the Croix de guerre, 4,071 the médaille de la Reconnaissance française and 4,615 the médaille des Epidémies.[7] In addition, approximately 10,000 nuns and 10,000 other women worked in war hospitals in various capacities, of which there were approximately 400 killed and wounded.[8] The categorisation of women as 'mutilées' (wounded) or 'réformées' (unfit for service) had important implications, even though the numbers involved were tiny in comparison to the numbers of men in these categories, as it explicitly placed women in the same category as ex-servicemen.

In principle, nurses who had been wounded or who had contracted an illness during their war service were entitled to a military pension by the law of 31 March 1919. However, because Article 64 of the law, which gave veterans the right to free surgical, pharmaceutical and medical care, stated that this article applied only to 'marins et militaires' (sailors and soldiers); nurses were excluded from this benefit. This inequity of treatment was more likely the result of omission than design, but it proved a rallying point for disgruntled nurses.[9] There was also a further discrepancy in that, unlike ex-servicemen, nurses who had been awarded a military pension were not entitled to a cost-of-living allowance. In practice, moreover, it was difficult for nurses to prove that they had contracted their injuries or illnesses in service. Like male veterans, many

---

[7] Evelyne Diebolt, 'Utile, utilitaire, utilise … Naissance et expansion du secteur associatif sanitaire et social (1901–2001)', *Connexions* 2002 (77): 7–24.

[8] Frédéric Pineau, *Les Femmes au service de la France: Vol 1, La Croix-Rouge Française 1914–1940* (Paris: Histoire et collections, 2006), p. 14.

[9] Minister of Pensions Edouard Bovier-Lapierre responded to a question from Humbert Ricolfi about Article 64 by stating: 'Concerning nurses declared unfit for service, there is a lacuna in the legislation which was undoubtedly an oversight on the part of the legislator.' *Journal Officiel*, 29 June 1924.

nurses were involved in appeals in order to try and claim their pensions. A key problem was that when they were wounded or became sick they were usually treated at the same hospital where they had been working and thus did not go through the admissions process and were demobilised without the required paperwork – the 'billet d'hôpital' (hospital card). Many nurses were obliged to try and find the doctors who had treated them in order to get certificates signed retrospectively, which were subsequently not necessarily accepted by the authorities.[10]

In response, Renée Guérin-Charvet founded the Association nationale des infirmières blessées et mutilées de guerre (AIBMG) (National Association for Wounded War Nurses) in 1923.[11] The AIBMG was a small association with only around 350 members, but fought hard to gain influence and an audience for their demands. It was also long-lived, and was still active after the Second World War.[12] Its leader, Guérin-Charvet, was the daughter of a general and a much-decorated disabled war nurse. She was therefore able to wield a certain amount of influence; she was on the first board, for example, of the Association des Grands Invalides de Guerre (Association of Seriously Disabled War Veterans). In 1924, the AIBMG persuaded General Paul Pau, president of the French Red Cross, to write an article on their behalf in a veteran journal.[13] The AIBMG also arranged a meeting with the King of Italy, who was photographed by the press shaking hands with Guérin-Charvet (Figure 3.1).

In 1923, Humbert Ricolfi, centre right deputy and UF member, proposed an amendment to the law allowing nurses to benefit from Article 64, and the AIBMG successfully appealed to both veteran associations and to the French women's movement for support. The 1924 annual congress of the Conseil National des Femmes Françaises (CNFF) (National Council of French Women), for example, included a report on the exclusion of pensioned nurses from free health care. This was described as 'a deeply unjust measure, affecting women who have the same right as soldiers to

[10] *Le Mutilé de l'Algérie*, 6 October 1929.
[11] (Jeanne Eugénie Paule) Renée Guérin-Charvet (1880–1961) was a trained nurse who was awarded the Croix de guerre, médaille d'honneur des Epidemies and Légion d'honneur. After the war, she was an active member of the Union des Françaises décorées de la Légion d'honneur (Union of French Women Decorated with the Légion d'honneur), whose potential propaganda value for suffragists and feminists was noted by Louise Weiss in the 1930s: 'her decorations, her injuries and her professions of faith touched many hearts.' Quoted in Célia Bertin, *Louise Weiss* (Paris: Albin Michel, 1999), p. 252. Another prominent member of the AIBMG was Louise Bader-Gruber (1886–1977), who was also awarded the Croix de guerre, médaille d'honneur des Epidemies and Légion d'honneur. She was awarded the Florence Nightingale Medal in 1949.
[12] *Revue Internationale de la Croix Rouge* 31: 366 (1949): 426.
[13] *Le Mutilé de l'Algérie*, 27 July 1924.

Le roi d'Italie serre la main de Mme Guérin-Charvet, présidente des infirmières blessées et mutilées de guerre et de Mlle de Baye, leur disant : « Je salue en vous les femmes de France dont j'admire le courage et la vaillance et remercie les infirmières héroïques qui ont si bien soigné nos soldats ». Le Saint-Père a accordé à ces « apôtres actives de la plus grande charité, celle qui s'exerce au péril de sa vie » une bénédiction spéciale.

Figure 3.1   Renée Guérin-Charvet meeting the King of Italy. Bibliothèque Marguerite Durand.

gratitude and respect'. The CNFF also supported the AIBMG's demands for a cost-of-living allowance.[14] The CNFF's support for disabled nurses was entirely consistent with their broader demands for equal treatment for women and men, as well as their strategic use of women's war service in their fight for female suffrage.[15] It was equally a discourse AIBMG members repeatedly used themselves. At an UF Congress in Cherbourg in 1924, for example, Guérin-Charvet addressed a veteran audience 'with tears flowing', according to a newspaper report, in which she 'recited the trials in peace of the nurses who had already suffered too much in the war', asking the Congress to urge the government to put nurses 'on exactly the same basis as combatants'.[16]

More surprisingly, perhaps, demands for equality of status for war nurses were repeated in articles published in the veteran press. The 1924 article by General Pau, for example, asks: 'Why should a difference be established between soldiers and the women who shared their fatigue

---

[14] CNFF, Report of the Congress in Lyon, 18–19 November 1924. 'Rapports sur les pensions des infirmières blesses ou mutilées pendant la guerre', BMD.
[15] Bard, *Les Filles de Marianne*, p. 84.
[16] *Ouest-France*, 24 February 1924; *Reading Eagle*, 4 January 1925.

and their dangers, who fell struck by the same shells or poisoned by the same gas? And the women who contracted illnesses in inglorious posts, at the bedsides of contagious patients, don't they also merit pity as well as justice?'[17] Similarly, in August 1925, the National Congress of the Association Générale des Mutilés de la Guerre (General Association of Disabled Veterans) in Niort passed a resolution stating that wounded or medically discharged nurses 'must be treated as combatants and benefit from all of the articles of the law of 31 March 1919'. Another resolution demanded that nurses be categorised as 'fonctionnaires' (state employees) in order to benefit from the employment advantages given to mobilised state employees in the 1924 'loi Sari'.[18] The cause of pensioned nurses was also taken up in the popular press. Le Petit Parisien, for example, claimed that '[a]ll Great War veterans who were cared for by these admirable women, and who know that a great number of them paid for their devotion to the wounded with their lives, are ready to protest.'[19]

The figure of the wartime nurse had widespread appeal, and was used as an idealised model of patriotic female identity by different constituencies of post-war French society. For this reason, the AIBMG had no difficulties in finding support amongst politicians, feminists and veteran associations for their campaigns to amend the 31 March 1919 law, and Ricolfi's amendment was passed.[20] More generally, French veteran associations, and the UNC in particular, tended to construct women as 'alien to the combatant spirit' and therefore as unfit for political power.[21] Yet nurses were treated as an exception. Their high public profile both during and after the war was based upon an association with chaste, nun-like virtue, which meant that, for veterans and others, former nurses were seen in some ways as exempt from the dominant gender imperatives that preached a return to home and family life for women. In addition, and unlike, for example, the hated non-combatant politicians, shirkers and profiteers, nurses could prove their service via their medals and proximity to the front, and were therefore generally accepted as a part of the broader veteran community.

The aims of the AIBMG were twofold: to lobby for improvements to nurses' financial and employment possibilities, and to offer a network of

---

[17] *Le Mutilé de l'Algérie*, 27 July 1924.
[18] *Journal des mutilés, réformés et blessés de guerre*, 5 September 1925. The 'loi Sari' was proposed by Corsican senator Emile Sari (1877–1927).
[19] *Le Petit Parisien*, 20 May 1923.
[20] The AIBMG also appealed later in the 1920s when a decree of 6 August 1926 modified the status of military nurses. Again, the veteran press supported nurses' demands to remain on an equal standing with pensioned ex-servicemen. *La Voix du Combattant*, 19 December 1926.
[21] Millington, *From Victory to Vichy*, p. 94.

mutual support for wounded or medically discharged nurses. As a 1929 article by one member put it: 'For the last five years, despite its meagre funds, the AIBMG has been able to help many of those in trouble. By offering advice, many have had their rights recognised, and it has also helped to heal many emotional scars.'[22] This dual aim was equally apparent in other French nurse veteran organisations, in which membership was open to able-bodied former nurses, and for which the membership figures were higher.[23] These included the Association Amicale des Anciennes Infirmières du Front (AAAIF) (Association of Ex-War Nurses), founded in 1920 with Jeanne Fiant, a former nurse, as general secretary, and Juliette Adam as honorary president. In addition to its head office in Paris, it had four regional branches.[24] Although the UNC generally only accepted women and girls as members of their youth groups and excluded women from its leadership, the AAAIF was designated as a UNC 'section'. In a 1921 article in *La Voix du Combattant* that introduces the AAAIF to the journal's readers, the UNC's position in relation to nurses is explained and justified:

War nurses were the sisters and comrades of the combatants. Many of them served in dangerous posts; they were combatants as far as their sex and the tasks they were carrying out allowed them to be. It was only natural that our valiant comrades would have the idea to form a group in order to preserve their memories of the hours spent together in the service of the Fatherland and of Soldiers, and in order to offer mutual aid once they had returned to their families or to civilian life. Many of them, moreover, just like many veterans, have experienced misfortune and public indifference which sometimes borders on ingratitude. ... We thank Mme Fiant and her colleagues and members, and we respectfully pay tribute to them here. They will always find in the UNC and at the *Voix du Combattant* a particularly warm welcome and fellow feeling.'[25]

This article, written by a UNC member, deliberately aligns the nurses with combatants, asking the predominantly male readership to accept and support them as fellow veterans. A similar level of acceptance is evident in a 1922 article written in support of the AAAIF by Gustave Durassier, editor of the conservative veteran journal the *Almanach du Combattant*:

[22] *Le Mutilé de l'Algérie*, 6 October 1929.
[23] As there are no extant records of the AAAIF it is difficult to gauge membership numbers. The existence of four regional committees as well as the Parisian branch, however, as well as the fact that membership was open to all war nurses, suggests higher membership than for the AIBMG. A similar nurse veteran organisation also existed in Belgium, the Amicale des Infirmières du Front 1914–1918 (First World War Nurses' Association), whose president was Pauline de Mot. See Eliane Gubin et al. (eds.), *Dictionnaire des femmes belges* (Brussels: Editions Racine, 2006), p. 433.
[24] *L'Almanach du Combattant*, 1922, p. 246.   [25] *La Voix du Combattant*, 6 May 1921.

The battlefield, for nurses, extended way beyond the military zone. They also battled, fought and died in hospitals behind the lines. Contagious diseases ... claimed many victims amongst the nurses. Yes, many nurses were combatants and several of our associations have deservedly opened up their ranks to receive nurses as members.[26]

On a local level, there are several references in *La Voix du Combattant* to nurses taking part in UNC social or committee activities, as well as reports of AAAIF activities. For instance, in September 1919, Mlle Mancheron is named as a member of the Senlis (Oise) committee, in June 1921 Gabrielle Stouque is described as having been an 'active member' of her section since the Armistice, and in July 1922 Mme Tauton was elected to the committee for one of the Parisian branches.[27] There is also evidence in the form of published letters that some nurses read the journal and turned to the resources of the UNC for support, asking for advice about pension claims, or expressing their anger at government policy.[28]

The acceptance of nurses as members of the veteran fraternity is also evidenced by the fact that certain nurses were awarded the coveted 'Carte du combattant'. The kinds of women who were awarded this status, however, is revealing of the extent to which such women were viewed as exceptional. The treatment of nurses by the main veteran groups should not therefore be interpreted as a broader recognition in France of the value of women's war service. The 'Carte du combattant' was created by the decree of 28 June 1927, and was administered by the Office national du combattant (ONC) that had been founded the previous year.[29] Individuals were entitled to the card if they had had three months of continuous service in a combatant unit or could provide proof of a war injury.[30] Another decree of 6 July 1929 specified that the majority of male medical staff were entitled to carry the Carte, but it was not made clear whether nurses

---

[26] *L'Almanach du Combattant*, 1922, p. 246.

[27] *La Voix du Combattant*, 21 September 1919, 19 June 1921, 23 July 1922. Gabrielle Stouque (1889–1921), was a trained nurse who was awarded the Croix de guerre and Légion d'honneur after the temporary hospital she was working in was bombed, leaving her with a serious head wound. She worked at the Ministry of Pensions after the war. She died as a result of her injuries, and UNC veterans attended her funeral. *La Voix du Combattant*, 21 August 1921; *Le Figaro*, 27 May 1921, AN LH/2553/63.

[28] For a letter asking about a pension claim, see *La Voix du Combattant*, 24 April 1924. See also an interesting letter from Jeanne Bonnet expressing her anger at the government's insensitive treatment of the exhumation of her son's body. Here, she uses her dual status as bereaved mother and war nurse to justify her anger: 'I was a volunteer nurse from the beginning to the end of the war, [and] I gave to my country, the most precious gift of all, my only son who enlisted at 17, and was killed aged 18 ½. I never failed in my duty as a French woman.' *La Voix du Combattant*, 15 March 1922.

[29] Monte, 'L'Office National des anciens combattants'.

[30] Prost, *Les Anciens Combattants*. By 1935, 3,630,000 had been issued the Carte, which represented 66 per cent of those mobilised.

would be entitled on the same basis.[31] In November 1929, one of the French Red Cross organisations, the Union des Femmes de France (UFF), asked the ONC if it would be possible for nurses to apply, to which the Office replied that the only nurses eligible were those who had been awarded the Croix de guerre, where the citations specified the exact circumstances in which these women had risked injury or death.[32] Ultimately, only a handful of the 905 nurses who were decorated with the Croix de guerre were awarded the 'Carte du combattant'. These were generally high-profile war heroines who were singled out as exceptional, embodying national virtues.

They included Marguerite Jourdan Cauchy, a bourgeois Red Cross nurse and future president of the UFF, who contracted a disease while working on hospital ships; Evelyn Garnaut Smalley, a wealthy American attached to the YMCA who remained in France after the war and founded the 'Foyer des Soldats Français'; and Nelly Martyl Scott, another volunteer Red Cross nurse who had been a famous opera singer before the war, and was the wife of Georges Scott, an artist who worked for *L'Illustration*.[33] Their ranks also included a few non-nurses, such as the surviving members of resistance networks Jeanne de Belleville, Marie-Léonie Vanhoutte and Louise Thuliez.[34] These women were clearly held in high regard by the veteran community, and were cast as emblems of the elite of French womanhood, elevated above civilian men as well as the majority of other women. This was made particularly evident in press photographs that showed two of the nurses who had been awarded the 'Carte du combattant', Marguerite Jourdan-Cauchy and Mme Brennetot, lighting the Eternal Flame beneath the Arc de Triomphe, surrounded by ex-servicemen (Figure 3.2).[35] The selection of women to carry out the most important of all symbolic gestures amongst the veteran community reveals the extent to which certain women's heroine status persisted into the interwar period. It also reveals that war nurses were often accepted as part of the veteran community, and that it was not at odds with their own identities as ex-servicemen for a woman to lead their act of remembrance.

[31] *Journal Officiel*, 19 September 1929.

[32] *Bulletin de l'Union des Femmes de France*, November 1929, pp. 401–02.

[33] *Le Petit Parisien*, 18 March 1927; http://champagne1418.pagesperso-orange.fr/recit/recit9.htm#smalley; Jean Guillermand, 'Nelly Martyl Scott (1884–1953)', *Revue de l'Infirmière* 163 (2010): 45–50.

[34] *Le Combattant du Poitou: Organe du Groupe Poitevin de l'Union Nationale des Combattants et des Sociétés affiliées du département de la Vienne*, 34, September 1934. I would like to thank Chris Millington for generously providing these references.

[35] *Ouest-France*, 3 April 1924; Photograph in BMD, 'Dossier Infirmière Militaire'; *La Voix du Combattant*, 10 February 1934.

HOMMAGE A L'« INCQNNU ». — Une infirmière qui fit toute la guerre, Mme Brennetat, a hier soir ranimé solennellement la Flamme en présence d'une délégation d'anciens combattants

Figure 3.2 Marguerite Jourdan-Cauchy and Mme Brennetot, lighting the Eternal Flame beneath the Arc de Triomphe, surrounded by ex-servicemen, 1933. Bibliothèque Marguerite Durand.

Nursing organisations, however, objected to the awarding of the Carte du combattant to only a very limited number of war heroines, and wanted war nurses more generally to be recognised as having veteran status. The UFF stated in 1929, for example, that 'we hope that soon all nurses will be able to receive the Carte du combattant under the same conditions as male members of the medical services.'[36] Similarly, an article appeared in the *Almanach du Combattant* in 1933 that stated:

---

[36] *Bulletin mensuel de l'Union des Femmes de France*, November 1929, pp. 401–02.

Those who object [to the nurses being awarded the Carte du combattant] say that nurses weren't in the trenches. Or that they weren't wounded! Were the male nurses wounded? Were the hospital orderlies who washed the floor while the nurses bathed wounds? It is a glaring injustice and a failure of our nation. All nurses attached to surgical teams, military hospitals or army corps should be awarded the card. And as the government hasn't rewarded them with the recompense that they deserve, it's soldiers who should demand it on nurses' behalf.[37]

Its author, Magdeleine Chaumont, was a middle-class novelist and jour-nalist who had taken up the nurses' cause in her role as president of Forces Féminines Françaises, a conservative women's organisation.[38] Her pleas were backed up by the journal's editor, Jacques Péricard, who responded: 'There are, we know, strict rules governing the awarding of the Carte du combattant. These rules are sometimes cruel and we must try to correct them when there are grounds to do so, but they are necessary. If we listened to every claim there wouldn't be a single mobilised individual who wouldn't receive the card. However, if there is one category for whom the strict rules appear to be unquestioningly unjust, isn't this military nurses?' For some veterans, then, at least by the early 1930s, war nurses were implicitly understood as worthy not only of respect and admiration but also of combatant status. The same pleas for nurses to be awarded the Carte du combattant appeared side by side with attacks on those who were perceived as the enemies of the veteran community: profiteers and shirkers, categories that could include women as well as men in their ranks. Although nurses constituted a low percentage of the total numbers of men and women involved in the veteran movement, their presence suggests that their gender was not an excluding factor. Post-war society was not exclusively divided on gender lines: service for the nation could sometimes override gender as the most important ele-ment in an individual's positioning in relation to the state. The veteran journalists who argued in favour of nurses being awarded the Carte du combattant were clear in their logic that military nurses were just as deserving of veteran status as male medical staff. In theory this had further implications: if nurses could be understood as veterans, then why not as citizens, with the right to vote? However, most nurse veteran organisa-tions were not directly linked to suffragist or feminist organisations. Although suffragist Juliette Adam was named as president of the AAAIF, such organisations were generally not run by women who had

---

[37] Magdeleine Chaumont, 'Les infirmières de l'avant et la Carte du Combattant', *L'Alamanach du Combattant*, 1933, pp. 189–91 (p. 191).
[38] Laurence Klejman and Florence Rochefort, *L'Egalité en marche* (Paris: des femmes, 1989), pp. 203–04.

political roles or leadership positions. Their public functions were therefore limited to lobbying for veteran benefits for their members.

Ultimately, while French nurse veteran associations sought to bolster their claims to veteran status amongst male veterans and the wider public, their primary function was to offer emotional and practical support to their members. As the AAAIF stated: 'The goal of our Association is solidarity. We seek to help by all means possible the needs of our colleagues.'[39] Another association that offered this kind of mutual aid was the Association Mutuelle des Infirmières de la Croix Rouge (AMICR) (Mutual Association of Red Cross Nurses). This Association was originally associated with the oldest of the three French Red Cross societies, the Société de Secours aux Blessés Militaires (SSBM) (Society to Aid Wounded Soldiers), but in September 1919 it opened its membership to the other two Red Cross societies.[40] The AMICR organised meetings, lectures and social events and opened a 'Nurse's Home' in Paris, which had a meeting room and inexpensive rooms to rent for its members. It also went on in the 1930s to set up a mutual insurance fund and a nurses' retirement home. Under the leadership of the aristocratic Marie de Caters, its president and an important figure in the development of the nursing profession in France, the AMICR charts in its journal the post-war development of the role of the Red Cross nurse, which included a new emphasis on public health, particularly the education of mothers, child health and the combating of diseases such as tuberculosis.[41] In this sense, it did not view itself as a 'veteran association' like the AIBMG and AAAIF. However, it is clear that many former Red Cross war nurses used the pages of the journal not only for practical advice and up-to-date information but equally as a means of constructing an 'imagined community' of female war veterans.[42] In the conception of the organisation's role after membership was opened to all Red Cross nurses, the president wrote: 'Many amongst you have been profoundly affected by your exhausting war service; your health has suffered and always will do. ... After the separations ... caused by the war, it seems to me that we need to meet with each other once again, we have the desire to be more united than ever, to support and help each other more than in the past.'[43]

---

[39] *L'Almanach du Combattant*, 1922.
[40] *Bulletin Trimestriel de l'Association Mutuelle des Infirmières de la Société de Secours aux Blessés Militaires*, September 1919.
[41] See Yvonne Knibiehler, *Histoire des Infirmières* (Paris: Hachette, 2008); Katrin Schultheiss, *Bodies and Souls: Politics and the Professionalization of Nursing in France, 1880–1922* (Oxford: Harvard University Press, 2001).
[42] Benedict Anderson, *Imagined Communities: Reflections on the Origin and Spread of Nationalism* (London: Verso, 1991).
[43] *Bulletin Trimestriel de l'Association Mutuelle des Infirmières de la Société de Secours aux Blessés Militaires*, September 1919.

It is possible, in effect, to interpret many of the letters and articles submitted by the Red Cross nurses about their war experiences as examples of what Jay Winter has referred to as a 'community of suffering'.[44] There were several obituaries, for example, of colleagues that served as reminders of the losses amongst their own profession.[45] In addition, many contributions focused on the traumatic nature of some of the nurses' war experiences. One example that illustrates well the use of the journal as a cathartic space in which traumatic experiences could be shared was written by M. Dagbert, an SSBM nurse, who recalled an incident in Liévin (Pas de Calais) in the occupied region. While she was bandaging the eldest child of a miner in the cellar, who had been injured by a shell two days previously, one of the miner's daughters slipped upstairs to comb her hair in front of a mirror, and was struck by another shell, which killed her. The description of the dying girl is graphic and medically detailed: 'An enormous wooden splinter, which had come off the door frame through which the shell had entered, had become embedded lengthways in the frontal bone and the arch of the eyebrow.'[46] The nurse is clearly haunted by this experience, and ends with an emotional and patriotic plea to remember those whom she refers to as the 'forgotten victims' of the war:

We certainly registered the victory in our hearts, perhaps more so than those who hadn't 'seen' with their own eyes, who hadn't smelt the odour of shells and lived with the hated Huns. . . . we would never forget! And very often, in our spare time, in quiet moments, the long line of little children, women and old people who died for their country, like our dear soldiers, advances once again to remind us never to forget.

This vision of civilian victims of war rising up to 'advance once again' is, like Helen Little's vision that I discussed in Chapter 1, redolent of the many cultural representations of the 'return of the dead' that were produced during the interwar period. Like the hero of Abel Gance's 1917 film *J'accuse*, the nurse-narrator presented herself here as the authentic voice of the embittered veteran, speaking in her case on behalf of the civilian dead, and claiming their right to respect and remembrance.

The AIBMG and AAAIF are clear examples of women strategically using their war status for specific political ends, demanding equal treatment for war nurses in terms of pension rights and other benefits given to

---

[44] Winter, *Sites of Memory*, p. 29.

[45] Many of these are listed as having died from influenza, which was presented in the journal as a war death. Many others list the cause of death rather more vaguely as 'les fatigues de la guerre' (war exhaustion).

[46] *Bulletin Trimestriel de l'Association Mutuelle des Infirmières de la Société de Secours aux Blessés Militaires*, September 1919.

ex-servicemen in the interwar years. Yet they also functioned as social networks, offering regular consultation hours for advice, meeting places, newsletters and social and commemorative activities. The content of the journal of the AMICR, moreover, points to another aspect of function of female veteran associations. The *Bulletin* provided a space in which women could share memories, which were often traumatic, of their war experiences. This not only had a cathartic function in some cases but equally cemented an understanding of their shared identity as war veterans who had the right, or even the duty, to speak about the war and its lessons for the civilian population. The identity of war veteran for these women, like the organisations of ex-war nurses themselves, therefore served dual purposes in the interwar years. In some cases it provided former nurses a public role, allowing them to accrue cultural capital through their appearance at remembrance activities, participating in veteran congresses and becoming the spokeswomen for other nurses in their claims for recognition and respect. In other cases, however, it served as an important identity hub for nurses on whom war service had had longer-term psychological impacts.

In Britain, there were no direct equivalents of the French ex-nurse associations. For nurses who were disabled during their war service, however, and who were entitled to a pension, there was some support. Letters exist from local branches of the British Legion in nurses' pension files, and they were also supported by the 'Officers' Friend', an organisation set up by the Ministry of Pensions in January 1919 to support officers through the complicated business of claiming a pension. In the letters preserved in the pension files both nurses themselves, and those who acted as their advocates, often presented them as entitled to compensation from the state as a result of their war service, and they are keen to underscore the difficult conditions in which they served in order to argue for their rights. For example, Mamie Ibberson, writing to a Colonel Millward from the local branch of the Officers' Friend about one VAD nurse, who suffered from ongoing depression and delusions after suffering a cerebral embolism while nursing on the Western Front, noted: 'It is a terribly sad case, as Mrs ... has evidently been most capable in the past, and her present sad condition is due to the War Service that she rendered.' The nurse herself wrote: 'I went out to France in Oct 1914, staying there until Jan 1919, when I got shell shock. ... I have been, and am, absolutely unfit for all work ever since.'[47] The Officer's Friend could also offer support to a nurse's family members when a nurse's health required them to act as carers. In another case, for example, the niece of

[47] TNA PIN 26/20233.

a former QAIMNSR nurse wrote that she had been forced to give up her studies to care for her aunt, and requested financial compensation.[48]

In addition to the groups of individuals who supported disabled war nurses with their pension claims, it is also possible to find evidence of attempts on the part of some able-bodied British nurses to meet with former colleagues and re-evoke the war years. Denise Poynter notes that 'both soldiers and nurses sought emotional security and safety in what they had been familiar with, which was ... the strange intimacy that was part of being on the Western Front, and in their search for solace, many nurses ... demonstrated a desire to remain in contact with those they had served with.'[49] This appears to have usually taken place on a local and informal footing. Local newspapers reported meetings and social gatherings of former nurses across Britain in the early 1920s. In 1923 in Dundee, for example, there was a 'second annual' Red Cross Nurses Reunion at Cupar for former nurses at Wood End Auxiliary Hospital.[50] The year 1924 saw an 'Ambulance Reunion' that took place in the YMCA hall in Bristol, and consisted of men and women who had worked for the St John's Ambulance. The speeches praised the 'valuable work of the citizens' carried out in the war, and it was followed by an 'enjoyable reunion supper'.[51] In 1925 in Thanet, Essex there was a report of the annual reunion of Ramsgate Nursing Division and Kent 2nd VAD in Christ Parish Hall, which gave the 'opportunity of meeting fellow workers and friends and talking over old times and experiences'. The president, Rachel Weigall, also commented that it was an opportunity for women no longer engaged in nursing work to 'keep in touch with the work'.[52]

Alongside these localised initiatives there were some national ones. In 1920 the United Nurses' Services Club was launched with an 'At Home' at 3 Grosvenor Place, Hyde Park Corner, hosted by the Countess of Airlee (who worked with the Red Cross in the war, and had lost a son and a daughter, who was killed while training horses for the army), Maud McCarthy and Ethel Becher. According to a newspaper article, the founding of the club was 'a response to the wish expressed by nurses working in France during the war to have such a club', and the hostesses were 'convinced that Queen Alexandra, who loved her nurses, would do everything in her power to forward it'. It was to be 'run on the lines of a first-class residential ladies' club with at least 20 bedrooms'.[53] The first members' meeting took place on 12 December 1923, and it was clear from the discussions recorded during the meeting that its expensive

[48] TNA PIN 26/20232.
[49] Poynter, 'The Report on the Transfer Was Shellshock', p. 211.
[50] *Dundee Courier*, 5 January 1923.   [51] *Western Daily Press*, 30 January 1924.
[52] *Thanet Advertiser*, 29 August 1925.   [53] *The Scotsman*, 17 July 1920.

fees was limiting its membership to the wealthy and socially elite. One of the speakers noted: 'The question of enlargement had caused the board no little anxiety, for nurses were not among the very idle or the very rich!'[54] In some ways, although it was set up specifically for nurses who had served on the Western Front, the United Services Nurses' Club was a socially elite version of the pre-existing 'nurses' clubs' that had been set up in the early years of the twentieth century as places of respite for trained nurses. Nurses' clubs in Britain were therefore not a wartime phenomenon, but they were given added impetus by the war. For example, a nurses' club in Edinburgh had first been proposed in 1907, but in 1920 Sir John Lorne Macleod declared that 'the idea largely took shape as a token of gratitude for the services rendered by professional and voluntary nurses. . . . During the last few years of the war the public had become more acquainted with the value of skilled nursing. As a nation they were proud and glad to show that they really appreciated the wonderful work the nurses had done. So many soldiers and sailors could not have got through their illnesses without the help . . . of these in the wards of our hospitals.'[55]

Finally, another way in which former nurses evoked their wartime identities was through commemoration activities. In the 1920s ex-servicemen and bereaved family members took several pilgrimages to the former battlefields, and hundreds of nurses were also involved. In 1928, the 'Great Pilgrimage', in which 3,000 women went as part of the British Legion's Expeditionary Force, included 300 nurses and VADs. One newspaper article stated that '[m]any of them have never met since and arrangements are being made for reunions on spots which are for them historic.'[56] For these nurse-pilgrims, the visits to the Western Front were not only an opportunity to pay tribute to the dead, including servicemen they had nursed but equally an opportunity to share it with the women they had worked with, and with whom they would have formed strong bonds in what Poynter termed the 'peculiar intimacy' of the Western Front. While nurse veteran organisations in Britain were more localised and informal than was the case in France, nurses clearly benefited from the networks of support in the same way. In both cases, it is important to acknowledge the difference between women who continued to nurse, and women who ceased to nurse at the end of the war. For women who went on to take up new roles as health professionals, nurses' clubs often had an ongoing function, and they were caught up with new challenges and the evolving contexts of their professional lives. For

[54] *Northern Whig*, 18 December 1923.   [55] *The Scotsman*, 6 May 1920.
[56] *Dundee Evening Telegraph*, 3 August 1928.

women who had taken on private domestic roles as wives or mothers, however, there was often a degree of nostalgia for a more public wartime role.

The WAAC Old Comrades Association

Veteran organisations provided spaces in which men and women could return to what was generally understood as a positive shared past as a member of the armed services, sometimes with a degree of affectionate nostalgia. This function of veteran organisations is particularly in evidence in relation to the British WAAC Old Comrades Association (OCA). The WAAC itself was founded in March 1917 as a result of government debates around the increasing shortage of manpower. These had culminated in Lieutenant General Henry Lawson's report, presented to the Army Council in January 1917, which recommended the replacement of men by women as ambulance drivers, clerks, storewomen, checkers, telegraphists, telephonists, postal employees, orderlies, cooks and domestic servants.[57] By the end of the war the WAAC employed around 38,000 women, of whom around 9,000 worked overseas.[58] Following Lawson's recommendations, the members of the Corps engaged in traditional support roles, the majority of which were in the domestic or administration sectors: cooking, cleaning, laundry and clerical work. Smaller numbers were employed as gardeners and mechanics, and a (well-publicised) few tended war graves.[59] After the majority of women were demobilised in 1919, a final group of WAACs remained in St Pol, France in 1920 and 1921 working for the War Graves Commission. This group returned for good in September 1921, after which point the Corps ceased to exist.[60]

As an organisation the ranks and structures of the WAAC were modelled on those of the British armed services. Its leaders were Mona

---

[57] Julia Margaret Cowper, *A Short History of Queen Mary's Army Auxiliary Corps* (London: Women's Royal Army Corps Association, 1966), p. 17.

[58] Sources vary in terms of the numbers of women enrolled in the WAAC. The official history of the WAAC states that 53,009 members were enrolled in the Corps. The *Old Comrades Association Gazette* states that 'during the first two years of the existence of QMAAC fifty-six thousand women were enrolled.' Cowper states, however, that at any one time 'there were never more than nine thousand women abroad or twenty-nine thousand at home.' See TNA WO162/6 *History of the Development and Work of the Directorate of Organisation August 1914–December 1918*, p. 591; *Old Comrades Association Gazette (OCAG)*, 1: 1 (July 1920): 1; Cowper, *A Short History*, p. 57.

[59] Haig insisted that women be employed as dilutees, proposing a ratio of 200 women to replace 134 men as clerks and in domestic service. Noakes, *Women in the British Army*, p. 68.

[60] *OCAG*, 2: 1 (July 1921).

Chalmers-Watson, who was chief controller based in London, and Helen Gwynne-Vaughan, who was controller in France. Gwynne-Vaughan's memoirs included as an appendix a 'Table of Relative Ranks', underscoring the extent to which she saw the Corps as an integral part of the armed services. In relation to the Army, WAAC Workers were the equivalent to Privates, Forewomen and Assistant Forewomen equivalent to Corporals and Lance-Corporals, and the various grades of Administrators equivalent to those of Army Officers. While the female leadership of the WAAC (many of whom were, like Gwynne-Vaughan, highly educated professional women who supported female suffrage) were keen to highlight commonalities between mobilised men and women, there was considerable resistance in government and army circles to any notion of direct equivalence between the women's auxiliary services and the armed services. Gwynne-Vaughan expressed her frustration, for instance, when the Corps was not permitted to call the upper ranks of women 'officers', but was instructed instead to use the term 'officials'. She also continually reaffirmed her desire to conform to the norms of the services in terms of communication, behaviour and discipline.[61] In this sense, Gwynne-Vaughan follows other suffragists in emphasising the equivalence of the contribution made by women's auxiliary services as a means of bolstering their claims for full citizenship.[62] The corps also, however, reproduced pre-existing class dynamics, which were embedded in its structures.[63] As Lucy Noakes rightly points out, then, it is important to emphasise the conservatism of the WAAC concerning relationships between women of different ranks/social classes, as well as its potential transgression of dominant gender discourses in terms of its attempts to 'militarise' women.[64] Moreover, the complications described by Gwynne-Vaughan in relation to discipline, where women were subject to the Army Act and some elements of military discipline, but would be tried in civil and not military courts for serious breaches in discipline, demonstrate the fact that however closely the structures of the organisation mirrored those of the armed services, WAACs remained civilians.[65]

In sum, although members of the WAACs were interpellated by the female leadership as 'female combatants', as far as the army authorities

---

[61] Gwynne-Vaughan, *Service*, p. 156.

[62] Gwynne-Vaughan formed the University of London Women's Suffrage Society in 1907 with Elizabeth Garrett-Anderson.

[63] This was also the case with other leaders of the auxiliary services, such as Katherine Furse, in charge of the VAD, who argued in 1916 that 'gentlewomen' needed to be recruited as Officers. Noakes, *Women in the British Army*, p. 68.

[64] Noakes, 'Demobilising the Military Woman', p. 146.

[65] In legal terms, WAACs stationed abroad were designated 'camp followers'.

and the mainstream French and British press were concerned, this was only ever a symbolic and temporary identity at most.[66] Commentators often focused on the auxiliary nature of their service, which was understood as an extension of women's traditional domestic roles as carers or nurturers of male relatives. This was an attempt to allay the anxieties aroused by the sight of *Eve in Khaki*, to borrow the title of Edith Barton and Marguerite Cody's 1918 laudatory account of the WAAC.[67] As the questions that were raised about the morality of servicewomen indicate, however, even their temporary presence behind the lines in France in support roles was unacceptable and unsettling to many.[68] Like many women war workers, the WAAC, particularly its working-class members, was faced with criticism 'for not being sufficiently attuned to ideas of honour and service to the nation'.[69] Rumours abounded about WAACs stationed across the Channel, who were tainted by well-worn and long-standing stereotypes that associated France with prostitution and illicit sexuality.[70] Hundreds of WAACs were said to have been shipped home to give birth to illegitimate children, and it was claimed that a maternity home had been established for unmarried WAAC mothers.[71] In her memoirs, Gwynne-Vaughan stated that the pregnancy rate amongst WAACs working abroad was lower than average at around 3 per cent, and suggests that the rumours of promiscuity were the result of misogyny, 'an excellent stick with which to beat a Corps of women'.[72]

For many of the women involved, though, their wartime identity as WAACs was a source of pride both during and after the war, and proved pivotal to their self-presentations in the post-war years. For some,

---

[66] Haig had clear conceptions of the lines that should be drawn between female civilian support workers and mobilised men. See Noakes, *Women in the British Army*, pp. 65–66.

[67] Edith M. Barton and Marguerite Cody, *Eve in Khaki: The Story of the Women's Army at Home and Abroad* (London: Nelson, 1918). Noakes, *Women in the British Army*, p. 70; Grayzel, *Women's Identities at War*, p. 199.

[68] Watson, *Fighting Different Wars*, p. 41.

[69] Janet Watson, 'Khaki Girls, VADs, and Tommy's Sisters: Gender and Class in First World War Britain', *The International History Review* 13: 1 (1997): 32–51 (p. 41).

[70] Lucy Noakes, '"A Disgrace to the Country They Belong To": The Sexualisation of Female Soldiers in First World War Britain', *Revue LISA* 4 (2008). Available online at http://lisa.revues.org/951. This criticism was not exclusively class-based, and to some extent was aimed at all women who were working close to the front or in proximity to mobilised men. Nurses' morality was also frequently subject to suspicion in the press and popular culture. See for example Margaret Darrow's discussion of 'true nurses' and 'false nurses' in *French Women*, chapter 5.

[71] Cowper, *A Short History*, p. 43.

[72] In contrast, Gwynne-Vaughan asserts that the presence of women in France was good for both sexes: 'It is not always realized how large a part Queen Mary's Army Auxiliary Corps played in bringing about the good comradeship and joint enterprise which is to be found today among working young men and women. They used only to "walk out", on active service they learnt to work and play together.' Gwynne-Vaughan, *Service*, p. 53.

networks they had established through the war, and that were maintained through the OCA, allowed them to shape their career paths in concrete ways. Others turned to the 'imagined community' of the demobilised corps in order to re-invocate their wartime roles, shoring up their identities as war veterans. The kinds of women who were active in the OCA tended to be those who were the most nostalgic about their war service, and in some of their writings they implied that had joined in an attempt to counteract the isolation or dissatisfaction that they were experiencing in relation to their peacetime lives.

The WAAC OCA was launched in 1919 during a meeting at which 600 officials and members were present.[73] It was organised and led by the middle- and upper-class leaders of the WAAC who, in common with many women involved in the leadership of the British women's auxiliary services, were keen to extend the life of the organisations into peacetime.[74] This is evidenced, for example, by the fact that the leaders of the WAAC, Helen Gwynne-Vaughan and Florence Leach, who replaced Gwynne-Vaughan in September 1918 when the latter left to become commander of the WRAF, were members of the Women's Reserve Sub-Committee that met at the War Office in 1920 to discuss the possibility of a women's reserve in peacetime.[75] In 1924, Gwynne-Vaughan also served on the Voluntary Aid Detachment Council as chairman of the mobilisation committee, again motivated by her avowed desire to 'keep in touch with ... the developments at the War Office in relation to the employment of women'.[76] In addition to sitting on government committees, the leadership of the women's auxiliary services including the WAAC met in the early 1920s to discuss the maintenance in peacetime of 'that feeling of corporate life and *esprit de corps* ... whose mainspring was patriotism and loyalty', which led to the formation of a Service Women's Association to which the WAAC OAC was affiliated (Figure 3.3).[77]

Both Gwynne-Vaughan and Leach were actively involved in the OCA, with Florence Leach acting as president and Gwynne-Vaughan as vice president, which they also viewed as a way of maintaining the life of the Corps, and of promoting the identity of the female war veteran in the interwar years. Unlike the French war nurse organisations, Gwynne-Vaughan was at least partly motivated by her political and feminist beliefs, and was keen for the women's services to remain visible and active in the

[73] *The Times*, 19 December 1919.
[74] Noakes, 'Demobilising the Military Woman', p. 150.
[75] The planned reserve was, however, never realised. See Noakes, 'Demobilising the Military Woman', p. 151.
[76] Gwynne-Vaughan, *Service*, p. 77.   [77] *The Times*, 3 March 1920.

Figure 3.3 Promotional article for the WAAC Old Comrades Association, 1928, Liddle Collection, University of Leeds.

interwar years in order to combat the notion that they had been a temporary solution to a manpower crisis, or an example of women temporarily replacing men in a national emergency. Other middle- and upper-class women who had been in prominent leadership positions in the WAAC also played key roles in the OCA. In the second edition of the OCA *Gazette* that appeared in August 1920, for example, Lila Davy, a wealthy upper-class woman who was promoted to chief controller (the equivalent of brigadier general) during the war, targeted her OCA recruiting plea specifically at her former supervisees:

I welcome the opportunity of sending a message to my old comrades who served under me in France when I was Deputy Controller, Rouen, and afterwards Chief Controller, GHQ. Those were strenuous days, days which inevitably make the routine of ordinary life seem trivial and uninteresting in comparison. We felt we were pioneers, and it was up to us to make good, and to prove what women could do. I am sure that the discipline, pluck and grit learnt then will help us in whatever the future has in store. Also we have learnt what comradeship means in the widest sense. [If you join the OCA] you will be helping others, and you will feel all the better for knowing that you are still in the ranks of the old Corps, though not on active service.[78]

After the war, Lila Davy took up once again the social action committee work that many unmarried women of her class engaged in.[79] Here, though, she expressed pride and pleasure in the value of her war work, contrasting wartime with 'trivial' and 'uninteresting' peacetime life. Equally in evidence in this excerpt, moreover, is her confidence in her role as leader as she rallied her troops, effectively underscoring the hierarchy in place that lies beneath her evocation of 'comradeship' amongst the female 'pioneers' of the WAAC.

Unsurprisingly, given their experience and the professional opportunities that were available to educated middle-class women in the interwar years, several of the Administrators whose letters or articles appeared in the *Gazette* continued to work in jobs that involved the supervision of other women. Another active committee member of the OCA, for example, was Hilda Horniblow, an assistant headmistress before the war who served as Deputy Commandant of the Cooking Section of the Women's Legion and became a chief controller when this was absorbed into the WAAC.[80] Horniblow continued to exercise authority over other women in her working life after the war, taking charge in 1920 of the Fair Street Women's Evening Institute in London, and becoming a staff inspector for the Board of

---

[78] *OCAG*, August 1920.
[79] *The Times*, 13 December 1928. Lila Davy (1873–1949) was the granddaughter of wealthy merchant George Thomas Davy (1803–74), who bought the estate of Colston Bassett in Northamptonshire in 1864, where Lila was born. Her mother, Martha Jane Mackay, was also wealthy, and the family became Scottish lairds at Spean Lodge, Spean Bridge, Inverness, where she lived pre-war and served on philanthropic committees. After the war Lila lived in London, and features in the *Times* in her role as organising secretary for the Magdalen College Mission.
[80] See Jane Potter, 'Hilda Horniblow', *Oxford Dictionary of National Biography*; *The Times*, 15 April 1935.

Education in 1935.[81] Similarly, former Assistant Administrator Muriel Reid wrote in October 1920 that she had secured a post as 'Patrol Officer at Rowntrees Cocoa Works, York, where I work single-handed with over 6,000 women and girls', adding that she 'liked it very much indeed'.[82] In the profile she produced for the *Cocoa Works Magazine* in September 1920, Reid deliberately linked her wartime and post-war roles. Not only did she deploy militaristic vocabulary in her evocation of her war work, stating that 'she was stationed in various parts of the Scottish, Eastern and Southern Commands' but she also selected a photograph of herself in WAAC uniform (Figure 3.4).[83]

The women who formed the upper echelons of the management structure of the WAAC usually belonged to a similar social group to the British women referred to in Chapter 1 who instigated commemorations to women who had died in the war. Either professional women like Muriel Reid, or philanthropic social activists like Lila Davy, who lived on a private income, and were usually unmarried or childless, they were committed to promoting women's achievements. Whereas some were prominent pre-war suffragists, others were concerned more broadly with improving women's social conditions, or encouraging 'citizenship' skills. Ex-Deputy Chief Controller Winifred Haythorne, for example, a Senior Student at Somerville College, Oxford, at the outbreak of the war, became in 1920 Secretary of the 'Women's Industrial League'. This middle-class feminist organisation fought for the rights of women workers who had been demobilised, but although it earned publicity, it achieved little in the way of concrete gains.[84] The fact that Haythorne became its secretary is indicative of the attitudes towards post-war female employment that had currency amongst many former WAACs. Another active member of the OCA, Blanche Ireland, a former Unit Administrator who became Secretary of the

---

[81] On the various short-lived schemes to encourage women from the auxiliary services to enter domestic service, see Noakes, *Women in the British Army*, pp. 86–87. *OCAG*, July 1920.

[82] *OCAG*, October 1920. Margaret Muriel Reid (1888–1950) was the daughter of a minor Scottish painter, Samuel Reid. When her father died in 1919 he left only £331, so unlike some of the unmarried female leaders of the WAAC she did not have a private income.

[83] *Cocoa Works Magazine*, September 1920. Rowntree archives, Borthwick Institute, University of York.

[84] Braybon, *Women Workers*, pp. 200–01. Winifred Scott Parsons née Haythorne (1891–1977) was the daughter of a Canadian surgeon. See IWM Misc 44 (754) for a small collection of items relating to her First World War and later service including an invitation to the funeral procession of the Unknown Warrior and Order of Service (11 November 1920) and two menus for WAAC reunions (25 June 1920 and 26 February 1938).

Figure 3.4 Assistant Administrator Muriel Reid in her WAAC uniform, *Cocoa Works Magazine*, Borthwick Institute.

Ex-Service Women's Club founded in 1923, also took on a role after the war relating to female employment, as organising secretary for a scheme promoting the federation of professional women.[85]

Although several members of the WAAC leadership were vocal in their support of women workers, in their professional or private lives many such women often administered or supervised women of a lower social class. They therefore operated, at least to some extent, according to the 'mistress-service' dynamic that Ann Summers identifies in relation to trained nurses, and that Lucy Noakes argues formed 'a framework for the foundation of women's wartime auxiliary services'.[86] It is notable that some of ex-officials drew on the OCA to find their own domestic staff, such as Alice Low, a prominent pre-war Scottish suffragist activist who worked as the Boulogne area WAAC Controller during the war.[87] She became Chairman of the Edinburgh Branch of the OCA, and in 1920 can be found in the *Gazette* advertising for a 'QMAAC Table Maid', having already found herself a 'QMAAC Cook'. Moreover, many of the leaders of the WAAC used the pages of the OCA *Gazette* to attempt to put into motion schemes that aimed to employ former members of the auxiliary services as domestic labour after the war, such as the Overseas Settlement Scheme that operated in 1919 and 1920. Some former WAACs were directly involved in these schemes, such as Chief Controller Edith Thompson, who after managing the England women's hockey team was appointed Chairman of the Executive Committee of the Society for the Oversees Settlement for British Women.[88] Middle- and upper-class women who had had leadership roles in the WAAC therefore mobilised the connections they made in the war in order to recruit their own employees, in order to achieve social mobility in terms of finding employment in management positions themselves, often in supervisory roles over other women and, finally, in order to gain positions of influence in the political organisations or government committees dealing with women's employment in the interwar years.

---

[85] *OCAG*, July 1920; *The Times*, 5 March 1923, 26 November 1955. Blanche Ireland (1891–1955) was the daughter of a policeman who in 1911 was working as a 'Wine and Spirit Merchant's Assistant'. Her social background differs somewhat from that of the rest of the WAAC leadership. It is suggested in her obituary that she was promoted on merit, as a result of her 'extraordinary gift for organisation and administration'.

[86] Noakes, *Women in the British Army*, p. 155.

[87] Alice Low (1877–1954) was the daughter of Lord Low, senator of the College of Justice, Scotland. An international hockey player before the war, she was on the Executive Committee and acted as organising secretary of the Edinburgh Society and Scottish Federation of Women's Suffrage Societies. She described herself as 'Political Organiser (Suffragist)' on the 1911 census.

[88] *The Times*, 12 June 1937. Edith Thompson (1875–1961), the author of *Hockey as a Game for Women* (1905), also served as governor of Bedford College.

However, that is not to say that WAAC Workers, who were recruited from the lower-middle and working classes, did not participate in and benefit from the OCA. After its launch and subsequent promotion by the elite women who formed its leadership, the OCA flourished in the early and mid 1920s, attracting at its peak more than 3,000 subscribers.[89] A hard core of between 1,000 and 2,000 members remained active throughout the interwar period. The OCA was initiated from the top down, but it was supported and sustained by women from all of the ranks, who participated in events and contributed to its journal. The uses these women made of the OCA and its *Gazette* reveal, on one hand, an investment in the identity of war veteran, and, on the other, the maintenance of networks created in the war that offered both professional and emotional support.

The *Gazette* records the trajectories of several women from the lower-middle or working classes who turned to the networks and affiliations with other women formed during the war in their quests for post-war employment. As several historians have noted, there was a widespread expectation for working-class women to re-enter domestic service after the Armistice.[90] However, domestic service proved increasingly unpopular after the war and women sought other forms of employment, resulting in debates in the press around the post-war 'servant problem'.[91] The pages of the OCA *Gazette* make clear that individual former WAACs drew on their war service as a means of following these non-domestic career paths. There are references to several individual members who clubbed together to form business partnerships, for example as tomato growers, poultry farmers or clerical workers. These were encouraged, and in some cases, financially supported, by the OCA, with the December 1920 issue reporting that '[h]elp, both in cash and kind, have been given to members starting enterprises of one kind or another.'

For some working women, it was new skills acquired during the war that led them to consider career changes. An article in *The Times* in December 1919 noted a number of ex-WRAF drivers who set up motoring businesses, and in the early 1920s, Ivy Macdonald and Frances Hodgson, both former WAAC Workers, used the pages of the *Gazette* to advertise their new business, 'The Remy Car Company Ltd', which offered a chauffeuring service.[92] In another example of WAACs joining forces in the pursuit of employment, Worker Rose Leeson wrote in the OCA *Gazette* in December 1920 that: 'I have such pleasant

---

[89] Membership numbers are taken from NAM, OCA Minutes in the 1920s.
[90] Noakes, *Women in the British Army*, p. 85.
[91] Noakes, *Women in the British Army*, p. 86; Watson, *Fighting Different Wars*, p. 141.
[92] *The Times*, 29 December 1919; TNA BT 31/25959/167849.

memories of my three years in the QMAAC, in fact it is among the members of that corps I made some splendid friends, several of whom are joining me very soon. I have two with me, in New York now, whom I sent for from England, and got positions for – Miss Ena Jones and Miss Annie Styles.' Leeson, born into a military family that was scattered after the early death of her mother, was listed as a twenty-two-year-old parlour maid in the 1911 census. In June 1920 she emigrated to the United States, describing herself on the ship's passenger list as a 'typist'.[93] In October of the same year, Annie Styles and Ena Jones made the same journey, stating that they were travelling to join their 'friend' Rose Leeson. Styles, the illegitimate daughter of a widowed char-woman, worked in domestic service in 1911, and Jones, the daughter of a widowed laundress, was described as a 'Paper stall attendant' in 1911. After the war Styles was listed on the passenger list as a 'lady's help' and Jones as a 'clerk'. All three settled in America: Leeson married and Styles trained as a nurse before being joined by her sister and mother. Like many young working-class women, then, two of these former WAACs left British domestic service after the war. To do so, they drew on both the widening of their horizons the war brought about, and, in Leeson's words, the 'splendid friends' that they had made in order to live and work abroad, travelling and initially living together in an extension of their wartime lives.

The *Gazette* records others who had taken advantage of the Overseas Settlement Scheme, publicised via the OCA, which granted free passage to colonies for 'women who have served for not less than six months as enrolled members of any recognised corps attached to a Government Department ... provided they are recommended by the Headquarters of their former corps, and are accepted by the Agent-General of the Dominion concerned'.[94] In 1920, more than 200 WAAC members suc-cessfully applied for the scheme, the majority of whom went to Canada, Australia and New Zealand.[95] Most women who took advantage of this scheme went out to work as domestic servants, although not all of them remained so. Two such women, who emigrated to Canada, were Daisy Minns and Catherine Findlay. Minns was the daughter of an estate worker who enrolled as a twenty-three-year-old cook in 1917 after 'seeing in the Daily Papers that several women are needed as Army Cooks for France'.[96] Initially posted to Boulogne, she was discharged on medical grounds after being treated for epilepsy. Having previously worked in

---

[93] TNA 1911 Census; *White Star* passenger log, Southampton to New York, 16 June 1920.
[94] *OCAG*, December 1920.
[95] TNA WO 162/54, *Overseas Settlement of QMAAC Members*.
[96] TNA WO 398/156, Initial enquiry letter from Daisy Minns, 1 March 1917.

Canada, she took advantage of the scheme to travel to Canada once again to work as a cook in 1919.[97] A keen member of the OCA, Minns wrote to the *Gazette* in December 1920: 'How can I ever thank you for those magazines? I devoured every word of them over and over again.' She equally expressed her regret in letters retained in her service record about having to leave the Corps, as well as pride in her war service.

Catherine Findlay was a Durham miner's daughter who in 1911 was working as a housemaid before enrolling as a WAAC Worker. She emigrated via the scheme to Canada in July 1920 in order to marry a wounded Canadian ex-serviceman, Terence Mosher, whom she had met in England.[98] In 1922, she proudly reported in the *Gazette* that '[w]e had a parade on Armistice Day, and as I was the only woman who had been overseas on war work I was asked to carry and place on the memorial the wreath of poppies. I felt shy about doing it, but it was a great honour.'[99] These examples suggest that it was not only the female leadership of the OCA who mobilised their wartime identities in the post-war years.

Like other women who had been involved in war work, the majority of former WAACs returned to pre-war lives of paid or unpaid domestic work, and some were keen to do so. It is striking, however, to read the degree of nostalgia evident in letters written to the *Gazette* during the 1920s. Like Daisy Minns and Catherine Findlay, many WAACs described their ongoing pride in their identity as female veterans. Even if the editor was likely to select such letters for publication in a desire to promote the OCA, the letters' very existence reveals the extent to which former WAACs used the Association to strengthen their wartime identities and to prolong their connections to former comrades. This is true of women across the social spectrum. Annie Bartlett, for example, evoked the joys of comradeship as well as the hard working conditions of her role as forewoman of a cookhouse: 'My days are not so strenuous and my nights are not vivid with nightmares as they were then, but though I firmly believe I should eventually have succumbed, and died on active service if the war had continued, I look back with regret on four glorious years of service, and would gladly do it all over again, even with the prospect of a military funeral.'[100] Rose Batty, a housekeeper for her clergymen brothers before and after the war, wrote from Alexandria in September 1920

---

[97] TNA, Passenger list, *Tunisian*, London to Quebec, June 1919.

[98] Catherine Findlay stated that her passage was paid by the Overseas Settlement Scheme on the Canadian Ocean Arrivals Form, and that she was engaged to marry Terence Mosher. Mosher was listed on the *Aragueya* in 1919, a troop ship returning to Canada, with a gunshot wound to his back.

[99] *OCAG*, January 1922.

[100] *OCAG*, June 1921. Annie Bartlett, who worked as a cook in a school in 1911, returned to domestic service in a household after the war.

that: 'I often think of the dear old days ... and wish very much that one could live them all over again. We certainly had very happy times and very interesting work, and I think we all miss the corporate life of the corps very much indeed.'[101] A former WAAC Official, Margaret Bradfield, who married a captain in the Indian Medical Service in 1920 and travelled with him to Madras where he became a professor of surgery, described her delight at the confusion her WAAC uniform wrought amongst her Indian servants:[102]

My old Waac tunic, which since demobilisation has been lovingly laid up in lavender, or to be strictly truthful, naphthaline, was unpacked the other day among other clothes. The 'chokra' took it for one of my husband's tunics, and a free fight ensured, ayah claiming it as mem sahib's. Finally it had to be broken to the 'chokra' that mem sahib had been a woman soldier in the great war, at which the chokra nearly fainted backwards over the parapet.[103]

Here, the uniform is presented a source of both pride and nostalgia, suggesting that, like her uniform, Bradfield had rather reluctantly 'laid up' her wartime identity.

A strong sense of nostalgia is also evident in the letter of Worker Edith Curtis, a shorthand typist, in which she articulated the importance of the OCA in a continuation of members' wartime comradeship:

By means of the OCA we shall feel we are still one big family, and able to get news of one another, and oftentimes meet again. I am proud to have belonged to the dear old corps, and only wish it were still in existence. The life was so open, free, and healthy, and a much more natural one than that which our return to civil life offers. ... As I look back I feel certain that the very happiest hours of my life were spent there. The glorious comradeship, the feeling that we were really up against things, and doing something that was really worthwhile, fired us with enthusiasm and interest, and gave us something to hold on it, that was true and real, and brought to the surface the highest and best ideals. ... These days of peace that we have looked forward to, and prayed for so long, seem to fall very short of expectations.[104]

A notion of 'glorious comradeship' was a key component of the qualities of the war veteran as constructed by many male veteran associations, as was the evocation of a superior existence that compared poorly with peacetime. However, it was one that in many cases assumed a uniquely male membership and that included women as part of the civilians in opposition to which their veteran identity was constructed. What the WAAC letters in the OCA *Gazette* prove is not only that women expressed similar emotions and sentiments, including a degree of

---

[101] *OCAG*, September 1920.   [102] *The Times*, 28 October 1963.
[103] *OCAG*, August 1921.   [104] *OCAG*, December 1920.

affectionate nostalgia for the wartime years, but also that they had no problem in aligning themselves with servicemen in doing so. The women who were active in the OCA were forthright in their desire to associate themselves with the war generation, were proud of their identity as women who had served, and used military metaphors and military language to describe their experiences. In short, the *Gazette* reveals the extent to which war experience remained a central component of many members' identities into the 1920s. Certain women turned to the networks formed in wartime to further their professional aims, whether as elite women keen to promote women's roles in public life, or as working-class women keen to embrace new employment opportunities and move away from life as a domestic servant. Other women used the pages of the *Gazette* as a space in which they could express their nostalgia for the comradeship of wartime life, and reaffirm their belief that their war service had been identity-forming, setting them apart from other civilians, both men and women.

Conclusions

An important way in which both ex-war nurses and ex-servicewomen maintained their identity as 'war veteran' in the interwar years was through their presence at remembrance activities. Although, as Lucy Noakes comments, the WAAC was rarely officially invited to participate in large national ceremonies, members of the OCA regularly played a part, both as groups and as individuals, in local commemorative ceremonies. These included the ceremonies in York for the Five Sisters' Window, and in Edinburgh for the Scottish National War Memorial that I discussed in Chapter 1. Letters and reports reveal the eagerness of ex-servicewomen to participate in these occasions. Adela Annikin, a civil servant from Leeds, urged all who attended the York opening ceremony in 1924, for example, to wear uniforms, medals and badges, and subsequently then reported that they paraded with Hilda Horniblow 'in command' before laying their own wreath.[105] Similarly, in 1927 Alice Low wrote to the Duke of Atholl on behalf of her branch of the OCA: 'We are most anxious that the organisation should be represented at the opening of the Scottish National War Memorial. I understand that the space is very limited but there were 52,000 of us serving with the armies in France from 1917 until after the armistice.'[106] The willingness of former WAACs

---

[105] *OCAG*, April and July 1925.
[106] Letter from Alice Low to Atholl, 8 April 1927. Box 25, 'Opening Ceremony'. Papers of the Duke and Duchess of Atholl concerning the Scottish National War Memorial, National Library of Scotland.

to play a part in national commemorative activities is also evidenced by their participation in the 'Great Pilgrimage' organised in 1928 to the battlefields in France. In the report in the *Gazette*, the writer aligns their journey with that of other veteran associations making similar pilgrimages 'ten years on'.[107] Finally, smaller groups or individual women, unable to participate in larger commemorative occasions, were also able to draw on their identities as WAACs, bolstered by the continuing activities of the OCA, in local remembrance activities. In October 1922, for example, thirty members of the Leeds local branch paraded at the unveiling of the Leeds war memorial, and in 1923 Marion Mackenzie reported from Middlesbrough that she 'represented the Corps at the unveiling of our local Cenotaph on Armistice Day. I paraded with my Girl Guide Company but wore [my] QMAAC uniform'.[108]

Reports and letters about these commemorative activities sometimes bear witness to the difficult relationship some ex-servicewomen had with male veterans. Alice Low's letter, for example, commented that '[o]ur secretary sent an application through the British Legion but it is more than likely that they will do nothing for us.' Her tone in relation to the British Legion matched that of a 1923 letter in the *Gazette*:

Some of us felt that we wanted more serious recognition by our male comrades in the Legion, who seemed only to remember that we were comrades when there was any entertainment at foot at which they required our help. In true Waac style (I should rather say true ex-Service style in this instance) we laid our 'grouse' before the Committee of the Legion, with the result that at the next General Meeting of the Dunfermline branch of the British Legion (to which the women members turned out en masse) ... three of us were nominated as members of the Executive.[109]

The OCA was affiliated to the British Legion, but regular letters and articles in the *Gazette* expressed dissatisfaction with male veterans' attitudes towards their membership. There was also disapproval of the suggestion that they should join the British Legion's 'Women's Section', that was not intended for ex-servicewomen but for female relatives of male veterans. Throughout 1924, there were debates in the *Gazette* as to what form their links with the British Legion should take, with many members wishing the OCA to remain an autonomous organisation. Niall Barr notes that the British Legion itself was similarly divided over the question of female membership, but it is clear from the OCA

[107] *OCAG*, September 1928. For descriptions of WAAC activities in York and Edinburgh, see *OCAG*, April 1923 and September 1927.
[108] *OCAG*, March 1922 and April 1923.
[109] Letter from Mrs H M Drysdale, Dunfermline branch of the OCA, *OCAG*, April 1923.

Gazette correspondence that on a local level many male veterans were resistant to the idea of former WAACs playing any kind of leadership role in their organisations.[110]

The reluctance of some British veterans to accept WAACs into their fold contrasts with the willingness of French veteran organisations to welcome former war nurses. It points, firstly, to a difference in the national contexts. In Britain, women had taken a step towards being 'militarised' in a way that was not the case in France. They had a greater claim to the identity of veteran, and in greater numbers, but equally came up against the criticisms of the 'women in khaki' that the WAAC had been subject to during the war, and that continued to be levelled against them in the post-war years. In France, however, women were not integrated formally into the armed services. Although there were also attacks on nurses' sexual morality, generally the nurse was a much more widely acceptable symbol of female service and sacrifice during the war, as the figure of the nurse could be either equated with that of 'male combatant' or presented as a 'natural' and temporary extension of women's domestic role, therefore presenting less of a threat to the status quo. Significantly, British pension files for disabled nurses reveal that wounded or sick British nurses tended to enjoy positive relationships with male veterans, with many turning to the British Legion for both practical and emotional support. The file of a Territorial Force Nursing Service Sister who was pensioned on the grounds of neurasthenia, for example, contains warm, personalised letters from the chair of the Eastbourne branch of the British Legion and the British Legion's Pension Committee, as well as from the College of Nursing, all supporting her claim to an increased pension.[111]

In the interwar period, sources reveal that male veteran groups admitted, collaborated with or supported both ex-servicewomen and former war nurses on both sides of the Channel.[112] However, the relationships between male and female veterans also point to the limits of acceptability for male veterans in terms of women's active wartime roles. Leaders of nurse organisations were invited to veteran congresses in France, and nurses, members of resistance organisations and former female prisoners of war who had enjoyed a high public profile during

---

[110] Barr, *The Lion and the Poppy*, p. 48.   [111] TNA PIN 26/20027.

[112] I do not consider war widows here, as they lie outside the scope of my study of female veterans. However, there are interesting parallels between the experiences of ex-servicemen, ex-servicewomen and activist widows in the interwar years that merit further research. On US and German widows, see Erika Kuhlman, *Of Little Comfort: War Widows, Fallen Soldiers, and the Remaking of the Nation after the Great War* (New York: New York University Press, 2012).

the war continued to be lauded by male veterans as heroines deserving of public gratitude and reverence. Some of these women were awarded the 'Carte du combattant' in recognition of their war service. In Britain, where the numbers of women who could claim veteran status were greater, however, the relationships with men's groups appear to have often been more fraught.

To conclude, despite the so-called reconstruction of a 'collapsed' system of gender norms in Britain and France that has been much commented upon by gender historians, it is important to recognise that alternative identity models for women, albeit on a more modest scale, circulated alongside dominant understandings of women's primary roles as those of housewife and mother. Although conservative gender discourses preached a return to the home and frequently attacked women who claimed a right to a more public role, the extent to which individual men and women internalised these gendered imperatives is much more difficult to gauge. The case studies highlighted in this chapter show us that women who promoted themselves as female veterans deserving of praise and gratitude came from a variety of social, political and ideological positions. Whereas some did so in a feminist bid to promote gender equality or to add weight to arguments for female suffrage, the majority were motivated by a combination of patriotic, psychological and economic reasons. The response to these women's claims to veteran status reveals a wider degree of acceptance by the male veteran community than might have been expected. French nurses, who continued to be perceived by many as the finest embodiments of patriotic femininity, were largely accepted as 'combatants' by veterans who were in other respects conservative in terms of their understanding of gender roles. In this sense, public life became more 'permeable' for women in some spheres, even though they remained formally excluded by their gender.[113] Female veteran associations also created imagined communities of women who were able to adopt and extend the identity of 'female war veteran', which gave them access to a privileged social role. Many women, however, did not join veteran groups to enter public life, but to strengthen the social bonds they had formed with other women. One anonymous WAAC ex-Forewoman who wrote to the *Gazette* in 1921 spoke for many when she stated: 'That spirit of comradeship which helped us in the past, is a present bond, and a surety for the future.'[114] In this sense, female veteran associations offered women a rare opportunity to articulate a collective identity

---

[113] Reynolds, *France between the Wars*, p. 156.   [114] *OCAG*, July 1921.

based upon a professional rather than a domestic identity. The powerful discourses preaching a return to the hearth and to the pre-war status quo could, at least to some extent, be circumvented by women who had been active during the war, and their wartime roles continued to be evoked, often with nostalgic pride, in the interwar years.

4   Writing as a Veteran
Women's War Memoirs

The previous chapters have noted that a hierarchy of war experience existed in the interwar years. Over time, 'the trench fighter's story' was received and understood differently to those of other participants in the war, such as non-infantry combatants, non-combatant support personnel, war workers and civilians.[1] A definition of 'war literature' that is limited to combat excludes many of the economic and social ramifications of 'total war' that civilian and non-combatant perspectives can bring to light.[2] However, in the interwar years, as well as in later decades, there was a moral economy of suffering associated with this conflict that privileged the combatant's war story above all others. As Leonard Smith argues in his persuasive study of French combatants' published testimonies: 'The war of 1914–18 became construed as a tragedy, and the hero in it, the soldier of the trenches, a tragic victim.'[3] Although they could not claim victimhood in quite the same way, the handful of women who took up arms were perhaps best placed to set themselves up as alternative heroes in this dominant cultural narrative of the war, drawing on long-standing 'she-soldier' figures such as the Amazons or Joan of Arc.[4] Some of these women were able to play on their heightened visibility during the war in order to publish their memoirs.[5] British woman Flora Sandes, for

---

[1] Margaret Darrow and Claire Buck both make this point in relation to France and Britain, respectively. Darrow, *French Women*, p. 40; Claire Buck, 'British Women's Writing of the Great War', in Vincent Sherry (ed.), *The Cambridge Companion to the Literature of the First World War* (Cambridge: Cambridge University Press, 2004), pp. 85–112 (p. 87).

[2] Margaret R. Higonnet, 'Another Record: A Different War', *Women's Studies Quarterly* 23 (1999): 85–96.

[3] Leonard V. Smith, *The Embattled Self: French Soldiers' Testimony of the Great War* (Ithaca, NY: Cornell University Press, 2007), p. 8.

[4] On the fascination with armed women soldiers, see Joanna Bourke, *An Intimate History of Killing: Face to Face Killing in Twentieth Century Warfare* (London: Granta, 2000), p. 294; Libby Murphy, 'Trespassing on the Trench-Fighter's Story: Re-Imagining the Female Combatant of the First World War', in Ana Carden-Coyle (ed.), *Gender and Conflict since 1914* (Basingstoke: Palgrave, 2012), pp. 55–68.

[5] In this chapter I use 'memoirs' to refer to a range of personal writings on the war, including published diaries and letters as well as autobiography.

example, a former captain in the Serbian army, published *The Autobiography of a Woman Soldier* in 1927. Her volume was praised by one reviewer for being 'unique among modern war books', with the Serbs described as 'fortunate in finding in Miss Sandes an excellent soldier' while Britain was 'fortunate in having such an excellent representative amongst that brave people'.[6]

This positive assessment of Sandes' memoirs, however, depended on her rarity as a female combatant. As I observed in my exploration of war heroines in Chapter 2, more broadly there was considerable resistance to the idea of militarised women, especially in France. Moreover, and more importantly, producing war memoirs in the direct mould of male combat narratives was not a possibility for the vast majority of women who wished to tell their war stories and thereby participate in broader post-war moral and political debates. And these women had a limited number of female models to draw on from male-authored war writing. As Pierre Schoentjes summarises in his survey of French war literature, female characters in ex-servicemen's literary evocations of the war tended to be two-dimensional in nature: 'Objects of seduction, unfaithful wives, sexually predatory creatures, *images d'Epinal* sweethearts: war literature only produced stereotypes of women.'[7] Given this, if women were not able to ape the male combatant role in the guise of a 'she-soldier', it tended to be via their relationship to the male 'trench fighter', and in particular to the tragically ubiquitous figure of the dead or wounded soldier, that some women were able to find an audience for their war stories in the interwar years. This was certainly the case for the female nurse, who could not only claim proximity to the front but also be seen as a vessel through which the male combatant's story was told. The nurse's story therefore 'counted' in the stories that shaped post-war accounts because nurses circulated close to what was understood as the 'real' war story: front-line combatant experience. As a result, the nurse was able to present herself as a 'moral witness' to the war in a manner akin to that of a front-line combatant.[8]

In the context of the cultural memory of the war in Britain, the perspective of the First World War nurse has tended to be transmitted via the voice of VAD nurse Vera Brittain. Her 1933 memoir *Testament of Youth* was founded on the notion of a 'Lost Generation', and is seen by many as

[6] Flora Sandes, *Autobiography of a Woman Soldier: A Brief Record of Adventure with the Serbian Army, 1916–19* (London: H., F. and G. Witherby, 1927); *Dundee Evening Telegraph*, 13 April 1927. As I noted in Chapter 2, however, the reception of female combatants was more mixed in the interwar years than it had been during the war.

[7] Pierre Schoentjes, *Fictions de la Grande Guerre: Variations littéraires sur 14–18* (Paris: Classiques Garnier, 2009), p. 195.

[8] Jay Winter, 'The "Moral Witness" and the Two World Wars', *Ethnologie française* 37: 3 (2007). doi: 10.3917/ethn.073.0467

a key text in the construction of the British 'disillusionment narrative' of the war, which charts the shift of an individual from a naïve pro-war to a pacifist anti-war stance through loss and trauma.[9] *Testament of Youth* was a best-seller at the time of its publication in 1933; subsequently, her role as *the* literary representative of women's war experience was further enhanced by the rediscovery of her story in the 1970s and 1980s, when her autobiography was republished and adapted into a television drama. While in the 1930s reviews of *Testament of Youth* focused on its frankness and 'authenticity', with I. A. Williams in the *Times Literary Supplement* describing it as 'tragic and noble', a 'wise chronicle of the war', it was received differently in the climate of second-wave feminism in the 1970s and 1980s, when it was interpreted as a woman's story of emancipation from the limitations of pre-war domesticity, as well as an anti-war 'disillusionment narrative'.[10] In a 1968 essay entitled 'War Service in Perspective', Vera Brittain justified her decision to publish her war memoir in the following terms: 'With scientific precision, I studied the memoirs of Blunden, Sassoon, and Graves. Surely I thought, my story is as interesting as theirs. Besides, I see things other than they have seen, and some of the things they perceived, I see differently.'[11] Here, she was positioning herself in relation to three of the most influential male veteran-writers whose war memoirs follow the 'disillusionment' model.[12] Her defensive tone also reveals her awareness of the extent to which a woman's war story was seen by many as trespassing on what was usually viewed as an exclusively masculine field of war literature.

Although Brittain's wartime nursing was often the focus of discussions of her memoirs, both at the time and in later dramatisations of her life story, she did not see herself primarily as a nurse, but as a politically

[9] For discussions of Brittain's role in the construction of British war memory, see Braybon, 'Winners or Losers', p. 8; Jane Potter, *Boys in Khaki, Girls in Print: Women's Literary Responses to the Great War 1914–1918* (Oxford: Clarendon Press, 2005); Watson, *Fighting Different Wars*.

[10] I. A. Williams, 'Testament of Youth', *Times Literary Supplement* 1639 (1933): 571. *Testament of Youth* was republished in paperback by Virago in 1978 and swiftly became a best-seller, assisted by its adaptation into a BBC drama series in 1979. Indeed, her story continues to attract attention, having been the subject of a recent BBC docudrama and a successful feature film. Its ongoing influence can also be seen in the fact that, as Dan Todman notes: 'In two thirds of the novels [about the war] produced in the period from 1978 to 1998, the principal activity for the main female characters was nursing, usually in France as a VAD.' Todman, *The Great War*, p. 183.

[11] Vera Brittain, 'War Service in Perspective', in George A. Panichas (ed.), *Promise of Greatness: The War of 1914–1918* (New York: John Day Co., 1968), pp. 363–76.

[12] Several historians have sought to show the extent to which such 'disillusionment' narratives should not be seen as representative of the wider experience of the war: see for example Todman, *The Great War*; Brian Bond, *The Unquiet Western Front: Britain's Role in Literature and History* (Cambridge: Cambridge University Press, 2002).

committed lecturer, novelist and journalist who had nursed during the war.[13] Motivated by Brittain's ideological beliefs and literary ambitions, and a product of her class and education, *Testament of Youth* is in some ways not a typical example of a First World War nurse memoir. Brittain's 1933 narrator was in fact markedly uninterested in the nursing work she was doing and focused instead on her own political, ideological and psychological development. The principal aim of her text was not to offer insights into wartime nursing (this, after all, was only a part of her autobiographical trajectory as detailed in *Testament of Youth*) but to write her own version of the now familiar interwar pacifist narrative of the journey from naïve idealism to bitter and painful disillusionment. This points to the driving force of Brittain's literary and political ambition to be, in her words, 'the woman ... who by presenting the war in its true perspective in her own life, will illuminate its meaning afresh for her generation'.[14] Brittain, as she stated in her later volume of autobiography, *Testament of Experience* (1957), wanted women to be taken seriously as witnesses of war, rather than to feature simply as the various stereotypical 'others' who peopled male war fiction and memoirs: 'Didn't women have their war as well? They weren't, as these men make them, only suffering wives and mothers, or callous parasites, or mercenary prostitutes.'[15]

However, despite the fact that she did not present her identity primarily in relation to her wartime medical work, the role of the nurse was vital for Brittain in her literary-political enterprise to write as a war veteran. As Sharon Ouditt argues, 'nursing was seen by many as women's nearest equivalent to that of the fighting male ... the Red Cross sign ... was the badge of their equal sacrifice.'[16] The fact that Brittain nursed, and especially the fact that she nursed overseas (and did not, for example, remain at Oxford), close to the front, became an entry ticket into what was for Brittain the much coveted and largely male world of published literature and public debate about the war in the interwar years. This chapter considers the ways in which two other women attempted to write women back into the war story via the publication of their war memoirs. More specifically, it examines the writings of a British trained nurse who wrote about the war: Kate Evelyn Luard, a member of Queen Alexandra's Imperial Military Nursing Service, who published *Diary of a Nursing Sister*

[13] For a fuller version of the argument I make here about Brittain's *Testament of Youth*, see Fell, 'Myth, Countermyth and the Politics of Memory'.
[14] Quoted in Paul Berry and Mark Bostridge, *Vera Brittain: A Life* (London: Pimlico, 1995), p. 241.
[15] Vera Brittain, *Testament of Experience: An Autobiographical Story of the Years 1925–1950* (London: V. Gollancz, 1957), p. 77.
[16] Sharon Ouditt, *Fighting Forces, Writing Women: Identity and Ideology in the First World War* (London: Routledge, 1993), p. 9.

on the Western Front anonymously in 1915, and *Unknown Warriors* under her own name in 1930. Luard's memoirs are very different from Brittain's. Her publications consisted of edited extracts from her letters and diaries rather than retrospectively constructed memoirs, and unlike Brittain her identity was firmly situated in direct relation to her nursing work. However, what both of these examples of British women's war writing share is an attempt to use the role of the nurse in order to present themselves as female veterans of the war whose perspectives had both cultural and political validity in the post-war world.

To some extent, nursing offered French women too the opportunity to publish their war stories. Madeleine Clemenceau Jacquemaire, for example, the daughter of the French prime minister, published *Les Hommes de bonne volonté* (*Men of Good Will*) in 1919, which equally presented the nurse as both a vessel through which male combatant stories could be told and as a kind of female war veteran.[17] In *Men of Good Will*, although the nurse-narrator was unstinting in her patriotic admiration for the poilus who suffered during the war, fulfilling a function as a mouthpiece for trench fighters' heroic narratives and sacrifices, she also frequently equated the nurses' role with that of the male combatants. In one episode, for example, the nurses, waiting for a convoy of wounded to arrive, are described as 'weary and stiff, with throbbing feet . . . Some of them haven't had any leave for seven months and this evening "le cafard" [depression] is making its way into more than one overworked brain'.[18] Here, the women are deliberately aligned to soldiers, suffering from the same complaints (no leave) and psychological symptoms (war-induced depression). Despite its title, Clemenceau Jacquemaire's narrative was as much a tribute to the nurses as it was to the soldiers they cared for, and was implicitly a plea for public respect and recognition for the value of their war work.

Unlike in Britain, the experience of occupation offered another role to French and Belgian women that allowed them to construct themselves in their post-war autobiographical writings as veterans of the war. The women

---

[17] For analyses of Clemenceau Jacquemaire's text, see Fell, 'Myth, Countermyth and the Politics of Memory'; Ruth Amossy, 'Argumentation, situation de discours et théorie des champs: l'exemple de *Les Hommes de bonne volonté* de Madeleine Clemenceau Jacquemaire', *Contextes* 1 (2006). Available online at: http://contextes.revues.org/index43.html; Ruth Amossy, 'L'image de l'infirmière de la Grande Guerre de 1914 à 2004. La construction de la mémoire', in Annamaria Laserra, Nicole Leclerq and Marc Quaghebeur (eds.), *Mémoires et anti-mémoires littéraires au XXe siècle. La première guerre mondiale.* Colloque de Cerisy-la-Salle 2005, 2 vols. (Bern: Peter Lang, 2008), pp. 273–96.

[18] Madeleine Clemenceau Jacquemaire, *Les Hommes de bonne volonté* (Paris: Calmann Levy, 1919), p. 234.

who participated in Resistance movements in occupied France and Belgium or who worked for the intelligence services in the First World War were often heroised, both during and after the war, as female combatants.[19] This was largely understood to have been a temporary role in exceptional circumstances, which of course is very different from a state-sanctioned, waged role as a member of an auxiliary corps of the armed services. Nevertheless, it allowed a handful of women to claim a form of 'combatant' war service in the post-war years. In this chapter I examine the war memoir published by a French schoolteacher who was active in the same escape network for Allied soldiers as Edith Cavell: Louise Thuliez. She published an article entitled 'Condamnée à mort' ('Condemned to Death') in 1919, before publishing a longer memoir, also entitled *Condamnée à mort*, in 1933. Thuliez's memoir was one of several examples of autobiographical writings by or interviews with women in the late 1920s and early 1930s who had been active in resisting German rule in occupied France and Belgium, including other women who had been associated with the Edith Cavell network, and can therefore be seen as part of a broader trend.[20] One of the reasons Luard's nursing memoir and Thuliez's resistance memoir have been chosen for comparison is that in both of these cases it is possible to compare their wartime or immediate post-war versions of their wartime activities with those they published more than ten years later. This reveals the changing cultural and political contexts in which they were seeking to publish their war memoirs, and equally reveals the different ways in which they adopted and adapted a literary genre that was dominated by ex-servicemen.

Writing the War in Interwar Britain and France

In both Britain and France, there was a public appetite for war literature, and particularly for first-person accounts in the form of war memoirs, which, in turn, provided a commercial opportunity for both authors and publishers. Hundreds of books about the war were published by individuals who had experienced it between 1915 and 1933 (and beyond).[21] Although the memoirs of well-known figures, such as military leaders or established writers, were more likely to be published by major publishers

---

[19] Proctor, *Female Intelligence*; Debruyne and Fell, 'Model Martyrs'.

[20] See Emmanuel Debruyne, *Le Réseau Edith Cavell: Des femmes et des hommes en résistance* (Brussels: Racine, 2015); Debruyne and Fell, 'Model Martyrs'.

[21] On Britain see Ian Isherwood, 'The British Publishing Industry and Commercial Memories of the First World War', *War in History* 23: 3 (2016): 323–40 (p. 326); on France (and Germany) see Smith, *The Embattled Self*; Nicolas Beaupré, *Écrire en guerre, écrire la guerre: France, Allemagne 1914–1920* (Paris: CNRS Editions, 2006).

seeking commercial success, the majority of war memoirs were by first-time 'amateur' authors. The war's legacy remained both important and contested in the post-war years, and writing about individual experiences provided the chance not only to gain 'cultural capital' from promoting an author's veteran status but equally to articulate opinions about the war's lessons and consequences to a wider public. In both nations it is possible to distinguish waves of war literature. In Britain, the first wave consisted of books published in the war's immediate aftermath, in the years 1919–20, which can be seen as an extension of the widespread publication of memoirs during the war years. War literature continued to be published throughout the 1920s, but there was an upsurge in the publication of books about the war from the tenth anniversary of the Armistice in 1928 until the early 1930s, a phase that included the canonical veteran memoirs Brittain refers to: Edmund Blunden's *Undertones of War* (1928), Robert Graves' *Good-Bye to All That* (1929) and two volumes of Siegfried Sassoon's autobiographical trilogy, *Memoirs of a Fox-Hunting Man* (1928) and *Memoirs of an Infantry Officer* (1930). War books continued to be published in the 1930s, but not in the same quantities as in the early years of the decade.

As in Britain, it is possible to divide French war writing into similar periods. The immediate post-war period of 1919–23 also saw a boom of war literature, including war memoirs, which largely echoed in style and content those published during the war. The next peak in war literature in France came a little later, in the early 1930s, which saw a new wave of books in which, as Catharine Savage Brosman notes, 'the Great War appears in a new light – that of failed peace-making, economic crisis, and fascism.'[22] Of the combat narratives published during the war, Henri Barbusse's *Le Feu* (*Under Fire*) (1916) was the most influential, both at the time and in subsequent assessments. In his autobiographical novel, Barbusse constructs the collective identity of a squad of stoical front-line poilus, presented as victims of high politics, an identity that the author-narrator implicitly claims to share. The early post-war years saw the publication of a range of fiction and memoir which equally focused on combatant experience but which espoused a broad range of political interpretations of the war, from combat novels reminiscent of Barbusse such as Roland Dorgelès' 1919 *Les croix de bois* (*Wooden Crosses*), to the glorification of military life in the works of Henry de Montherlant, who published *Le Songe* (*The Dream*) in 1922, to the detached and ironic treatment of the theatricality and illusions of war in Jean Cocteau's

[22] Catharine Savage Brosman, 'French Writing of the Great War', in Sherry, *The Cambridge Companion*, p. 171.

Thomas l'imposteur (*Thomas the Imposter*), published in 1923. Much of the war writing published by ex-servicemen in the 1930s can be understood as *littérature engagée*, or politically engaged literature, which offers both left- and right-wing interpretations of the war and its consequences, often in relation to key events in 1930s politics such as the Spanish Civil War and the Popular Front in France.[23] In all of the male-authored canonical texts of French First World War writing, however, the depiction of women rarely departs from cliché.

Historians and literary scholars alike have examined the social, cultural and political contexts in which war memoirs and fictionalised accounts of the war were published in both Britain and France in the 1920s and 1930s. In relation to Britain, there has been a debate about the extent to which a concentration on high-profile memoirs has contributed to a 'disillusionment narrative' which has distorted popular memory of the conflict. Historians have suggested that the prominence of 'disillusionment' veteran narratives, not only in the popular memory, but equally in Paul Fussell's enormously influential study *The Great War in Modern Memory* (that saw in a modernist mode of 'ironic' war writing a more generalised response to the war), created a false narrative of veteran resentment that belies the diversity and complexity of veterans' feelings towards the war in the interwar years.[24] Rosa Bracco's study of 'middlebrow' novels in the 1920s, alongside Jay Winter's analysis of European memorial culture, demonstrates the extent to which there was a considerable amount of cultural resistance to an 'ironic' interpretation of the war. Bracco and Winter show that in many cases writers and artists turned to more conservative narrative frameworks in their evocations of the war.[25] The construction of a canon of war memoirs, however, has meant that the range and variety of war memoirs that were published is rarely acknowledged. Ian Isherwood concludes in his study of British war memoirs that the 'vast commercial catalogue of war reflections reveals ambiguity on the war's broader meaningfulness to its generation ... the war's published experiences reflect an overall culture of war-consciousness, but no uniform or dominant war memory'.[26] Jessica Meyer, Janet Watson and Jane Potter have also explored the print culture that existed after the war, the study of which

---

[23] Eliane Tonnet-Lacroix, *La Littérature française de l'entre-deux-guerres 1919–1939* (Paris: Nathan, 1993), pp. 35–51.

[24] Todman, *The Great War*; Deborah Cohen, *The War Come Home: Disabled Veterans in Britain and Germany 1914–1939* (Berkeley: University of California Press, 2001).

[25] Rosa Bracco, *Merchants of Hope: British Middlebrow Writers and the First World War* (Providence, RI: Berg, 1993); Winter, *Sites of Memory*.

[26] Isherwood, 'The British Publishing Industry', pp. 326–38.

gives a much more nuanced picture of the ways in which the war was evoked in veterans' writings.[27] This scholarship reminds us that, despite the prominence given to front-line fighting, 'there was no typical participant, no single, authentic voice', and it remained possible for other participants, including women, to use war memoirs as a platform from which to express their own war experiences.[28]

In France, the traditional genre of war memoirs produced by military and political leaders and tacticians remained in evidence, but as in Britain was overtaken in both number and influence by the large wave of 'témoignage' (testimony) by front-line combatants which responded more closely to the public's desire for 'authenticity', which was largely dependent on the writer's proximity to the front.[29] Whether autobiographical fiction or war memoir, male-authored combat writing published in French sought to persuade its readers of its authenticity, for example through prefaces emphasising an author's war service.[30] As in Britain, there was an enormous variety of French war writing, and veteran testimony 'does not tell a single story of experience'.[31] The critical reception of war writing also revolved in the interwar years around the notions of authority and authenticity, most famously in relation to Jean Norton Cru's publication in 1929 of *Témoins* (*Witnesses*). Norton Cru offered a prescriptive definition of what constituted a 'bon témoin' (good witness) of the war: one who offered both a valid tribute to the sacrifice of the dead and an appropriate 'moral' response. His book provoked a heated debate amongst male war writers, in particular Dorgelès and Barbusse, both of whom Norton Cru had attacked in his book. Women did not feature in this debate, however. They were necessarily excluded from Norton Cru's understanding of 'bon témoignage', as along with other non-combatants

---

[27] Jessica Meyer, 'The Tuition of Manhood: 'Sapper's War Stories and the Literature of War', in Mary Hammond and Shafquat Towheed (eds.), *Publishing in the First World War: Essays in Book History* (London: Palgrave Macmillan, 2007), pp. 113–28; Jane Potter, 'For Country, Conscience and Commerce: Publishers and Publishing, 1914–1918', in Hammond and Towheed, *Publishing in the First World War*, pp. 11–26; Watson, *Fighting Different Wars*.

[28] David Taylor, 'Fiction and Memoir of Britain's Great War: Some Further Thoughts', *European Review of History* 22: 5 (2015): 814–18.

[29] Jean-Louis Jeannelle, 'Une guerre des Mémoires', in Annamaria Laserra, Nicole Leclercq and Marc Quaghebeur (eds.), *Mémoires et antimémoires littéraires au XXe siècle: La Première guerre mondiale*, second volume (New York: Peter Lang, 2008), pp. 107–28.

[30] Pierre Schoentjes, 'Les véritables écrivains de guerre ont-ils "rarement dépeint ce qu'ils avaient vu"', in Pierre Schoentjes (ed.), *La Grande Guerre: Un siècle de fictions romanesques* (Geneva: Droz, 2008), pp. 17–43.

[31] Smith, *The Embattled Self*, p. 1.

they were classified as the 'spectators' of war, whether they were 'a few kilometres from the action or sitting behind a desk in Paris'.[32]

Despite the emphasis on front-line experience in both Britain and France, scores of women wrote about the war, both during the conflict and in the 1920s and 1930s. In Britain, women's war memoirs followed the same trends as men's in terms of the 'waves' of publication. The ten-year anniversary of the Armistice saw the publication of several women's memoirs and works of fiction, including Mary Borden's *The Forbidden Zone* (1929), Evadne Price's (writing under the pseudonym Helen Zenna Smith) *Not So Quiet ...: Stepdaughters of War* (1930), Irene Rathbone's *We That Were Young* (1932) and Storm Jameson's *No Time Like the Present* (1933), as well as Brittain's *Testament of Youth* in 1933. It is true, as Angela Smith notes, that these writers were necessarily exploring the war 'from the marginal gendered position of women's experience'.[33] That said, the same issue about which memoirs became canonical and which were forgotten and sidelined was also at play in relation to women's memoirs of the war. The focus on, and republication of, a few key authors such as Brittain, Borden, Price and Rathbone has tended to over-simplify an understanding of the nature of 'women's war writing' more broadly. The consequences of this process of canonisation have been addressed, especially in relation to writing published during the war. Sharon Ouditt, Jane Potter and Angela Smith's work, for example, has revealed a fuller range of largely forgotten literary works by women published during the war, but (with the exception of Bracco's study of middlebrow writers) there has been less concentration on non-canonical women's war writing published in the interwar period.[34] The republication of women's inter-war writing by feminist publisher Virago in the 1970s and 1980s, for example, tended to favour not only those memoirs that foregrounded the bleak horror of the war but equally those that appeared to question the patriarchal and heteronormative culture in which it was fought, thereby echoing the political concerns of their new readership.[35] Luard's publications are not easily assimilated into this feminist version

[32] Jean Norton Cru, *Témoins: essai d'analyse et de critique des souvenirs de combattants édités en français de 1915 à 1928* (Nancy: Presses universitaires de Nancy, 2006), p. 9. For discussions of Norton Cru's notion of 'witnessing', see Smith, *The Embattled Self*; Beaupré, *Écrire en guerre*; Frédéric Rousseau, *Le Procès des témoins de la Grande Guerre: L'affaire Norton Cru* (Paris: Seuil, 2003).
[33] Angela K. Smith, 'How to Remember: War, Armistice and Memory in Post-1918 British Fiction', *Journal of European Studies* 45: 4 (2015): 301–15.
[34] Bracco, *Merchants of Hope*; Ouditt, *Fighting Forces, Writing Women*; Potter, *Boys in Khaki, Girls in Print*; Angela K. Smith, *The Second Battlefield: Women, Modernism and the First World War* (Manchester: Manchester University Press, 2000).
[35] The texts by Brittain, Borden, Price and Rathbone were all republished in the 1970s and 1980s by Virago in its Modern Classics series.

of the disillusionment narrative, but they were more typical in many ways of First World War nursing memoirs.[36] In this sense, their analysis here helps to redress the balance of the focus on the canon of women's war writing, and helps to complicate the picture of the ways in which British women understood and represented their war experience.

There was no equivalent rediscovery of women's war writing in the 1970s and 1980s in France. The works chosen by publishing houses such as the feminist publishing house Editions des Femmes in the 1970s and 1980s did not tend to include women's war memoirs.[37] Pioneering work by literary critics Nancy Sloan Goldberg and Catherine O'Brien has revealed, however, that French women published a wide range of auto-biographical prose, war fiction and poetry during and in the immediate aftermath of the war.[38] As Goldberg notes, these women presented themselves as much as the mouthpieces of the trench fighter as 'moral witnesses' to the war in their own right:

> [French women] presented the frontline experience ... through indirect means, and the women characters learned about the war in much the same way as noncombatant readers then and now, through the testimony of soldiers. By concentrating on women's experiences, the French novelists avoided the charges of pretense and impropriety that plagued other women war writers, and they did not challenge the notion of combat as a definitively male activity.[39]

These works are now largely forgotten; traditional in terms of form, and not fulfilling the criteria of Norton Cru's 'bon témoin', no woman's texts or memoirs, even if written from an autobiographical perspective, entered the French canon of war literature. Most bibliographies of war literature, including Jean Vic's five-volume annotated list of French works, *La Littérature de guerre* (1918–23), do not include any female authors.[40] And while writing *about* women in the aftermath of the war has been the subject of numerous studies, interwar French women's war writing itself has equally been largely ignored in studies of war writing.[41] This does not

---

[36] Fell and Hallett, *First World War Nursing*.

[37] Jennifer E. Milligan, *The Forgotten Generation: French Women Writers of the Inter-War Period* (Oxford: Berg, 1996).

[38] Nancy Sloan Goldberg, *'Woman Your Hour Is Sounding!' Continuity and Change in French Women's Great War Fiction 1914–19* (New York: St Martin's Press, 1999); Catherine M. O'Brien, *Women's Fictional Responses to the First World War: A Comparative Study of Selected Texts by French and German Writers* (New York: Peter Lang, 1997).

[39] Sloan Goldberg, *'Woman Your Hour Is Sounding!'*, p. xvii.

[40] Jean Vic, *La Littérature de guerre: manuel méthodique et critique des publications de langue française*, 5 vols. (Paris: Payot, 1918–23).

[41] Diana Holmes argues that the dismissal of women's writing as too focused on 'women's issues', such as relationships and the domestic space, to be of relevance for the under-standing of social, political or economic change was common throughout the first half of

mean, however, that there were no French women writing about the war in the interwar years. Jennifer Milligan's study of interwar French women's writing, *The Forgotten Generation*, notes that the rise in education levels amongst women gave more women than ever before the opportunity to write during this period, and women from all social backgrounds were published.[42] However, she equally points to the extent to which access to publishing was more difficult for women writers, who frequently faced obstacles and discouragement: 'Penetrating the interwar literary world, far less flourishing in it, was by no means straightforward, as at every stage in the process of promoting, producing and distributing fiction, the role played by women was restricted.'[43]

Established writers such as Colette, who had worked hard to carve out a career as a journalist and novelist, were able to trade on their existing reputations. Colette published her war journalism in 1917 under the title *Les Heures longues* (*The Long Hours*). After the war she offered her own vision of a society transformed by war in her 1926 study of a traumatised returning soldier, *La Fin de Chéri* (*The Last of Chéri*), in which a neurasthenic soldier is unable to reintegrate into the post-war world while his wife has flourished.[44] War experience was one possible route to publication for amateur women writers too, just as it was for hundreds of male veterans. Several accounts of wartime nursing were published, both during and after the war, as well as female-authored memoirs that focused on the war as one of the transformative episodes in their lives.[45] In this chapter, however, I focus on the popular memoirs of a woman who helped Allied soldiers to escape from the occupied zone. Writing as a female 'resistance heroine' was not without its reputational risks: while, as I suggested in Chapter 2, women who died, such as agent Louise de Bettignies, continued to be seen as war heroines after the war, other women who had been active in resistance networks were viewed more ambiguously, as they could be associated with female spies, largely viewed as sexually promiscuous and untrustworthy. To counter this, many former female resisters who wrote about their war experiences, such as

the twentieth century. See Diana Holmes, *French Women's Writing 1848–1994* (London: Athlone, 1996).
[42] Milligan, *The Forgotten Generation*, p. 15.
[43] Milligan, *The Forgotten Generation*, p. 35.
[44] Alison S. Fell, 'Life after Léa: War and Trauma in Colette's *La Fin de Chéri*', *French Studies* 59: 4 (2005): 495–507.
[45] Examples of French nurse memoirs include Clemenceau Jacquemaire, *Les Hommes de bonne volonté*; Geneviève Duhamelet, *Ces dames de l'hôpital 336* (Paris: Albin Michel, 1917); Juliette Dyle, *Au Fils de Mars: Journal d'une infirmière* (Paris: Editions 2 rue Guersant, 1926); M. Eydoux-Démians, *Notes d'une infirmière 1914* (Paris: Plon, 1915). For an example of interwar autobiographical writing of this type, see Weiss, *Mémoires d'une Européenne*.

Louise Thuliez, turned to the positive posthumous reputation of Edith Cavell in order to disassociate their own war stories from those of female spies.

Kate Evelyn Luard and British Interwar Nurse Memoirs

Thousands of First World War nurses wrote about their experiences: in letters, diaries and memoirs, and in works of autobiographical fiction published during and after the war. Although there has been a concentration on those whose writings most closely meshed with the 'disillusionment narratives', including Brittain and the powerful post-war narratives written by American nurses Mary Borden and Ellen La Motte, in reality there was a diversity of perspectives in nurses' writings which reveals the different ways in which nurses experienced the war and conceptualised their role within it.[46] While both historians and literary critics have become increasingly interested in what these accounts tell us about the development of nursing practice, women's war experiences or women's life-writing, scholars have rarely considered the question of how nurses themselves viewed their roles as chroniclers of the war and its consequences in their writings. Nurses played dual roles during the First World War, and this duality was reflected in their memoirs.[47] On one hand, they functioned as witnesses to men's war, acting as a link between home and front, for example by writing letters on behalf of their patients to families and loved ones at home. On the other hand, they were active participants in the conflict, offering vital medical care, and operating closer to the front than the majority of their sex. The narrators of nurses' war memoirs often oscillated between these two roles. While they used their memoirs to present themselves as veterans, referring to their front-line war experience in order to be able to speak publicly about the war and its legacies, they rarely questioned the primacy of combat experience. This stance can be conceptualised in relation to literary critic James Campbell's term 'combat gnosticism', which he defines as:

[46] On British nurses see Fell and Hallett, *First World War Nursing*; Christine Hallett, *Containing Trauma: Nursing Work in the First World War* (Manchester: Manchester University Press, 2010); Smith, *The Second Battlefield*; Watson, *Fighting Different Wars*. On French nurses see Darrow, *French Women*; Darrow, 'French Volunteer Nursing'; Yvonne Knibiehler, *Cornettes et blouses blanches: Les infirmières dans la société française* (Paris: Hachette, 1984); Thébaud, *La Femme au temps de la guerre de 14*.

[47] This section develops the argument about nurse memoirs I make in an earlier article. See Alison S. Fell, 'Witness or Participant', *Knjizenstvo* (2015). Available online at www.knjizenstvo.rs.

[An ideology] that gives us war experience as a kind of gnosis, a secret knowledge which only an initiated elite knows. Only men (there is, of course, a tacit gender exclusion operating here) who have actively engaged in combat have access to certain experiences that are productive of, perhaps even constitutive of, an arcane knowledge. Furthermore, mere military status does not signify initiation, but only status as a combatant. It is not the label of 'soldier' that is privileged so much as the label of 'warrior'.[48]

The presence of the ideology of combat gnosticism helps to contextualise and to explain the choices made, and some of the hesitations nurses expressed in relation to their roles as war writers.

This tension between the roles of a woman on active service – who can therefore present herself as a war veteran – and as a channel or scribe for combatant war stories is particularly evident in Luard's memoirs. Luard's publications in 1915 and 1930 are based on the same primary material, and in both texts the narrator has a dual voice. At times, Luard presents herself as a vessel through which her warrior-patients' voices may be heard, but at other times she presents herself as a 'moral witness' to the war, and as a guide for the uninitiated civilian reader. Further, it is possible to chart an evolution in Luard's understandings of herself and her role as war writer in the fifteen years between the two publications. Whereas the account in 1915 was published anonymously, the full title of the 1930 publication – *Unknown Warriors: The Letters of Kate Luard RRC and Bar, Nursing Sister in France 1914–1918* – not only stated the author's name, but emphasised her war decorations and the fact that she was nursing in France, thereby reinforcing her identity as a female veteran. This shift, I argue, was due to the changing contexts in which the memoirs were edited and published.

Luard's wartime and post-war autobiographical writings have more in common with the diary of Australian army nurse Kit McNaughton, recently examined by Janet Butler, than with Vera Brittain's authorial voice as an Oxford graduate, journalist and committed pacifist. Butler argues that the war gave Australian trained nurses like McNaughton access to new identities beyond those usually circumscribed by their social class and profession, but that these new identities were not easily assumed, and writing the self therefore involved a degree of hesitation and negotiation:

Kit's record . . . provides us with a window on the manner in which she negotiates her unconventional position [as a woman in a war zone]. For her, the diary is a tool in this process of negotiation. Viewed in new ways, it can also tell us about the

---

[48] James Campbell, 'Combat Gnosticism: The Ideology of First World War Poetry Criticism', *New Literary History* 30: 1 (1999): 203–15 (p. 204).

effects that her movement outside the boundaries begin to have upon the identities of the woman she had once been.[49]

Luard's wartime nursing also took her 'outside the boundaries' of her
pre-war life. She was born in 1872, the tenth of thirteen children born
to Rev Bixby Garnham Luard and Clara Isabella Sandford née
Bramston.[50] Like many trained British nurses, her entry into the profession chimed with an understanding of the importance of public service
and quasi-religious vocation that she had imbibed from her father and
other family members. She trained at King's College Hospital and in
1900 joined the Army Nursing Service, serving in the Second
Anglo–Boer War. In the decade preceding the outbreak of the First
World War she was working as the matron of a sanatorium.
As Christine Hallett summarises, in many ways, she was a 'typical
member of the early-twentieth-century British nursing elite', a highly
experienced medical practitioner with a strong sense of vocation, and
a woman who was used to having a degree of authority over other nurses
and, at least to some extent, over her patients.[51] In 1914 she was first
posted to No 1 British General Hospital, and worked throughout the
war at various general hospitals, stationery hospitals and casualty clearing stations, as well as on ambulance trains, which are the setting for her
1915 publication (Figure 4.1). Luard's anonymous *Diary of a Nursing
Sister on the Western Front*, published early in the war, takes its place
alongside other trained or volunteer nurses' eyewitness accounts published during the war, such as Violetta Thurstan's *Field Hospital and
Flying Column* (1915), Kate Finzi's *Eighteen Months in the War Zone*
(1916), Olive Dent's *A V.A.D. in France* (1917) or Grace
McDougall's *A Nurse at War* (1917).[52] It was based on journal entries
included in letters that she sent home to her family in Essex.[53] Her early
published response to the war has much in common with male war
memoirs of her class and background. The descriptions of the patients'
wounds and illnesses that she treated are not sanitised, but the tone of

[49] Janet Butler, *Kitty's War: The Remarkable Wartime Experiences of Kit McNaughton*
(Brisbane: University of Queensland Press, 2013), p. 10.
[50] For biographical information, see Christine E. Hallett, *Nurse Writers of the Great War*
(Manchester: Manchester University Press, 2016), and Christine Hallett and Tim
Luard's introduction to the 2014 edition of *Unknown Warriors*.
[51] Hallett, *Nurse Writers*, p. 100.
[52] For an exploration of the full range of nursing memoirs, see Hallett, *Nurse Writers*.
[53] Many of the letters are preserved in the Essex Records Office. Her letters were often sent
to other family members and to members of the local community. In this sense, even if
she hadn't originally intended to publish her diary entries or letters, she was nonetheless
writing her account for unknown civilian British readers as well as for her close family
members.

Figure 4.1 Kate Evelyn Luard. Reproduced with permission of Caroline Stevens.

the diary remains patriotic throughout, especially in her descriptions of the bravery of her soldier-patients.

The text functioned, firstly, as an initiation into front-line nursing for what was assumed to be an uninitiated reader from a woman who describes herself as being 'on Active Service'.[54] From the outset the narrator of the *Diary* embraces her role as authentic eyewitness to the war, and at the beginning of her account there is a sense of excitement about being close to the action when she was first posted to work on the trains: 'It was worth waiting five weeks to get this; every man or woman stuck at the Base has dreams of getting to the Front, but only one in a hundred gets the dream fulfilled' (25). Once there, she emphasises her

[54] Anon [Kate Evelyn Luard], *Diary of a Nursing Sister on the Western Front* (London: William Blackwood and Sons, 1915), p. 30. All subsequent page numbers are included in parenthesis.

proximity to the front, and her exposure to the sounds and weapons of industrialised war:

Shells are coming in at intervals into the village. I've seen two burst in the houses, and one came round over our train. Two French soldiers on the line lay flat on their faces; one or two orderlies got under the train; one went on fishing in the pond close by, and the wounded Tommies got rather excited, and translated the different sounds of 'them Jack Johnsons' and 'them Coal-boxes' and 'Calamity Kate' and of our guns and a machine-gun popping. There is a troop train just behind us that they may be potting at, or some gunners in the village, or the R.E. camp. There have been two aeroplanes over us this afternoon. You hear the shell coming a long way off, rather like a falsetto motor-engine, and then it bursts (twice in the trees of this wood where we are standing). (33)

In addition to functioning as a translator for her civilian audience of the British Tommies' war slang, she peppered her text with French expressions, adding to a sense of place and authenticity. She sometimes corrected the *Times* correspondents in relation to troop movements, stating that one journalist 'never found out that Havre has been a base for over a fortnight', and exclaims that the press 'gives the British public no glimmering of what [the fighting] really is' (43). This educative function of her text as an initiator into the war zone for the British civilian reader is reminiscent of male combat narratives keen to differentiate themselves from journalistic versions of the war in order to underscore the authenticity of their own accounts. It is also in evidence in relation to Luard's descriptions of the treatment of the wounds and illnesses from which her patients suffered, as well as the functioning of ambulance trains:

I thought things were difficult in the hospitals at Le Mans owing to lack of equipment, but that was child's play compared to the structural difficulties of working a hospital on a train, especially when it stands in a siding several days. One man will have to die on the train if we don't move soon, but we are not full up yet. (34)

This function of the text was also emphasised in some of the press reviews. A review article in *The Sphere*, for example, in May 1916 appeared next to photographs of ambulance trains and lengthy descriptions of equipment and treatment. The reviewer recommended Luard's text in relation to its usefulness at filling a gap in knowledge: 'it records experiences which have not been recorded elsewhere and which is, therefore, especially welcome.'[55]

The reviewer also commented on the second function of the nurse's memoir: the description of the soldiers' experience via the nurse's

---

[55] 'Life on a British Ambulance Train', *The Sphere*, 6 May 1916.

narrative: 'The nursing sister bears witness to the extreme reticence of the wounded not to give trouble.' In Luard's *Diary*, the descriptions of the conditions in which the nurses worked, and the suffering of the patients, are vivid and moving: she did not hesitate to describe the 'carnage' (40) wreaked by 'this modern perfection of machinery killing' (25). Yet the *Diary* remained resolutely pro-war in tone, and the patients remained admirable examples of courage and stoicism, uncomplaining and not questioning their duty to fight: 'The biggest wonder of it all is all the grit there is in them, and the price they are individually and unquestioningly paying for doing their bit in this War' (20). The British soldiers were presented according to the stereotypical qualities of British 'pluck': 'brave and angelic and polite in their uncomfortable and unwonted helplessness' (45). Luard's patriotism is also made evident through her anti-German sentiment. She stated that 'it is quite difficult to nurse the Germans, and impossible to love your enemies' (44), and passed on atrocity stories – 'instances of unprintable wickedness' – that she heard from her patients (45).

Thus, in the 1915 *Diary*, it was the role of war witness that was prioritised. Luard was keen to emphasise the extent to which she had a privileged position in relation to the battlefield, unlike newspaper journalists and her civilian readers: '[The soldiers] get awfully sick at the big-print headlines in some of the papers – "The Hill 60 Thrill"! "Thrill, indeed! There's nothing thrilling about ploughing over parapets into a machine-gun, with high explosives bursting around you – it's merely beastly." said a boy this evening, who is all over shrapnel splinters' (125). Her proximity to the action, and her attempts to differentiate her version of events from a sanitised or journalistic vision of war, bolstered her role as a participant in the war. But it equally foregrounded the importance of her role as transcriber of the 'authentic' soldier's voice, which she presented uniformly as expressing courage, stoicism and a willingness to serve:

Their conversation to each other from the time they are landed on the train until they are taken off is never about their own wounds and feelings, but exclusively about the fighting they have just left. If only one had time to listen or take it down it would be something worth reading, because it is not letters home or newspaper stuff, but told to each other, with their own curious comments and phraseology, and no hint of a gallery of a Press. (47)

Thus, although the tone was modified and was significantly more sombre in the later entries as she dealt with higher death rates and more difficult conditions in which to work, Luard's *Diary* supported a patriotic vision of a brave, united and praiseworthy fighting force. In this sense, the text had a morale-boosting function for its wartime readers.

Luard's 1930 publication *Unknown Warriors: The Letters of Kate Luard, RRC: Nursing Sister in France 1914–1918* belongs to the second wave of war writing. As one of its reviewers noted, however, it did not use the horrors of war in order to communicate an anti-war or pacifist message to its readers: 'there is none of that deliberate attempt to shock one's senses that one can spot in some of the most recent widely acclaimed war books.'[56] Its title makes clear that Luard in 1930 still saw one of her functions as a writer was to be a witness to the 'warrior's' story as much as a witness to her own war. This acceptance of the ideology of 'combat gnosticism' was reinforced in the choice of illustration with which she opened her text: a reproduction of a watercolour painting by Harold Sandys Williamson entitled 'Removing the Wounded' (rather than a photograph of herself in nursing uniform, for example).[57] Yet, as I noted earlier, the inclusion of her name, her titles and the preface by Field-Marshal Viscount Allenby equally set up Luard herself as the heroine of her story. Allenby's preface positions Luard's wartime role in familiarly gendered terms, describing the nurses as 'gentle women' full of 'self-sacrificing devotion' in their 'work of mercy'. However, including a preface by a high-ranking military officer also foregrounded her 'feminine' brand of heroism in a way that the anonymous *Diary* did not. Other reviews also cast Luard as the heroine of her war story, praising her 'quiet heroism' and calm under shellfire, and describing her memoir as a 'fine record of duty performed'.[58]

Unknown Warriors is more edited than the 1915 publication, covers a longer period of time and is based on extracts from her diary as well as letters home. Christine Hallett observes that there is a perhaps surprising continuity in tone with the earlier text, arguing that there is no sense of the 'hindsight that is a feature of many memoirs of the late 1920s and early 1930s'.[59] However, in the editing choices that Luard makes, as well as in the para-textual elements of her publication, subtle differences remain between the two. As in the 1915 text, the darker passages were interspersed with more light-hearted, humorous or pastoral episodes in which both nurse and reader temporarily escape from the war, such as the three-year-old French civilian victim of a bomb who when recovering 'demands beer and refuses everything else, so he's had some and has gone to sleep'

[56] *Dundee Evening Telegraph*, 4 April 1930.
[57] Harold Sandys Williamson attended Leeds School of Art until 1914. He enlisted as a private in the King's Royal Rifle Corps and after being injured worked as a theatre orderly in the No 6 General Hospital. The original of his watercolour is in the Imperial War Museum, Art.IWM.ART 1477.
[58] *Yorkshire Post*, 22 March 1930; see also *The Scotsman*, 9 April 1930.
[59] Hallett, *Nurse Writers*, p. 106.

(38). But in relation to the destruction and devastation caused by the war itself the tone of the 1930 text was more sombre. This may, of course, be due as much to the fact that the diary entries date from the later years of the war as to its later publication date. But it is nonetheless striking that within a page the reader is told that on inspecting an officers' hospital that had been set up in an infant school, Luard notes: 'It seems to be quite as well done as it could be in existing circumstances, but it makes you all the time wonder, more than ever, the Why of it all, and the When it will end.'[60] A later entry in March 1916 commented: 'Snowing hard this morning and to-night, and men are lying out in the cold slush the better to kill each other. Isn't it insane and immoral beyond description' (48). The emphasis on the keenness of the soldiers to fight for King and country has been replaced by a more muted praise of the sacrifices of 'weary, trench-worn' (35) combatants, which is redolent of the context of 1930. In a context of political policies of reconciliation with Germany, including the Locarno Treaties (1925) and Kellogg-Briand Pact (1928), anti-German sentiment was more absent from the text (or had been edited out). There were still frequent references to the 'Boche' and the 'Hun', but the examples of German atrocities and objections to nursing German patients that were present in the 1915 text were replaced by a greater and more universalised sense of reverence for the suffering and uncomplaining tenacity of combatants, both officers and men.[61]

In *Unknown Warriors* Luard continued to present herself as a conduit for the war stories of the men she treated, whose illnesses and wounds had often robbed them of a voice. Some of these stories had particular resonance in relation to interwar veteran culture, such as the exchange she related with an amputee 'wonderin' how I'm goin' to keep me family'. Luard's comment – 'I told him what splendid new arms soldiers get now, and how everyone would give them the best possible jobs, like messengers and commissionaires, before civilians, and his brow cleared at the rosy visions. I only hope it's true. Is it?' (50) – seems to be aimed at a 1930 readership as much as an original 1916 readership. Another important way of passing on men's stories was through letters. Nurses often did write letters to patients' relatives, acting as a vital communication channel between front and home. In some entries, Luard discussed the difficulties she found in her role as writer of 'Break-the-News Letters' (106). After describing the death of an underage soldier, who related his desire to see

---

[60] Kate Evelyn Luard, *Unknown Warriors: The Letters of Kate Luard, RRC and Bar, Nursing Sister in France 1914–1918*, ed. by John and Caroline Stevens (Stroud: The History Press, 2014 [1930]), p. 27. Subsequent page numbers are included in parentheses.

[61] Some German patients are described sympathetically, and it is noteworthy that the German mothers were also written to by nurses when German patients died (125).

his mother before he died, she repeated his final words to his mother in a letter, something she described as 'the most upsetting thing that has happened of all the upsetting things' (63). In a later passage, she expressed some frustration at female relatives' responses to her letters:

[Mothers] almost invariably write and ask if he 'said anything under the operation' or if he 'left any message' when you've carefully told them he was unconscious from the time he was brought in. And when you've said the Chaplain took the funeral they write and ask, 'If he was buried respectable?' Some of them write most touching and heart-broken letters. (75)

There is clearly a difference of social class at work here: Luard's mimicking of the working-class mothers' language betrays a sense of frustration with their inability to understand the medical realities of their sons' cases. However, there is also a sense of responsibility expressed in the passing on of news, on the need to act as a bridge between front and home. This chimes with other nurse-writers, who often presented themselves as a channel of communication between combatant and family, rather than as narrators of their own war experiences, in a manner reminiscent of the way in which early female religious autobiographers presented themselves as a vessel through which the word of God might be communicated, rather than as women daring to speak as individuals in their own right.[62]

Yet in *Unknown Warriors*, Luard's desire to tell the stories of her patients existed side by side with a narrative of pride at nurses' contributions as participants. This emphasis on the importance and efficiency of trained nurses was much more in evidence in her 1930 version of her war memoirs:

For efficiency in this sort of work give me the average British trained nurse, Scotch, English or Irish. When there's work to be done she goes about it without any noise or fuss or flurry, gets unemployed patients or orderlies to work, has eyes all over her head, and brains behind them, and her hands and feet never stop. (45)

The uncomplaining nature of the nurses – they are described as going to their billets 'hungry, tired and cheerful' – echoed the qualities of stoicism and cheerful perseverance she praised in her soldier-patients. Individual feats of nursing work were also praised in the memoir. When working at a casualty clearing station in the Somme, for example, she highlights the importance of nurses' work in terms of patient survival. She gives the example of 'A little Night Sister in the Medical last night' who 'pulled

[62] Leigh Gilmore, 'Policing Truth: Confession, Gender and Autobiographical Authority', in Kathleen Ashley, Leigh Gilmore and Gerald Peters (eds.), *Autobiography and Postmodernism* (Boston: University of Massachusetts Press, 1994), pp. 54–78.

a man round who was at the point of death, in the most splendid way' (30) through her initiative and nursing skill when dealing with a patient with bronchitis and acute Bright's Disease. Another entry states:

Of course we ourselves have learnt a great deal. There is no form of horror imaginable, on any part of the human body, that we can't tackle ourselves now, and no extreme of shock or collapse is considered too hopeless to cope with, except the few who die in a few minutes after admission. Some of the most impossibly pulseless people have 'done' (the slang word for recover) after hours of coping with every known means of restoration, most of which can be got going in five minutes as we have everything ready for these efforts in every ward. (90)

Here, Luard praises the contribution of nurses to the war effort, and suggests that they have gone through a 'learning curve' alongside the rest of the British army, leading to better outcomes with patients.[63] She also notes the toll their war service takes on the nursing staff, commenting on their loss of weight (70), lice (110, 116) and long hours (120), and the psychological toll of working in a casualty clearing station, that in one entry she calls 'brain fag' (137): 'It is sometimes rather overwhelming to all our nerves. The Sister (Miss D.) ... is made of real gold of a quite rare kind, and was made especially for [abdominal care], but it will wear her out in time' (72). She also mentions nurses under fire, including five nurses who were awarded the Military Medal (85) and a sister who was killed in 1917 (150). Given the frequent descriptions of shelling nearby, here Luard was implicitly placing both herself and her colleagues under fire, and positioning them as war heroines, embodying what she refers to as 'true Active Service spirit' (100). To underline this, she quotes a cavalry officer who describes nurses as quasi-combatants – 'our uniforms, our work, our hospitality, our tin hats, roaring guns' – who put civilian women to shame – 'the beastly women at home selling flags' (143). In similar vein she quotes a colonel who comments, 'I don't know how you women stick it', to which Luard responds, '[w]ell we've got to stick it'. ... I am amazed at the [level of calm] of the Sisters sometimes. They'd rather die than show any windiness, though everyone hates it' (148). In this way, and including the voices of senior male military leaders to back up her stance, she constructed the nurses as embodying the same 'pluck' that she singled out for praise amongst her combatant patients.

Luard's nurse memoirs crystallise the ethical ambiguities and liminality of women's position as female war writers. As nurses, they often wrote as participants – or, in post-war texts, as female veterans – claiming their

---

[63] Luard also mentions the importance of cooperation between medical staff, for example between surgeons and nurses (139).

right to speak, and placing themselves in the category of participants who could educate, inform and remind their civilian readers of the lessons of the war. In a climate of 'combat gnosticism' they were positioning themselves as quasi-combatants rather than as civilians. This was particularly the case, I would argue, in *Unknown Warriors*, in which Luard was keen to foreground the nurses' valuable contributions to the war effort, and in which she described the advanced casualty clearing station during the Battle of Passchendaele as itself being 'very like a battlefield' (146). On the other hand, as witnesses to men's suffering, they presented themselves as channels for communicating male warrior heroism, or for lamenting the dead. In this sense, they were not questioning the hierarchy in which male combat experience was placed at the top of war narratives, but taking up the role of comforter, nurturer and supporter that was illustrated in countless popular images of the war nurse. In the tension that existed between these dual roles of participant and witness, these nurse memoirs illustrate perfectly what literary critic Dorothy Goldman calls the 'different and complex double function' of women war writers, being simultaneously 'actors in their own war and spectators of the soldiers' war'.[64] It is a tension that is not resolved within their writings; rather, it reveals the difficulties of being taken seriously as female chroniclers of the war in a post-war climate in which the myriad of diverse war experiences was largely condensed into a culturally dominant war story in which the central protagonist was a warrior-hero.

Louise Thuliez and Interwar Resistance Memoirs

Hundreds of British, French and Belgian women participated in resistance movements in occupied France and Belgium.[65] Some worked as agents for the secret services, while others were involved in distributing underground newspapers, or in hiding and facilitating the escape of Allied soldiers.[66] As I noted in Chapter 2, some of the most prominent French and Belgian war heroines who were revered in the interwar period were members of the resistance movements who had died or been killed. Alongside the memory cults that developed around Edith Cavell, Frenchwoman Louise de Bettignies and Belgian Gabrielle Petit, other women as well as male resisters such as the French teenager Léon Trulin

---

[64] Dorothy Goldman, *Women Writers and the Great War* (New York: Twayne, 1995), p. 102.
[65] Antier, Walle and Lahaie, *Les Espionnes*; Van Ypersele and Debruyne, *De la guerre de l'ombre*.
[66] It is estimated that around 1,760 women worked as agents, many of whom were recruited by male relatives. Ten women were executed out of a total of 277 executed resisters. See Debruyne and Fell, 'Model Martyrs', p. 147.

were also remembered by their towns and nations in the interwar years.[67] Statues, ceremonies and hagiographic publications sanctified their deaths and transformed them into martyrs. As Sophie de Schaepdrijver notes in her study of the memory of Gabrielle Petit, the deaths of these resistance heroines and heroes had political, religious and emotional resonance, and their commemoration was taken up by different interest groups as a means of 'thinking through post-war issues: women's public role, paternal authority, the social order ... the theme of post-war reconciliation with Germany'.[68]

The remembrance and heroisation of surviving resisters was less public and more muted in the interwar period, but they too were not forgotten in French and Belgian commemorative culture. In 1919 and 1920, decorations were awarded to former resisters by the Belgian, French and British governments. The largest number was awarded by the latter, because of the dominance of the British intelligence services in the occupied territories in a context of fierce rivalry between the Allied secret services. In January 1920, there was a large commemorative ceremony in Lille, along with similar ones in Ghent, Brussels and Liège, during which hundreds of Belgian and French citizens were appointed to the Order of the British Empire, of whom approximately one in six was a woman. This context provided a ready-made audience for women who wished to write their war memoirs. However, writing as a female resister was an enterprise fraught with ambiguity in the interwar years. While wartime nursing largely retained its public reputation as an appropriately feminine patriotic task in the interwar years, women who were active in resistance movements were sometimes seen as morally ambiguous and subject to suspicion. They were accused both during and after the war of being 'francs-tireurs' (free-shooters, or unlawful combatants) and therefore of having broken the international rules of warfare. Further, if they worked as agents for the secret services (or were thought to have done so), they risked association with long-standing negative stereotypes of female spies as untrustworthy and sexually promiscuous *femmes fatales*, a myth that the First World War successfully revivified. Thus, the memory cult of Edith Cavell provided female resisters who wished to publish their war stories with an unimpeachable female role model as well as with a market for their writing.[69] A connection to Cavell and to the escape network for Allied soldiers in which she participated functioned as an entry ticket for a number of women into the publishing world, either as accounts published in the press or as longer published war memoirs.[70]

---

[67] See for example the *Monument aux fusillées lillois* in Lille.
[68] Schaepdrijver, *Gabrielle Petit*, p. 155.   [69] Pickles, *Transnational Outrage*.
[70] See Debruyne, *Le Réseau Edith Cavell*, chapter 12.

Louise Thuliez's first published version of her role in the Cavell network and subsequent imprisonment appeared in April 1919 as a journal
article, shortly before Cavell's body was repatriated from Belgium to
Britain with great ceremony. On 14 March 1919, Thuliez had received
from Clemenceau the Légion d'honneur and Croix de guerre, along with
several other network members. August 1919 saw the trial of Georges
Gaston Quien, the French man who was accused of having betrayed the
Cavell network.[71] Thuliez was one of the key witnesses at the trial, and
appeared 'wearing the ribbon of her Legion of Honour on her chest'.
In a dramatic moment, the prosecuting and defending counsel 'rose to do
[her] honour', and Colonel Camus, 'a veteran of five years of war, in
a voice full of emotion, begged Mlle Thuliez to accept the respectful
homage of his colleagues and himself, representing the French army'.[72]
Her identification, both by herself and by others, during the trial as a war
heroine who deserved respect and whose version of events could be
trusted bears witness to the wave of gratitude for and recognition of the
services of the men and women who had helped Allied soldiers to escape
that was in evidence in 1919. After the trial, there was a push to award
Thuliez and her fellow network members British decorations, and they
were amongst the recipients of OBEs in Lille in January 1920. There is
a reference in Quien's MI5 file to the fact that Thuliez was about to
publish her memoirs, and had asked a fellow network member, Henri
Baron, to write to ask advice about mentioning the transmission of
military intelligence to the British authorities in her account.[73] She was
discouraged from publishing as the British authorities were anxious that
no information implicating Cavell in espionage activities appear in the
public domain. The version that appeared was therefore an edited one as
a result of the advice she had received. Thuliez may have been motivated
to publish her memoirs in 1919 because she was subject to particular
suspicion, having been accused by the widow of Philippe Baucq, executed
alongside Cavell, of betraying him to save her own skin, accusations

---

[71] See TNA KV2/844 for reports and statements regarding Quien. This file confirms
Thuliez's role in the network, including for example witness statements from her sister,
Aubertine Thuliez, with whom she was living. A statement from Captain Miller, an MI5
officer, however, suggests that he did not consider Thuliez herself a reliable witness:
'I must add that Madame Thulliez's [sic] statements at the witnesses' bar were not nearly
as categoric as the ones she made when interrogated by an officer of our service.' He also
recommends that all the network members be awarded British medals.
[72] *Hull Daily Mail*, 30 August 1919.
[73] TNA KV2/844. After Thuliez's arrest, Henri Baron and his brother continued to be
active in resistance activity in order, according to their post-war statement, 'to avenge
their friend Louise Thuliez and to serve their dear country again'. Working for the British
intelligence services, they procured, for example, the plans for the station at
Valenciennes. Debruyne, *Le Réseau Edith Cavell*, p. 178.

repeated in the press.[74] More generally, however, like other women who published their war memoirs, she manifested a desire to collude in her public construction as a female combatant and war heroine, and presented her war activity as patriotic and dangerous active service. Her account was first published in the journal *La Revue des deux mondes* and was entitled 'Condamnée à mort par les Allemands: Récit d'une compagne de Miss Cavell' ('Condemned to Death by the Germans: Story of a Companion of Miss Cavell').[75]

The journal introduces Thuliez by referring to three essential elements of her construction as war heroine: her connection with Edith Cavell, her two death sentences and her decorations. Henriette Moriamé, Thuliez's neighbour and companion in St-Waast-la-Vallée, the village close to the Belgian border where they lived, is equally introduced as 'one of the heroines of the following narrative'.[76] Her narrative begins with a condemnation of the Germans, referring to the plight of Belgian refugees after the 1914 invasion, and to the 'horrors committed in the invaded villages'.[77] The Germans are described as arriving 'ready to shoot at anyone who appeared', and immediately loot shops and destroy property (648–49). They aggressively interrogate Moriamé about the number of British wounded she is sheltering, threatening her with being shot; the women, however, do not admit how many soldiers they are hiding. Thuliez's 1919 account thus closely resembled those of the 'invasion heroines' I referred to in Chapter 2, such as Soeur Julie, in which heroic women embodied the 'spirit of France' in the face of 'German barbarism' (649). On discussing their decision to hide the soldiers in the forest, Thuliez assumes an uninformed readership, and stresses the risks they took: 'Those who haven't suffered under German occupation cannot imagine the difficulties experienced by those who hid [A]llied or French soldiers. There were incessant requisitions, the continual fear of denunciation' (651). She equally stresses the risk to life that network members undertook: 'The most severe punishments were passed on those who

[74] Debruyne, *Le Réseau Edith Cavell*, p. 209. In March 1921, several network members published an open letter expressing their support for Thuliez.

[75] Extracts were translated into English and published in the *New York Times* publication *Current History and Forum* 10 (1919): 146–50.

[76] Henriette Moriamé became a nun in 1915 and died in 1918. Thuliez noted in her 1933 text that 'I have always considered the entrance of Henriette Moriamé into religion as another sacrifice added to all those which had gone before, and I am convinced that I owe it to her in great part that I came back safe and sound after the war' (131).

[77] Louise Thuliez, 'Condamnée à mort par les Allemands. Récit d'une compagne de Miss Cavell, *Revue des Deux Mondes*, 50 (1919): 648–81 (p. 648). Further page numbers are in parentheses. Available online at https://fr.wikisource.org/wiki/Condamn%C3%A9e_%C3%A0_mort_par_les_Allemands._%E2%80%94_R%C3%A9cit_d%E2%80%99une_compagne_de_miss_Cavel.l

were hiding or feeding soldiers, or who didn't denounce them. Anyone who contravened these instructions was threatened with death: in more than one Kommandantur, people were threatened with hanging' (654). She offers a defence to those who may have accused her of giving away information during her trial, stating for example that her statements were not accurately transcribed or mistranslated from French into German (659) and that her German interrogators successfully played one network member off against another (660). She admits having given away names and having had incriminating documents in her possession when arrested, but claims to have saved one French host who had hidden four soldiers by a convincing lie to her German interrogators. She also claims that, alongside Cavell and Baucq, she was purely motivated by patriotism, and that only a few 'workers' were motivated by economic gain (662). In this way she constructs herself as a patriotic heroine who risked her life for her country: 'The women who had just heard the terrible sentence pronounced against them did not give any sign of weakness. . . . As far as I was concerned, I had sacrificed my life' (662). Finally, she also presents herself as a Catholic martyr, a victim of the 'Teutonic race' (663), and aligns her calm and dignified response to her potential death directly with that of Edith Cavell.

After having her sentence commuted to hard labour, she is then accused of espionage (of passing on information about a munitions depot). She claims her innocence in this, despite evidence to the contrary.[78] This reveals the extent to which being part of the Cavell network afforded her heroic status in a way that being an agent for the French and British secret services did not. The remainder of the account focuses on the time she spent at the women's prison at Siegburg, where she was kept alongside 'other heroines' including Louise de Bettignies (672). Here, she describes the continuation of her resistance, including refusing war work on the basis of her status as a political prisoner of war. She pays homage to the women who died in the prison, and claims that children and those who were frail or sick were maltreated by the Germans.

Another female witness at the 1919 Quien trial was Ada Bodart, who also published multiple versions of her role in the Cavell network.[79] Ada started hiding soldiers in her home in 1915, for financial as well as

---

[78] Antier, Walle and Lahaie, *Les Espionnes*; Pickles, *Transnational Outrage*; TNA KV2/844.

[79] Born Ada Docherty in Newry in 1881, Bodart aged seventeen had worked as a governess for the wealthy Capelle family in Belgium, and fell pregnant by a thirty-seven-year-old Belgian man, Louis Joseph Bodart. She married him in 1898 and gained Belgian nationality. She had a son, Philippe, in April 1899 and a daughter, Hilda, in 1900. From the beginning of the twentieth century the family settled in the outskirts of Brussels. Louis died in 1908 leaving Ada a widow, and she survived financially by renting out rooms to boarders in the family home.

patriotic reasons. She probably also served as a guide, along with her son Philippe, on the first stage of the escape route. Like Thuliez, Bodart capitalised on her connection with Cavell in order to publish multiple accounts of her life, many of which are fictionalised. In August 1919 she published a highly coloured account in *La Gazette de Liège* in which she claimed that the network had helped 1,600 soldiers to escape, and claimed to have also been condemned to death (whereas in reality she was condemned to hard labour).[80] In 1923 she published another semi-fictionalised account in the Scottish *Sunday Post*, in which she expands her role and emphasises her connections to Cavell. Her attempts to present herself as a war heroine were given a further boost when she was cast to play herself in the 1928 film *Dawn*, which dramatised Cavell's death, directed by Herbert Wilcox. This led to further newspaper articles, and in 1927 Bodart was sued by D. C. Thompson, the publishers of the *Sunday Post*, for publishing another article when they had paid her for exclusive rights in 1923.[81] This points to another motivation for Bodart; after the war she was in dire financial straits, and was at least partly motivated to publish her war story for economic reasons.[82] The film *Dawn* offers a pacifist interpretation of the Cavell execution with Sybil Thorndike in the leading role, and was controversial: it caused diplomatic tension with Germany, and led poet Gottfried Benn, the army doctor present at the execution, to publish his account of Cavell's death. The controversy reveals the extent to which the climate had changed from the dominance of Allied anti-German propaganda, as can be seen in Thuliez's 1919 text, to policies of reconciliation and the normalisation of the relationship with Germany.

By 1933, however, this had begun to change with the rise of fascism in Germany and mounting fears of the possibility of another war. The early 1930s also saw a wave of spy fiction and spy memoirs, including the publication of other female-authored spy narratives, such as the memoirs of Marthe Cnockaert, a Flemish woman who operated in an intelligence network working for the British and who married a British officer after the war. In 1932, she published her memoir, *I Was a Spy*, in English under her married name of Marthe McKenna; her husband, John McKenna, may have co-authored them.[83] Their link with the real war experience of

---

[80] Ada Bodart, 'Une collaboratrice d'Edith Cavell', *La Gazette de Liège*, 9 and 12 August 1919.

[81] *Dundee Courier*, 7 December 1927.

[82] This is confirmed by the fact that after her death in 1936 her funeral was paid for by ex-servicemen. See 'War Heroine Dies Penniless', *Hartlepool Northern Daily Mail*, 11 February 1936.

[83] On *I Was a Spy* and its genesis, see Roger Quaghebeur, *Ik was een spionne. Het mysterieuze spionageverhaal van Martha Cnockaert uit Westrozebeke* (De Klaproos: Coxyde, 2000).

Cnockaert was quite tenuous, as their content was very different from the activity report she wrote just after the war.[84] Nevertheless, the colourful narrative of her book certainly contributed to its success, and the book, prefaced by Winston Churchill, was soon translated into French, Italian and Romanian, and was made into a film in 1933.[85] Both Ada Bodart and Marthe McKenna made public appearances at cinemas for showings of the films depicting their war stories, usually wearing their war medals as proof of their heroism.[86] In 1932, French woman Marthe Richard published *Ma vie d'espionne au service de la France* (*My Life as a Spy in the Service of France*) published in the wake of a fictionalised biography of her by her employer, Georges Ladoux, entitled *Marthe Richard: Espionne au Service de France* (*Marthe Richard: Spy in the Service of France*) both of which heroised Richard as both patriot and 'female combatant' of the First World War.[87]

It is therefore not surprising that it was in 1933 that Thuliez published a longer version of her account (Figure 4.2). In the same year, another prominent member of the Cavell network, Belgian princess Marie de Croÿ, also published her memoirs.[88] De Croÿ's memoirs were nationalist in tone and reflected the changing political situation as well as her own political beliefs as they included a strident attack on German militarism. She also made a claim, moreover, for the importance of the contribution of the civilian men and women who resisted German occupation, arguing that '[m]odern warfare spares neither age, nor sex, nor profession, nor situation; it is this which constitutes its chief horror.'[89] Thuliez's 1933 memoirs made a similar claim. The 1919 text was repeated verbatim in places, but the narrative was expanded and edited, along with the addition of a preface by General Weygand, who made direct reference to Antoine Redier's 1923 book *La Guerre des femmes*, that I discussed in relation to Louise de Bettignies in Chapter 2. Like Redier, Weygand set Thuliez up as a model for France to emulate: 'It will do good, as truth must always do. Like all

Marthe McKenna published a dozen books, including novels, about spying in the following years, until the couple separated in 1950.

[84] AGR, *Archives des Services patriotiques*, no. 27.

[85] *I Was a Spy* (1933) was directed by Victor Saville and starred Madeleine Carroll as Marthe. It was a box office hit and was voted the best British film of that year.

[86] See for example *Dundee Evening Telegraph*, 2 November 1928; *Sunderland Daily Echo*, 27 October 1933.

[87] See Philippa Read, 'Female Heroism in First World War France: Representations and Lived Experiences', unpublished PhD thesis, University of Leeds, 2017, chapter 4. Richard's autobiography was made into a film, *Marthe Richard, au service de la France*, in 1937.

[88] Marie de Croÿ, *Souvenirs de la princesse Marie de Croÿ* (Plon: Paris, 1933).

[89] Marie de Croÿ, *War Memories* (London: Macmillan, 1932), p. vii.

LOUISE THULIEZ AT THE DOOR OF HER CELL AT SIEGBURG

Figure 4.2 Louise Thuliez. Photograph taken from Louise Thuliez, *Condemned to Death* (London: Methuen, 1934).

good examples, it should breed strength.'[90] Thuliez's text retained the virulently anti-German tone of her 1919 account. There are frequent

[90] Louise Thuliez, *Condemned to Death*, trans. by Marie Poett-Veltichko (London: Methuen, 1934), viii. References are to the English translation. Further page numbers are included in parentheses.

references to German brutality and to German 'Kultur' (60), and she offers sweeping assessments of the German 'race': 'The German is as servile and cringing before somebody who resists him, as he is arrogant and cruel towards a defenceless being' (203). Her text was equally impregnated by right-wing Catholic nationalism, which she enthusiastically espoused after the war; the contributions of Catholic clergy and French aristocrats, such as Marie de Croÿ and Jeanne de Belleville, were described in particularly positive terms, and her German interrogator Pinckoff was described as a 'loyal servant of German Kultur' who 'tried hard to pass for a gentleman, though his every move betrayed his common origin' (120–21).

In the early pages of the text, Thuliez stresses the importance of the Franco–Prussian War in the development of her patriotic love for France, and describes her desire to be 'mobilized' in August 1914 when her services as a Red Cross nurse were not needed (xi). This theme of quasi-military mobilisation for her country is continued in the text when she claims that Captain Preston, one of the British men she is hiding, 'gave me entire charge of the [twenty-nine] men, naming me their "captain"' (23). Edith Cavell is similarly described as 'declaring that she had no more right to leave her post than a soldier had to desert his colours' (95). She also emphasises the risk to life she undertook in hiding the soldiers, commenting that she risked being shot if she were to be betrayed (31). She pays tribute to three French women who were executed for their resistance activities, Flore Lafrance, Georgina Danel and Angèle Lecat, who were shot for having used carrier-pigeons to send messages to the Allies: 'It is my duty to mention here the names of three heroic Frenchwomen who paid with their lives for the services they rendered to the country and I regret deeply that their names are not more widely known' (69).[91] Martyr-heroines Louise de Bettignies and Gabrielle Petit are also included in her narrative, the latter's death in the women's prison being described as the fault of a botched operation by German army doctors (117, 193–96). She is keen to distance herself from the negative stereotype of prostitute-spy, differentiating Cavell from Mata Hari, and declaring her own innocence from such accusations: 'The Germans knew only too well that these women that they named "spies" were not of those who can be bought with money or with favours. . . . They knew it was the pure love of our country alone that inspired us and led us to sacrifice all, even life itself, in her cause' (150). In this way Thuliez used her memoirs to make a plea, using the discourse of right-wing Catholic nationalism, for

---

[91] For details of the executions of these and other civilian resisters, see Philippe Nivet, *La France occupée 1914–1918* (Paris: Armand Colin, 2014).

the importance of remembering 'so many valiant soldiers, so many obscure heroes' (241) active in resistance networks in occupied France and Belgium, including, implicitly, her own contribution.

Like many veterans, Thuliez's dissatisfaction with interwar Republicanism had led her to engage with politics, and she was associated with right-wing nationalist organisations and networks, as well as with several veteran groupings. Thuliez was also a committed suffragist; but unlike, for instance, Vera Brittain or Germaine Malaterre Sellier, her feminism was nationalist rather than pacifist in nature. The drive to memorialise Louise de Bettignies was largely motivated by Catholic nationalist political aims, and this can equally be seen in relation to Thuliez's own self-presentation in her memoirs as a war veteran. *Condemned to Death* was praised in the right-wing press, and used as an example of exceptional heroism with which to attack contemporary social and political failings. The reviewer in *L'Action française* for example described Thuliez as 'a worthy sister of Joan of Arc', claiming that she had 'served her fatherland in a way which was more than virile', and that her work proved the 'immortal shame' of Germany's wartime atrocities.[92] Despite the conservatism of many veteran associations in terms of women's social roles, female resisters' transgression of gender norms as 'active combatants' during the war was celebrated because of their symbolic weight, the way in which they were made to embody the superior qualities of a nation. Veteran organisations, especially those on the political right, frequently made a clear distinction between 'deserving' and 'undeserving' women in order to score political points. For example, in the February 1929 edition of the journal *La France Héroïque*, the organ of the right-wing Association des décorés (Association of Those Awarded Honours), the editor stated: 'Today, many women wear medals on their chests: actresses, Ministers' secretaries, authoresses, dancers and even ... heroines. ... It is to the latter that our organisation has opened its doors.'[93] He went on to praise Louise Thuliez, deliberately contrasting her veteran-heroine status with frivolous or promiscuous 'civilian' women:

Those who lived under German oppression; those who, in broad daylight, under the hostile gaze of sentries, or during dark nights ... hid French soldiers and procured information by carrier pigeon and other difficult and dangerous means, will guess what great and sublime acts are implied in her short citation. At a time when so many women ... are assassinating their husbands, when magazines and journals are publishing the photo of Mme Hanau[94] dripping with jewellery stolen

---

[92] *L'Action Française*, 2 January 1934.
[93] *La France Héroïque: Revue mensuelle du courage civil et militaire*, 3 (1929): 56.
[94] Daughter of a Jewish industrialist from Lille, Marthe Hanau was a speculator and newspaper owner who was imprisoned for fraud in 1929. She committed suicide in 1935.

from the *Gazette du Franc*, let us bow before a real French woman, for there are, thank God, a few left!

It was on the basis that French women could carry out 'sublime acts' in times of peril that Thuliez called for the vote for women, writing in the right-wing journal *L'Intransigeant*, for example, that '[i]t is regrettable that the country of ... Joan of Arc is one of the last countries of Europe not to recognise the aptitude of women as collaborators with the government and, when necessary, as saviours of the country.'[95] In the interwar years, Thuliez consistently presented herself as an exceptional war heroine deserving of public praise and recognition. A journalist visiting her in 1926 noted that she had hung a framed copy of the announcement of her death penalty in the front room of her house. In the interview she bemoaned the fact that she had not been able, as a 'woman of action', to find a role in interwar France, her wartime deeds having been forgotten.[96] After the publication of her memoirs in 1933 she gave a series of talks to veteran organisations, with titles such as 'Female Heroism during the War' and 'Women's Energy during the War'.[97] In 1934 she gave a talk entitled 'How I Was Condemned to Death' alongside Marthe Richard, whose title was 'Should We Despise Women Spies or Recognise Their Courage?' Both women were keen at this point to capitalise on the success of their memoirs in order to represent themselves as exceptional female veterans. The review of these joint talks by novelist and journalist Michelle Deroyer is particularly telling of French post-war attitudes towards women's wartime resistance activity:

I went to the Club Faubourg to see and listen to two female spies. They were Madame Thulliez [*sic*], who was sentenced to death by the Germans at the same time as Edith Cavell ... she told us her misfortunes and her adventures in a simple style. It was very moving. Then Madame Marthe Richard appeared. She's still a beautiful, young and seductive woman ... who alas didn't tell us how she conquered the heart of Ludendorff's nephew before stealing his secrets. But, between us, I felt a little uncomfortable seeing Madame Richard on a public stage. Hasn't it been said that she was a double agent? Her Legion of Honour can't make us forget about her duplicity.[98]

Whereas Marthe Richard had a mixed reception, and was frequently accused of fabrication and of sexual misconduct by her critics, the association with Edith Cavell meant that Louise Thuliez was less vulnerable to such criticism, and she was able to maintain her reputation as a war

---

[95] Quoted in Binot, *Héroïnes*, p. 192.   [96] *L'Intransigeant*, 29 August 1926.
[97] *Le Journal de Fourmies*, 9 February 1935; *L'Ouest-Eclair*, 1 January 1938.
[98] *L'Africain: hebdomadaire illustré*, 18 February 1934.

heroine – even if, as she frequently noted, her service remained largely unrecognised and financially unrewarded in the interwar years.

Conclusions

The accounts published by both nurses and female member of resistance movements in occupied France and Belgium were part of the larger waves of 'war memoirs' and 'war fiction' that was published in both Britain and France. Whereas, especially in Britain, only a limited number of these texts are still read and studied, and have become emblematic of a broader response to the war in the public imagination, in reality a much wider range of men and women were able to tell their war stories in the post-war years. However, in order to interest both publishers and a potential readership, it remained important for women to emphasise their proximity to the front and to outline the connections between their own stories and the culturally and politically dominant male combat narrative. This relationship could be one of equivalence, as in the case of Louise Thuliez, who emphasised the risk to life and patriotic service to the nation of the women who risked their lives helping French and British soldiers to escape from occupied territory. Or it could be one of bearing witness to the combatants' war, which was at the forefront of Kate Luard's nursing memoirs.

Although these women positioned their narratives in relation to the male combat narrative, however, they also staked a claim for the importance of their own roles as 'moral witnesses' to war.[99] They dismissed what they saw as sanitised or propagandistic versions of the war in order to offer their readers the authority of direct experience. They claimed the status of 'truth-tellers' in the same way as male veteran-writers often did. In so doing they were also offering political interpretations of the war. Luard's accounts were both faithful to the tenets of British patriotic conceptions of the heroism of the ordinary 'Tommy'; Thuliez's espousal of right-wing Catholic nationalism is readily apparent, especially in her 1933 memoir. An analysis of their memoirs proves that in both nations women as well as men were able to use the publication of war memoirs as a means of having a voice in the cultural constructions of war memory, and in political debates about the war's meanings and legacies.

[99] Winter, 'The "Moral Witness"'.

5   Women's Wartime Industrial Action and the Limits of Female Veteran Identity

My previous chapters have demonstrated that some women who had been active during the war were able to claim 'war veteran' status more easily than others. In the post-war years, spies and female combatants were often viewed ambiguously, working-class members of the British auxiliary services were accused of sexual immorality, and even middle- and upper-class nurses' morality and motivations were sometimes questioned. In this chapter I consider in more detail the limits of a veteran identity for women in the interwar period, as well as some of the differences between France and Britain in this context. My focus is on female industrial workers who were leaders of episodes of wartime industrial unrest, particularly the widespread factory strikes amongst women workers that took place in 1917 and 1918. To some extent, industrial war work could be claimed as constituting a form of war service, involving a degree of sacrifice. In left-wing political and trade union circles claims could be made in relation to workers' 'patriotic sacrifices' for the nation in opposition to the 'selfish individualism' of factory owners and managers who were presented as 'shirkers' and 'profiteers'. In France, as John Horne notes, French munitions workers were presented in some circles as 'an alternative type of combatant', paying their 'impôt de sang' (blood tax) on the factory floor.[1] Horne focuses on male politicians and union leaders, but this rhetoric of national service and sacrifice was also deployed – albeit in a different context – by labour and feminist activists in relation to women workers.

However, participation in industrial action complicated this picture for former women war workers. In addition, there was a difference between national contexts. In France, many saw strike activity as a threat to national defence in a time at which the nation's survival was at stake, and strikers were often portrayed as dangerous revolutionaries. Strikes were not reported in the press, and *munitionettes* were frequently criticised

---

[1] John Horne, 'L'impôt de sang: Republican Rhetoric and Industrial Warfare in France, 1914–1918', *Social History* 14: 2 (1989): 201–23.

as selfish profiteers. Participation in strike action was therefore a problematic legacy to claim for both men and women, akin in some respects to the difficult legacy of the 1917 mutinies. In Britain, the nation was not under threat of survival in the same way. Although strikers were still routinely portrayed as traitors, defeatists or anti-patriotic revolutionaries, as was the case in France, strikes were reported in the press, and there were open disagreements on the streets and in the letters pages of newspapers between striking and non-striking workers about the morality of industrial action during the war. Christabel Pankhurst, for example, when speaking in 1918 in Glasgow about the WSPU's opposition to a compromise peace to end the war, competed with one set of women munitions workers attempting to drown her out by singing the 'Red Flag' while another set supporting her approach sang 'Rule Britannia'.[2] These differences between the political situations in France and Britain had an impact on the ways in which female strikers narrated their war experiences in the post-war years. An analysis of their post-war rhetoric demonstrates which aspects of their war experiences could have broader public resonance, and which aspects needed to be avoided to garner broader support. Whereas both French and British women workers were sometimes able to position themselves as having patriotically contributed to the war effort via their war work, their leadership of episodes of industrial action generally only brought them a degree of credibility and cultural capital amongst narrower audiences of socialists, trade unionists and communists in the years following the Armistice, especially in France. Thus, while rhetoric that spoke of revolution and class warfare, and that looked back with pride on the revolutionary year of 1917, could be deployed in trade union congresses and left-wing political meetings, for other audiences French women labour activists either avoided mention of their active roles during the war, or turned instead to broader discourses of patriotism and service, making more general claims about the inequalities of sacrifice and levels of suffering amongst different sections of the population.

In both nations, the war saw high levels of women employed in industry. In some cases it was the first time women had entered the workplace, but for many others it was a case of moving from one sector to another, often for (temporarily) higher wages.[3] France had seen high levels of

[2] Gullace, 'The Blood of Our Sons', p. 135.
[3] See Thom, Nice Girls and Rude Girls; Braybon, Women Workers; Evelyne Morin-Rotureau, 1914–18: Combats de femmes (Paris: Editions Autrement, 2004); Thébaud, Les Femmes dans la guerre; Darrow, French Women; Laura Lee Downs, Manufacturing Inequality: Gender Division in the French and British Metalworking Industries 1914–1939 (New York: Cornell University Press, 1995); Laura Lee Downs, 'War Work', in Jay Winter (ed.),

waged female labour in industry before 1914; the 1906 census states that women accounted for 33.9 per cent of France's industrial labour force. By 1918 this had increased to more than 40 per cent.[4] In Britain, the Standing Joint Committee of Women's Industrial Organisations estimated that the percentage of female employees in the total workforce increased from 26.5 per cent in 1915 to 46.7 per cent in 1918, representing an increase of around 1.4 million.[5] War work in industry for women was not without its risks. Several hundred female munitions workers died in both France and Britain from explosions or toxic poisoning.[6] However, a relatively small minority of women were employed in this high-risk work. Out of the 372,000 women who worked in the British metal trades in June 1916, for example, about 12,000 were employed in shell making and shell filling.[7] For most factory workers during the war, as had been the case in the pre-war years, industrial labour involved long hours of monotonous and strenuous repetitive tasks. On the other hand, the war years saw increased opportunities, higher wages and a new mobility. Wages were still lower than those of men, and did not keep pace with the rising cost of living, especially from 1916 onwards. Yet they were higher than they had been pre-war, especially for women who had moved from, for example, domestic service to factory work.[8] Because of the need to encourage mothers to work as well as younger or childless women – something which previously had been seen as a social ill by employers, unions and reformers alike – there was also some state provision for childcare in both nations, although in practice this was patchy and inadequate. The war also accelerated changes in production methods. As Laura Lee Downs has shown in her study of female metalworkers in Britain and France, the influx of female workers from 1915 onwards coincided with experimentation in new technologies of work. This brought opportunities for women, but it did not end gendered divisions of labour. On the contrary, French and British employers 'reorganized productive hierarchies and allocated tasks between the sexes in accordance with their understanding of the ways in which male-female

The Cambridge History of the First World War, vol. 3 (Cambridge: Cambridge University Press, 2014), pp. 72–95; Keith Mann, *Forging Political Identity: Silk and Metal Workers in Lyon, France 1900–1939* (Oxford: Berghahn, 2010).

[4] Mann, *Forging Political Identity*, p. 18.

[5] IWM, EMP 4.282, Standing Joint Committee of Women's Industrial Organisations, *The Position of Women after the War*, p. 4. Reproduced in Thom, *Nice Girls and Rude Girls*, p. 34; Norbert C. Soldon, *Women in British Trade Unions 1874–1976* (Dublin: Gill and Macmillan, 1978), p. 80.

[6] Woollacott, *On Her Their Lives Depend*, p. 9; Downs, *Manufacturing Inequality*, pp. 50–52.

[7] Thom, *Nice Girls and Rude Girls*, p. 38.

[8] Thébaud, *Les Femmes*; Braybon, *Women Workers*, chapter 2.

difference manifested itself on the assembly line or at the machine'.[9] This resulted in effect in a crystallisation of existing inequalities in the workplace, with decisions about rates of pay related to new gendered understandings of levels of skill.

The early years of the twentieth century had seen high levels of industrial action amongst workers in both nations, including women workers. The numbers of strikes and protests increased in the context of new economic and industrial conditions that prevailed during the war, particularly in 1917 and 1918.[10] A significant percentage of these wartime episodes of industrial action involved not only female workers but were also led by women, some of whom had been involved in strikes in the pre-war years, and others for whom the war was an initiation into industrial action. These female strike leaders acted as spokespeople for other workers and negotiated with union leaders, factory owners, politicians and the mediators who were commissioned by the government in both nations to act as arbitrators. For the working-class women whose writings, speeches and activities I examine in this chapter, this entry onto a public stage during the war led to longer-term political careers in the post-war years. I concentrate in particular on female strike leaders who went on to have careers in Britain as trade union organisers and, in France, as communist party leaders. The years 1917–21 were marked by a series of political developments that had a long-term impact on employer–employee relations and on workers' political identities: the waves of industrial action in 1917 and 1918, the Russian Revolution, the splits in pre-existing socialist groupings and formation of the PCF (French Communist Party) and CPGB (Communist Party of Great Britain) in 1920. These developments not only shaped the way women understood their labour and their relationship to production and to the state but equally provided opportunities for a select cohort of activist women to gain positions of leadership and influence.

The reasons these women's wartime experiences mattered in left-wing and trade unionist circles in the post-war years was that, as Keith Mann points out in relation to France, during the 1920s and 1930s 'competing socialist, anarchist, revolutionary syndicalist, and communist organizations vied for working-class support'.[11] In general terms, there was ongoing opposition to women's presence in what had traditionally been men's professions by trade unions on both sides of the Channel, as female labour (alongside foreign labour) was largely viewed as competition for male workers which might lead to the driving down of wages and conditions. The ideal of a 'family wage', to allow married women to remain at

---

[9] Downs, *Manufacturing Inequality*, p. 2.   [10] Thom, *Nice Girls and Rude Girls*, p. 109.
[11] Mann, *Forging Political Identity*, p. 1.

home, remained at the heart of much union rhetoric around female labour in both Britain and France. Nevertheless, in order to increase their political clout and financial sustainability, the leadership of unions and political parties were keen to recruit more members amongst women workers. Their policy, in other words, was to seek to enrol women in order to control them as workforce rivals.[12] The difficulty of doing so was a constant theme in their publications and congresses. The women who had led strikes during the war years could claim to be valuable assets in this goal, as they were able to argue that they could tap into the concerns and psychology of female war workers, and therefore act as recruiters in a more effective way than their male colleagues. Before the First World War, working women were not only disenfranchised but were also largely excluded from shop floor struggles, as either male skilled workers or the philanthropic middle classes tended to act as the mouthpieces of both male and female workers.[13] The highly charged atmosphere of the war in which women fought their employers and the state in a struggle for higher wages, improved conditions and, in some cases, an end to the fighting, led some women to gain a new sense of their political identities, and a new-found confidence in speaking on a public stage. Charles Tilly argues that 'political identities are relational and collective; they therefore alter as political networks, opportunities and strategies shift.'[14] The First World War was a moment in which networks and opportunities shifted for female industrial workers. The war and immediate post-war years saw large increases in unionisation, and increased power for trade union leaders, both male and female, as war production made the cooperation of organised labour essential to the state in both nations.[15] The war years thus saw the start of a rapidly evolving climate that certain women were able to take advantage of – despite the ambiguous public legacy of strike action in the post-war years – in order to gain positions of power and responsibility within unions and political parties. Although only a handful of women benefited in this way, in the pre-war years the possibilities for working-class women to have access to public life, and thereby to have their voices heard, were extremely limited.

French Women in the CGTU

The years 1915–16 saw a limited number of strikes, including eighteen by women workers in the capital, as well as a handful in other

[12] Sheila Lewenhak, *Women and Trade Unions* (London: Ernest Benn Ltd, 1977), p. 156.
[13] Mann, *Forging Political Identities*, p. 5; Thom, *Nice Girls and Rude Girls*, p. 107.
[14] Tilly, *Stories*, pp. 66–67.
[15] Richard Hyman, *The Workers' Union* (Oxford: Clarendon Press, 1971).

regions.[16] At the same time, in September 1915, anti-war unionists and socialists met in Zimmerwald, Switzerland, and began to organise a more effective opposition to the Sacred Union. Their stance became increasingly influential in the final months of the war, but unionists and socialists remained divided between a minority pacifist/revolutionary position, and a majority one which broadly supported the war effort. The situation changed dramatically in 1917. January of that year saw the introduction of the 'Thomas scale' of wages, introduced by the minister of munitions to raise the minimum rates of pay for both sexes and rationalise the calculation of piece rates. In spring 1917, many employers were refusing to implement the scale, in spite of the wartime inflation which had cut wages by an average of 23 per cent.[17] Employees became increasingly desperate and dissatisfied, and by May their grievances were being expressed in incidents of industrial action. There was a wave of strikes: in 1917 as a whole, there were 696 strikes involving almost 300,000 strikers, which was more than double the number of the previous year. Many of these strikes involved women, especially in the early period from May to June. In the metal-working trade, for example, female workers were at the forefront of the spring 1917 strikes.[18] The tone and nature of strikes shifted as the wave of strikes spread, and some became more markedly political, accompanied by demands for peace, and sometimes by support for the Russian Revolution, such as the large strikes that took place in armaments factories in Saint-Etienne, Lyon and Paris.[19] Public attitudes towards female strikers varied. Despite some public sympathy for war workers in relation to the rising cost of living, many commentators, including some trade unionists, represented striking women as grasping individualists at a time when selfless sacrifice was the order of the day. Yet the role of women in wartime labour protests had left its mark on male activists, and there were more concerted attempts to recruit women. As early as 1916, trade unionist Jules Bled had argued that: 'Given that to a certain extent women will be called upon to replace men in the factories after the war, it is their duty to join their respective trade unions.'[20] In May and June 1917 the CGT intervened in an attempt to organise what had originally been spontaneous strikes

[16] Jean-Louis Robert, *Les Ouvriers, la patrie et la Révolution. Paris 1914–1919* (Besançon: Annales littéraires de l'université de Besançon, 1995).
[17] Downs, *Manufacturing Inequality*, p. 129.
[18] Mann, *Forging Political Identity*, p. 129; Downs, *Manufacturing Inequality*, chapter 4.
[19] Mann, *Forging Identity*, p. 71.
[20] AN, F7, 13366. Jules Bled, secretary of the Union des Syndicats de la Seine, quoted in Downs, *Manufacturing Inequality*, p. 123.

by women workers. Their interventions had as objectives to recruit more women members and to negotiate directly with Albert Thomas. In some areas women strikers were even seen as role models for male workers. In a meeting of workers from Berliet's factory in Lyon in January 1918, for example, a skilled male worker pointed to the struggle of striking female workers as an example to be emulated.[21]

The period of strikes and social agitation did not end with the Armistice. In fact, rising prices and frustration with slow demobilisation led to high levels of industrial action in the early post-war years, some of which was highly politicised, such as the 1920 railway strikes. As far as women were concerned, thousands were made redundant from their wartime roles, although this varied in different sectors. French unions continued to prioritise women's roles in the home as wives and mothers rather than as workers or as political activists. After the war, the two tendencies that had developed in relation to the support of the Sacred Union crystallised into an anti-war minority that aimed to defend and extend the Russian Revolution, and a pro-war majority that espoused a more gradual, 'economic' revolution. At the 1921 CGT convention held in Lille, the CGT split, mirroring the split in the French socialist party that had led to the formation of the PCF in December 1920. Debates were bitter and revolved around independence from the Communist Party and Moscow, on one hand, and failures to bring about real change in workers' conditions, on the other. This led to the founding of the Confédération Générale du Travail Unitaire (CGTU), which formally joined the Internationale syndicale rouge (ISR) in 1923, underscoring its pro-Moscow stance. It was in this breakaway union, closely aligned with the PCF, that the French former strike leaders I focus on in my case studies – Martha Desrumaux and Alice Brisset – found a home.

French communists and trade unionists redoubled their efforts in the period to recruit women to their ranks in the post-war years, including campaigns to encourage female industrial workers to join the CGTU. This was partly due to the influence of Moscow, which in the early 1920s espoused a policy of sexual equality, and partly due to their desire to find more support amongst working-class women, who could then help to propagate their political message.[22] A police report discussing the PCF's 'Sous-Commission féminine du Travail' (Work Sub-Committee), of

[21] Mann, *Forging Identity*, p. 130.
[22] Christine Bard and Jean-Louis Robert, 'The French Communist Party and Women 1920–1939: From "Feminism" to Familialism', in Helmut Gruber and Pamela Graves (eds.), *Women and Socialism. Socialism and Women. Europe between the Two World Wars* (Oxford: Berghahn, 1998), pp. 321–47.

which Alice Brisset was a member, stated that its aim was to 'intensify communist propaganda amongst women and to get them to urge their husbands to join the party'.[23] Relationships between women and the PCF were, however, fractured in this period. In her 1968 history of the PCF, Annie Kriegel argues that the interwar male leadership treated the issue of women with 'total indifference', and shared the wider public dismissal of, for example, single communist women teachers who had 'little of the aura of respectability generally accorded wives and mothers'.[24] In addition, many women who had joined in the early years handed in their party cards because of disagreements over membership of other organisations, including feminist ones, or because of ideological disagreements with the party line. The head of the Women's Commission, Suzanne Girault, was a particularly authoritarian figure who was responsible for some of the departures of some of the women who had joined in the early 1920s.

Women as a whole made up a very small percentage of total membership of the PCF: in 1924 they constituted 4 per cent of total membership, and this fell to around 2 per cent later in the decade. Given these low numbers, women were over-represented in leadership positions in relation to other political parties. For example, in 1926 8.6 per cent of delegates to the PCF National Congress were women.[25] In the 1920s, women were also present on its Central Committee, although their numbers dwindled to zero in the early 1930s. This context demonstrates that only a small number of women were able to have political careers within the PCF in the decade following the Armistice. As was the case with other political movements, it was largely educated middle-class women who had leadership positions. The exceptions were female workers who had been politicised during the war years, and who had become leaders of industrial action in their workplaces. Kriegel argues that the 'génération du feu' were one of four specific groups of men who joined PCF in the early 1920s, who 'came to communism from the war or because they had been against it'. She considers in particular shop stewards in munitions factories, three of whom when interviewed indicated that their experience in the war both 'provided a favourable educational opportunity' and 'initiated them into the trade union movement'.[26] Although Kriegel refers only to men, Martha Desrumaux and Alice Brisset also belonged to the communist 'war generation' that Kriegel identifies, for whom the war

[23] AN F7 1386, Report, 4 March 1922.
[24] Annie Kriegel, *The French Communists*, trans. by Elaine P. Halperin (Chicago: University of Chicago Press, 1972), pp. 67–68.
[25] Bard and Robert, 'The French Communist Party', p. 323.
[26] Kriegel, *The French Communist Party*, pp. 100–02.

provided educational opportunities. They had both led strikes during the war, and became prominent members of the CGTU as well as the PCF in the 1920s, gaining leadership positions in both organisations. This, I argue, was not a coincidence. The war initiated them into political life and gave them training in negotiation, political rhetoric and public speaking. They presented themselves as experts in the mobilisation of women workers, largely possible because of the opportunities the war presented. However, they did not present their experiences as 'war service' in the same way as ex-nurses or ex-servicemen when attempting to persuade their audiences. Rather, they tended to refer to a more acceptable image of wartime women as suffering civilians whose male relatives were at the front.

Martha Desrumaux

In August 1917, twenty-year-old Martha Desrumaux was working in the Hassebroucq munitions factory in Lyon having been one of thousands of textile workers evacuated from Comines in the occupied area of northern France in August 1914 (Figure 5.1).[27] She had already been introduced to socialist and trade unionist politics, but it was the First World War that initiated her into industrial action, and that enabled her to take on a leadership role. She led a strike of female workers demanding better pay and conditions, and was chosen to represent her fellow workers in negotiations. The strike was successful, and as the workers' representative she was asked to sign the agreement. At this point in her life, Martha was illiterate, and risked being humiliated and having her authority undermined by admitting in public that she was unable to read or write. Undeterred, she demanded that the agreement be read out loud so that everyone was aware of its contents, thereby masking her illiteracy.

The successful strike in Lyon marked the beginning of a life committed to the trade union movement and, from 1921 onwards, to the PCF. Returning to the textile industry in the north of France in 1921, Desrumaux attempted to persuade her fellow textile workers, the majority of whom were female, to join the CGTU and the PCF. She was at the heart of a series strikes of textile workers in 1921, 1924 and 1928, in which she became skilled at leading episodes of industrial action and in negotiations with both management and other political groupings. She also engaged in more traditional forms of education: a colleague taught her to read and write, and in 1924 she attended a kind of communist Sunday school, studying Marx and Lenin

---

[27] Pierre Outteryck, *Martha Desrumaux: Une femme du nord. Ouvrière, syndicaliste, déportée, Féministe* (Paris: Comité Régional CGT Nord-Pas-de-Calais, 2006).

Figure 5.1 Martha Desrumaux.

under Madeleine Devernay.[28] In 1925 Desrumaux wrote several articles for the communist journal *L'Enchaîné* praising women's anti-war activism, discussing maternity leave and the protection of working mothers, and denouncing both the impact of the Caillaux taxes on households, and the Rif War by evoking the 'slaughter of 1914–18'.[29] In this way she was presenting herself both as an expert on 'women's issues' and as somebody who could speak with authority on the consequences of war, but tellingly her focus was not on women as war workers or as strikers, but on family and domestic life.

As a female activist who was now literate and educated in communist ideology, but who was still engaged in factory work and who was regularly to be found at the front line of industrial action, Desrumaux was in an ideal position to present herself as a leadership candidate, as both the French and Russian communist parties were keen to encourage the political engagement of 'authentic' women workers. In 1927, Desrumaux was chosen as

[28] Outteryck, *Martha Desrumaux*, p. 69. In 1931 she spent sixteen months in Moscow attending the communist international school, which was set up in order to disseminate revolutionary communism across the world.

[29] *L'Enchaîné*, 26 September 1925; *L'Enchaîné*, 19 December 1925.

one of the French delegates who attended the second Soviet Congress of Women Workers and Peasants, to celebrate the tenth anniversary of the Russian Revolution. This was quite a feat for a woman of her social background; notably, the middle-class pacifist feminist Gabrielle Duchêne had to pretend Desrumaux was her domestic servant in order to secure her a passport. When Desrumaux addressed the delegates at the Congress, in response her Russian hosts expressed pleasure in the fact that a 'real' woman worker was present representing French women workers.[30] This ability to claim 'authenticity' as a representative of the working woman explains to some extent Desrumaux's rise to power in communist circles. In an intervention at the 1927 CGTU congress, for example, Desrumaux played on her many years of front-line experience in offering her analysis of the question of how to recruit more women workers: 'In the Nord region, where we have a very powerful consortium, unionisation is still weak amongst women workers. Even so, we have tried to do good work and we have managed to do so. . . . I have been a militant activist for many years on the factory floor, and I know how severe the repression of activists is.'[31] During this period she also honed her talents as an orator – an essential skill for women labour activists keen to have a prominent public role. She was frequently the only female speaker at communist and trade unionist meetings, and made regular interventions at congresses.[32]

Desrumaux's political activism was not without its risks; like many communist leaders and revolutionary trade unionists she was arrested and briefly imprisoned twice, in 1930 and 1931, for her part in episodes of industrial action.[33] This added to her reputation as, in the words of her critics, an 'agitatrice mouscoutaire' (communist agitator loyal to Moscow) and as 'la camarade rouge de Comines' (the red comrade from Comines).[34] But it also gave her a degree of authority in certain networks. In February 1928, for example, she was a speaker at the annual congress of the feminist pacifist organisation the Union Fraternelle des Femmes contre la Guerre (Fraternal Union of Anti-War Women). In her speech she began by passing on the 'fraternal greeting of Russian women workers' when she went to Russia to 'celebrate the tenth Anniversary of the Russian Revolution', thereby cementing her authority as a woman who could speak on behalf of other female workers, and whose engagement

---

[30] Madeleine Charpentier, 'La délégation féminine française est arrivée à Moscou', *L'Humanité*, 16 October 1927.
[31] *Congrès national ordinaire (4e congrès de la CGTU Bordeaux 19 au 24 septembre 1927)* (Paris: CGTU, 1927), p. 608.
[32] See for example *L'Humanité*, 6 December 1930, in which she is the only woman in a long list of advertised speakers at a meeting in Valenciennes.
[33] *Le Temps*, 17 February 1930; *Le Matin*, 17 June 1931.
[34] *Le Journal*, 19 August 1930; *Le Journal*, 21 May 1931.

dated back to the beginnings of the communist party in the war years.[35] By the mid 1930s she was spoken of in the communist press as a great orator and leader – she was credited, for example, in the communist journal *Regards* in 1934 for leading a strike of the workers of Saint-Omer: 'It is our comrade Martha Desrumaux ... who led them in their struggle against their grasping boss and whom they love like a sister.'[36] As her biographer Pierre Outteryck suggests, Martha Desrumaux was unusual in that as an uneducated and illiterate young female worker in 1917 she gained high profile and influential roles in interwar communist and trade unionist networks in France. She was, moreover, very aware of her importance as a representative of what a working-class woman could achieve; in a much later interview she argued that communist publications such as *L'Ouvrière*, a journal directly aimed at female workers in the 1920s and which she helped to distribute, were essential in 'consciousness raising [amongst women], in making women aware that they were not alone ..., in pushing women too to intervene'.[37] However, although it was not something she played on in her post-war writings and speeches, it was essentially her initiation into direct action as a war worker in Lyon in 1917 that first gave her the experience, the skills and the reputation to achieve the positions of leadership and responsibility in the post-war years. This was equally the case for her fellow communist and trade unionist activist Alice Brisset.

Alice Brisset

The strike of the 'midinettes' (dressmakers) in 1917, was one of the most visible and mediatised strikes of the First World War (Figure 5.2). The strike was triggered initially by the redundancy on 11 April of two workers who were told they were not needed for the Saturday afternoon shifts. In response the workers went out on strike demanding a full day's pay for Saturday in addition to an extra franc a day as a cost-of-living allowance. The strike quickly spread, the number of strikers rising to 2,000 the following day, and the garment industry ground to a halt. By the end of the month, it is estimated that 31,000 female workers from the dress, textile, fur and leather industries had joined in order to demand higher wages.[38] The demonstrators took to the Parisian streets, in a series of marches and public displays, wearing smart fitted suits that both showed

[35] *L'Humanité*, 20 February 1928.   [36] *Regards*, 29 June 1934.
[37] Quoted in Outteryck, *Martha Desrumaux*, p. 84.
[38] Maude Bass-Krueger, 'From the "union parfaite" to the "union brisée": The French Couture Industry and the Midinettes during the Great War', *Costume* 47: 1 (2013): 28–44.

Figure 5.2 Strike of the midinettes, 1917. Photo 12 / Alamy Stock Photo.

off their needlework skills and gave them elegance and dignity in the public eye. They sang, reminding spectators of previous parades for St Catherine's Day, but this time their lyrics were political. For twenty-three-year-old furrier Alice Brisset, it was an initiation into trade union politics and industrial action that changed the course of her life. It was her first strike, and in an interview many years later, she presented it as an example of women's appropriation of public space: '[T]he streets had always been a little bit the midinettes' domain. In happier days, we paraded there, singing, to celebrate St Catherine's Day. But now, the street belonged to us.' Brisset equally referred to a contrast between immoral 'war profiteers' and the 'sacrifice' of the female workers in her evocation of the strike in her interview: 'Everyone had a relative at the front and every morning the first question was: 'Have you had any news?' . . . Paris offered the double spectacle of hunger (bread and sugar ration cards) and immoral luxury . . . the wives of profiteers and the *nouveaux riches* were also our demanding and capricious clients.'[39]

---

[39] Interview in Madeleine Colin, *Ce n'est pas aujourd'hui: Femmes, syndicats, luttes de classe* (Paris: Editions sociales, 1975), p. 75.

The strike of the *midinettes* was a success: the textile industry employers met the women's conditions and work resumed. The strike was generally reported sympathetically in the French press. Many were already sympathetic to dressmakers' working conditions, and fellow Parisians equally viewed *la vie chère* as a real problem. The charm and appearance of the workers was noted, and their actions were viewed much more sympathetically than those of the *munitionettes*. Both Downs and Darrow point to the positive images of the striking women in popular memory ever since, the concentration on their 'singing charm', serving to some extent to depoliticise their industrial action.[40] A July 1917 article sent by an anonymous female participant in the 'midinette' strike to the American journal *The Ladies' Garment Worker*, however, couched the strike in more overtly political terms: 'The war has ushered in a new state of affairs, almost a revolutionary spirit amongst the French women workers. ... The war has given French women a deeper insight into the grim realities of life and they seem to realise their position. ... These young women have now realised the self-help principle of unity and organization.'[41] For some of the female strikers at least, the *midinettes* strike revealed the potential for organised industrial action amongst women workers.

Amongst communists, socialists and trade unionists, this strike continued to be associated with the successful mobilisation of working-class women. Indeed, Jean-Louis Robert argues that this women's strike, more than any other, 'entered collective memory' in France to such an extent that it attained the level of a 'mythology'.[42] Brisset's close links with the strike therefore endowed her with a degree of political authority in left-wing political circles in the interwar years. She joined the newly formed PCF in 1920, and took on important roles in a period in which both communism and trade unionism were dominated by men. In 1923, Brisset became Secretary of the Communist Federation of the Seine-et-Oise region, as well as becoming a member of the women's commission of the CGTU. In 1924, she became a member of the Women's Commission and delegate of the executive Commission of the CGTU. In 1926, she became a member of the Central Committee of the PCF and went to the congress at Lille. However, her influence faded in the later 1920s. In 1927, she resigned from the Executive Commission of the CGTU in a protest against Suzanne Girault's leadership. She was not re-elected to the Central Committee of the PCF or the Executive Commission of the CGTU, and did not gain another influential position until the unification of the unions in 1936. Until 1927, however, she was one of the most

---

[40] Downs, *Manufacturing Inequality*, pp. 136–37; Darrow, *French Women*.
[41] *The Ladies' Garment Worker*, July 1917.   [42] Robert, *Les Ouvriers*, p. 123.

influential communist women in France, and one of the few to come from
the ranks of the workers.

Brisset benefited in particular from the attempts in the early years of the
PCF to recruit more female members. However, in her interventions in
the 1920s congresses of the CGTU we can sense her frustration at the
lack of commitment for the recruitment of women amongst her male
colleagues. She enthusiastically took on the task of attracting a larger
female membership, but felt that this was hindered by 'outdated' male
views that insisted on the primacy of women's roles as wives and mothers
at home. In the 1925 congress, for example, she declared:

> We have emphasised and need to emphasise here the fact that even amongst trade
> union members certain prejudices remain. Our male comrades don't really realise
> that the current situation of women workers is a definitive one, that women will
> be ... increasingly industrialised. Comrades who still hold to these outdated
> principles 'Women are made to stay at home, and men must demand higher
> salaries to support their families' are mistaken. The bourgeoisie have been fond of
> saying that women are indifferent, that their brains are too small, that they are
> passive, not interested in the realities of life, or if they were interested, that it
> was not for them. Well now, we mustn't repeat what bourgeois morality has
> taught us![43]

For Brisset, women workers should not have been seen as a 'special case'
but as workers who deserved 'equal pay for equal work'. Given the
dominance of the 'breadwinner' model in which male union leaders
prioritised a 'family wage' for skilled male workers, this was not
a mainstream view. But Brisset commanded a degree of respect because
of her activist background, including during the war, and her extensive
experience of working alongside other women. In the same congress,
when she was elected onto the Parisian committee, she was praised in
the following terms: 'The Paris region thinks that Alice Brisset, who has
long experience of struggle, who really knows the working classes
because she has worked and suffered alongside them, ... is of all of us
the most capable of speaking on our behalf and expressing our ideas. ...
You know how eloquently she speaks of the exploitation by bosses that
she suffered herself, and also how much she has shown in her articles
that she understands working-class mentality.'[44] Brisset also frequently
advised her male comrades how to attract more women into the movement, and how to use post-war discourses of suffering and sacrifice most
effectively:

[43] *Congrès national ordinaire (3e congrès de la CGTU Paris 26 au 31 août 1925)* (Paris: CGTU, 1925).
[44] *Congrès national ordinaire*, 1925.

Comrades have explained to us the feelings of women in relation to the war. If we know how to exploit these feelings to bring women into the class struggle, we can in this way bring large numbers of women into revolutionary organisations against fascism. . . . We see in the bourgeois press that women tend to be given less and less space in public life. They are only addressed by playing on a sentimental note: in the name of mothers and widows, people speak to them about their dear departed ones, they are told that they went to war to win peace, but that in this country there are those who would prevent peace by calling for Revolution. . . . It doesn't always persuade men, when they are told a Revolution is worse than a war with an external enemy, but it certainly persuades women, whose brains haven't been trained to tackle political and economic questions. . . . So speak to them about the war, about their wages, about the high cost of living.[45]

Here, she argued that it was a risky strategy to evoke the notion of a potentially violent social revolution amongst women workers, and that the rhetoric of economic and personal sacrifices was safer ground. In so doing she was differentiating herself from what the majority of her audience would have understood as women's limited capacity for understanding and engaging with politics. But she was also, and crucially, presenting herself as somebody who understood working women's mentality – in contrast, for example, to middle-class school-teachers who also formed part of the female leadership – and who had lived through the same hardships, particularly during the war, and was therefore able to communicate with and persuade women to join the revolutionary movement.

Brisset's 1920s articles for *L'Ouvrière* also reveal the extent to which she saw herself as somebody who was able to directly address and engage with women workers. Her articles were all variations on the themes of class struggle, the exploitation of women workers, and the need for solidarity and industrial action. She also followed her own advice, and referred to workers' sacrifices and hard work in contrast with profiteers and shirkers. In an article in 1926 for example, she evoked women's wartime suffering, claiming that 'women have accepted a life of suffering for many years: grief, worries, shortages', in an attempt to establish common ground and a sense of shared experience with her readers.[46] When the war was evoked in communist and trade unionist circles in the 1920s, moreover, it was not only the sacrifices of the workers and soldiers that were remembered but equally the Russian Revolution and birth of communism. A frequent point of reference, especially in events related to the 'International Week of Women' organised by the PCF in the mid-1920s, was the Russian women's protest of 8 March 1917, demanding bread and the

---

[45] *Congrès national ordinaire*, 1925.
[46] Alice Brisset, 'Les grévistes de Larroque-d'Olmes', *L'Ouvrière*, 5 August 1926.

return of their men from the front. For example, in the police report of a meeting organised on 8 March 1927, Brisset's speech to the 2,200-strong audience reminded them that: 'In 1917 it was the women who went out into the streets to call for peace and for bread; in 1927 French women should be making the same declarations.'[47] Similarly, in an article for *L'Ouvrière* she described the 1917 action as providing a 'precious lesson' for French women of the 1920s. This set up the Russian women's 8 March protest as a model to emulate. Notably, the model was not that of her own experience of leadership on the factory floor. Rather, it consisted of women going onto the streets to demand bread and a return of their menfolk in an extension of their domestic roles, closer in spirit to the 1789 October days than to women's wartime strike action. Once again, this is telling of the limits of what was possible to refer to in relation to her own war experiences.

The PCF, despite the enthusiasm of female activists like Brisset and Desrumaux, was not successful in recruiting more female members. In addition, the unionisation of women workers, despite increases from a low base, remained relatively weak in the interwar period. As Laura Frader has shown, communists, socialists and trade unionists in France remained committed to the dominant 'breadwinner' model, in which women were viewed as wives and mothers to be supported by male wage earners, subsidised by the state if necessary.[48] This helps to explain the 'domestication' of women's roles in the class struggle in CGTU discourse as suffering wives and mothers rather than exclusively as exploited workers. However, as Geoff Read and Siân Reynolds have both pointed out, this generally hostile climate in France did not prevent certain women from becoming prominent activists in their political circles, particularly on the far right, something that Brisset refers to directly in another intervention in the 1925 CGTU congress. Women were more involved in French political parties during the interwar years than ever before. They spoke regularly in public, wrote articles for the political press, and helped shape the direction of policy, and, in some cases, took on leadership positions. For the French communist women whose stories I have resurrected here, it was their political education undergone during the war that was a catalyst for the post-war political lives.

---

[47] AN F7 1386, 'Semaine Internationale des Femmes', organisée par le PCF. Meeting, 33 rue de la Grange aux Belles.
[48] Geoff Read, *The Republic of Men: Gender and Political Parties in Interwar France* (Baton Rouge: Louisiana State University Press, 2014); Frader, *Breadwinners and Citizens*; Reynolds, *France between the Wars*.

Britain Women Organisers in the Workers' Union

The situation in Britain regarding the situation of women workers, and their relationship to trade unions, shared many characteristics with the situation in France in that the war years saw a series of strikes. The frequency of strikes increased in 1917 and 1918, with 730 stoppages in 1917, and 1,165 in 1918, as opposed to 582 stoppages in both 1915 and 1916.[49] Many of the strikes involved and were led by women workers in Britain, and, as in France, these strikes were different in nature to those led by men. Women workers were generally more likely to strike than their male counterparts, and some used tactics borrowed from the suffrage movement, such as leaflets, songs, postcards, ribbons and badges, in order to garner sympathy for their cause.[50] There was also a degree of hostility towards women workers amongst male members and leaders of trade unions in Britain, although this varied according to the industry and union concerned, and the threats (real or perceived) to the wages and conditions of their male members. All trade union leaders, including women, were keen to ensure that the thousands of unorganised and inexperienced women who entered the workforce during the war should not be permitted to undercut wages; a slogan of women's trade unions was: 'Don't blackleg your man in Flanders.'[51] There were key differences in attitudes towards women workers amongst general labour unions, who included large numbers of less skilled workers, and craft unions. The latter were most concerned with maintaining their members' industrial status, and a few, such as the Amalgamated Society of Carpenters and Joiners and the Amalgamated Society of Engineers, did not allow women to join.[52] For these unions, women workers remained primarily a threat to the wages and livelihoods of their members. However, the largest numbers of unionised women workers belonged to the general unions: the Workers' Union (WU), the General Union of Municipal Workers (GUMW) and the National Federation of Women Workers (NFWW), which had been founded in 1906 to cater for women not accepted into other unions, or for whom no union existed. Union membership amongst women workers rose steeply during the war, from 437,000 in 1914 to 1,342,000 in 1920, and although it fell again during the economic slump, unionisation remained significantly higher amongst women workers throughout the interwar period than it had been

[49] H. A. Clegg, *A History of British Trade Unionism since 1889, Volume 3, 1934–1951* (Oxford: Oxford University Press, 1994), p. 240.
[50] Thom, *Nice Girls and Rude Girls*, p. 105.
[51] Lewenhak, *Women and Trade Unions*, p. 147; Sarah Boston, *Women Workers and the Trade Union Movement* (London: Davis Poynter, 1980), chapter 4.
[52] Braybon, *Women Workers*, pp. 68–69.

pre-war.[53] As Sheila Lewenhak summarises, a significant percentage of demobilised women war workers 'took their initiation into trade unionism with them into their new employments' in the post-war period.[54]

In the incidents of industrial unrest that took place in 1917 and 1918, dozens of women were involved in negotiating with employers, managers and politicians in a bid for improved wages and conditions for women workers, either as representatives of other workers, or as leaders or organisers of trade unions. Some of these women were already well established as mouthpieces for the plight of working women, such as Mary Macarthur, the leader of the NFWW. Macarthur was a middle-class woman who had originally worked as a union organiser for shop workers before working for the Women's Trade Union League and then the NFWW. Frustrated with the limitations of smaller unions, Macarthur set out to recruit women from a wide range of industries to its ranks, and provided practical support such as strike pay.[55] Macarthur believed that the organising of women, and improvement of their conditions as workers, was a social good. For her, unionised women would be 'better citizens, living a fuller life . . ., more fitted mentally and physically to be mothers of the coming race'.[56] In this sense, her rhetoric was similar to that of reformist feminists of the turn of the century, and was one that resonated widely. She became a highly influential figure during and after the war, sitting on government committees discussing the question of female labour, such as the Munitions Labour Supply Committee and Women's Training and Employment Committee, during the war, as well as advocating on behalf of women in trade union congresses. She was thus seen by many as 'the voice of all women workers', and she continued to represent women workers on national committees after the war, for example on the NEC of the Labour Party in 1918, until her death from cancer in 1921.[57]

However, the context of women's industrial action during the war also provided opportunities for working-class women to have their voices heard, and in some cases to gain positions of influence within unions by becoming union organisers. An important factor in women's influence in disputes was the growth in arbitration, brought in by the government to ensure the continuation of production during wartime. The 1915

---

[53] Thom, *Nice Girls and Rude Girls*, Table 6.1, p. 140. Based on A. H. Halsey, *Trends in British Society since 1900* (1972), p. 123.

[54] Lewenhak, *Women and Trade Unions*, p. 166.

[55] Cathy Hunt, *The National Federation of Women Workers 1906–1921* (Basingstoke: Palgrave Macmillan, 2014), p. 1.

[56] Quoted in Hunt, *The National Federation*, p. 3.

[57] TNA LAB 5/1; Thom, *Nice Girls and Rude Girls*, p. 117.

Munitions of War Act made arbitration compulsory, and in theory made strikes and lock-outs illegal. But in practice, the legislation was limited by the power of rank-and-file union members, who could not all be jailed if they struck, and so strikes still took place.[58] Appointed arbitrators dealt with complaints from women workers, as well as with walk-outs and stoppages, usually in response to the lack of 'equal pay for equal work' that women workers had been promised by the government.[59] The arbitration files held at the National Archives contain letters and transcripts of agreements in which working women's voices can be seen to have had influence, given the importance to the government of keeping war production going. For example, in 1917 around fifty women weavers at Cumledge Mills in Duns, on the Scottish borders, who were employed making army blankets, went out on strike for higher wages 'in view of the high cost of living'.[60] They wrote several collective letters to Sir George Askwith, who was chairman of the Government Arbitration Committee under the Munitions of War Acts from 1915 until 1917, outlining their complaints. Their rhetoric is reminiscent of the 'double sacrifice' rhetoric deployed by French female munition workers, in which they present themselves as both war workers and as the female relatives of mobilised men:

In accordance with your suggestion the Blanket Weavers who were out on strike for a fortnight resumed our work on May 3 [1917]. We started work in order to give our Employers every opportunity to make a settlement failing a settlement we understand your Department would send down an official to arbitrate between the parties. ... We cannot make a wage to keep ourselves and some of us has our own near and Dear friends away to France.[61]

In a later letter, the weavers played on the stereotypes of 'sacrifice' of the workers versus the idle selfishness of the 'profiteering' and 'shirking' bosses in order to attempt to garner sympathy for their cause:

We are women weavers and many has a house to keep up with their Brothers and other friends fighting in France. ... One of our masters is lying in a helpless state with drink ... the other Master ... tends to go Motoring for golf and leaves us struggling on. They don't know what the War is and doesn't even ask for the Men that are away we are only fighting for a just cause for our wages.[62]

---

[58] Lewenhak, *Women and Trade Unions*, p. 152.
[59] In February 1916, the government made Circular L2 (requiring a minimum wage of £1 for substituted women workers) mandatory, but employers found ways of reducing the increase. Boston, *Women Workers*, p. 109.
[60] *The Berwick Advertiser*, 26 and 27 April 1917. See also *The Berwick Advertiser*, 27 July 1917 for the publication of the arbitration decision. The arbitrator, Sir Richard Lodge, raised the women weavers' wages.
[61] Letter, 11 May 1917, TNA LAB2/206/IC2882/1917.
[62] Letter from 'All Weavers', Cumledge Mill, Duns, 22 June 1917. TNA LAB2/206/IC2882/1917.

In this case, there are no individual women named, and the letters are signed collectively from 'All Weavers', but for many other files it is individual women who speak on behalf of other women workers, usually in their roles as union organisers. For the remainder of this chapter I focus on two other women whose names also appear in the arbitration files in their roles as organisers for the Workers' Union, and who went on to forge political lives in the interwar period.

The Workers' Union (WU) was founded in 1898, and at its peak in 1920 represented around 100,000 women from a broad range of industries, including textiles, metal, food, tobacco and rubber, as well as female domestic servants and agricultural workers.[63] At the start of the war, only one female organiser was employed, Julia Varley. Varley was a working-class woman with several years' experience of leading industrial disputes in the engineering and metal trades in the Birmingham area, negotiating and speaking on behalf of women workers, and who became the first full-time officer of the WU in 1912.[64] The primary function of organisers was recruitment, often in districts in which it was thought there was good potential for a growth in membership.[65] The influx of female workers during the war provided an opportunity to increase membership. As the male organisers were either not inclined or not able to commit to recruit more female members, in 1915 and 1916 a further nineteen female organisers were recruited, which represented nearly a quarter of the union's staff in 1918.[66] A further reason for employing these new women organisers during the war was the competition for the recruitment of women workers with other unions, particularly the NFWW and the GUMW. By the end of the war, the WU had the largest number of women in their ranks (80,000 as opposed to the NFWW's 76,000 and the GUMW's 60,000), but the majority of women workers remained unorganised.[67] In the 1920s, moreover, in the face of falling trade union membership more broadly, caused by high unemployment and sharp falls in wages, the recruiting and maintaining of female members remained a key concern of the general unions, including the WU.[68] This was exacerbated in the case of the WU by the financial difficulties of the union caused not only by falling membership but also by a disastrous insurance scheme, which in 1920 saw the loss of a sum equal to a third of

[63] Barbara Drake, *Women in Trade Unions* (London: Virago, 1984 [1920]), pp. 181–84.
[64] Thom, *Nice Girls and Rude Girls*, pp. 94–118; Soldon, *Women in British Trade Unions*, p. 120; Hyman, *The Workers' Union*, p. 30.
[65] Hyman, *The Workers' Union*, p. 36.
[66] Hyman, *The Workers' Union*, p. 87; Drake, *Women in Trade Unions*, p. 183.
[67] Soldon, *Women in British Trade Unions*, p. 85.
[68] Lewenhak, *Women and Trade Unions*, chapter 12.

the union's assets.[69] This decline eventually led to amalgamation with the Transport and General Workers' Union in 1929.

The role of paid women organisers, operating at a regional rather than a national level in the interwar period, has been recently analysed in articles by June Hannam, who examines Labour Party organisers, and Cathy Hunt, who focuses on the women organisers of the WU.[70] Hamman emphasises the development of skills amongst Labour Party organisers, for example as propagandists and public speakers, which 'not only increased their effectiveness in organizing women but also helped them to gain respect and loyalty from other activists'.[71] She points too to the extent to which female organisers' working-class backgrounds were evoked to lend them credibility, and to compete with 'bourgeois' women's groups in attempts to recruit working-class women. As I show through an analysis of my case studies, these insights are also important in an analysis of the interwar WU organisers. The WU was careful to employ women organisers with working-class credentials who, they believed, would appeal to and be able to effectively recruit women workers. Hunt's article argues that women organisers were not on an equal footing with their male comrades, and that the union's interest in women workers was, in line with other unions, largely in terms of their potential to strengthen it in terms of numbers and finances. Nevertheless, the opportunity to work as an organiser gave working-class women a rare opportunity to enter the public sphere, to speak in public meetings, intervene in negotiations in episodes of industrial unrest, and thereby construct a political identity. The particular context of the First World War, which created a new cohort of women workers that trade unions were keen to attract and control, thus allowed these working-class women to enter public life. And, for the two case studies I focus on here, their appointments marked the beginning of political careers that lasted well beyond the interwar period.

Florence Saward

In the 1938 obituary notice in the *Essex Newsman* of seventy-six-year-old Harry Saward, who had worked on Essex farms as a horseman all his life,

---

[69] Hyman, *The Workers' Union*, p. 131.

[70] June Hannam, 'Women as Paid Organisers and Propagandists for the British Labour Party between the Wars', *International Labour and Working Class History* 77: 1 (2010), 69–88; Cathy Hunt, '"Her Heart and Soul Were with the Labour Movement": Using a Local Study to Highlight the Work of Women Organisers Employed by the Workers' Union in Britain from the First World War to 1931', *Labour History Review* 70: 2 (2005): 167–84.

[71] Hannam, 'Women as Paid Organisers', p. 72.

half of the article is given over to a description of the only one of his eleven children who is mentioned by name:

> One of their daughters is Miss Florence Saward, who came into prominence during the strike of the work girls at Messrs Courtauld's Silk Factory 30 years ago. Afterwards, Miss Saward having been the leader of the strikers, she became a Trade Union official. . . . She was made a Justice of the Peace for Essex, and sat for some years on the Witham Bench.[72]

In fact, Florence Saward's initiation into industrial action had come earlier, in 1912 when she successfully led the silk workers' strike. However, it was not until the war that she, as she proudly remembered in a later letter, 'was appointed the second woman organiser of the old Workers' Union'.[73] Saward was the fifth of eleven children born to Harry and his wife, Alice. Her siblings were all manual workers – weavers, stokers, drivers and workers in sawmills and bakeries – and they remained so after the war. Like most young women in the area, after leaving school Florence worked at a local silk mill, Courtaulds, and took a leading role in the twelve-day strike in 1912, in which the majority of strikers were female. Her prominence as a strike leader led her to study at Ruskin College, and then in 1915 to be one of the new women organisers recruited by the WU during the war in response to the large increase in membership amongst female workers.

During the war she was an active professional union organiser, recruiting new members, giving public speeches and intervening in episodes of industrial action. In her speeches, she referred frequently to her working-class background in order to endow herself with 'authenticity' and authority. She gave an impassioned speech in 1917 for example on the impact of the war on rural workers, and on the need for agricultural labourers to organise:

> Miss Saward said she was proud to be the daughter of an agricultural labourer. . . . In years gone by the agricultural worker had been the 'scum of the earth'. Everyone had ignored him, but when war comes along; when huge armies have got to be fed; when the civilian population had got to be fed by our own production; then the agricultural worker came forward; then the agricultural workers' wage was brought before the public's eye. . . . It was their duty as English men and women to fight for better conditions on the land, better conditions in the homes of agricultural workers, and better education for their children.[74]

---

[72] *Essex Newsman*, 10 December 1938.
[73] Letter from Florence Balaam née Saward to Jack Jones, 1 January 1965. Warwick Records Centre, MSS 51/3/1/6.
[74] *Bury Free Press*, 15 September 1917.

Here, she confidently delivered the union's political line on the war economy, as well as including a consideration of the positions of the wives and families of male workers, and a plea for the value of education. In the same year, she also spoke on behalf of women war workers at an Essex brush manufacturers, J. West & Son, in a dispute over equal pay for the female workers who had replaced mobilised male workers. The local newspaper, which introduces her as 'Miss Florence Saward, formerly a Braintree woman worker who took part in the mill girls' strike a few years ago', cites her declaring that 'in future girl workers mean to do less work and to get more money for it, and intend to demand more liberties in factories where they are employed.' The newspaper condemned this statement, stating, '[t]his is not the spirit that any section of the community should bring to bear upon the problem', and warning against what they saw as the political exploitation of the war effort by women workers.[75] This reveals the extent to which Saward's example could be viewed as potentially threatening to the war effort and to the status quo.

After the war, Saward continued in her role, encouraging women to organise and speaking on their behalf during strikes. In a letter written in 1965 she remembered helping to recruit 1,000 women cleaners who worked in offices in Whitehall towards the end of the war years, an achievement which was enthusiastically reported on in *The Workers' Record*, and which led to an agreement on improved wages and conditions being signed in 1924. She also recalled with pride a 1925 strike of 'all women and girls, both members and non-members' who worked at Tollemache's brewery in Ipswich, in which they worked alongside the Women's Cooperative Guild, the Women's Section of the Labour Party and male trade unionists, which resulted in 'a great victory for the women both with wages and working conditions'.[76] As a respected and experienced union official, she chaired meetings, gave speeches, and offered advice to male union members in local branches, as well as talking directly to women workers.[77] The WU records reveal the amount of travelling she did during this period: in 1925, she received £51.13.6 in wages and £31.17.8 in expenses relating to rail and tram fares.[78] Reports of her speeches also reveal that she had developed her skills as an orator, and was able to capture

---

[75] *Chelmsford Chronicle*, 23 March 1917.
[76] Letter to Richard Hyman, 25 August 1965, Warwick Records Centre, MSS51/3/1/6 Balaam, F.
[77] Interview with Richard Hyman, 1965, Warwick Records Centre, MSS 51/3/1/6 Balaam, F.
[78] 'Wages and Expenses of Organisers for 1925', Warwick Records Centre, MSS51/4/14.

MISS F. SAWARD, SPEAKING AT CHICHESTER, July 24th, 1921.

Figure 5.3 Florence Saward, *The Workers' Union Record*, Modern Records Centre, University of Warwick.

the attention of large crowds (Figure 5.3). One of her recruitment methods for example was, after two or three days of leafletting at lunchtimes, she would hold a public meeting outside factory gates in order to catch women workers as they left work in the evening. Reports of her speeches also show that she often referred both to her previous experience as a strike leader and to her own working-class roots in order to appeal to her audience. In a 1927 report of a speech she made in Scotland, for example, published in *The Workers' Record*, the union's journal, she emphasised the progress that had been made, and used her own social mobility and politicisation as evidence to persuade her audience of the benefits of union membership:

After leaving school at the early age of thirteen, she was employed in the silk trade for several years. ... In 1912 the wages of silk workers in the South for adult women were anything from 5 shillings to 10 shillings a week for fifty-six hours. ... [After the war] there was a National Joint Industrial Council for the Silk Trade. This year she had the honour of being elected Chairman of the Council. At the time of election she was very proud of this honour.

She felt that it was a credit to the textile workers all over the country who were members of the union, because she had also been a textile worker.[79]

In an interview given in 1965, Saward also mentioned the importance of her background in persuading women workers of the benefits of trade unionism. She explained that she would 'visit girls and their parents' and argued that it was 'necessary to keep in personal contact with girls, and show them you were one of them'.[80] As was the case with Desrumaux and Brisset, then, Saward was keen in her self-presentations to emphasise her 'authenticity' as a working woman, and as one who has succeeded in effecting change in women's working lives, in order both to find solidarity with other female workers, and to endow herself with authority amongst male union leaders. Although Florence Saward had cut her teeth in the pre-war silk workers' strike of 1912, it was the particular economic and political conditions that prevailed during the war, which persuaded the WU to recruit women organisers, and which gave female strike leaders more sway with government arbitrators, that served to provide her with a platform and with a voice as a political activist. It was the war years, in other words, which allowed her to develop a long and successful post-war political career. Yet it tended not to be her activism as a representative of striking workers to which she made reference in her speeches, letters and interviews, but her working-class background and her knowledge of working peoples' lives.[81]

Rose Wyatt/Rosina Whyatt

The Workers' Record published regular 'biographical sketches' of their leaders, and from 1916 onwards they included sketches of their prominent women organisers. In May 1923 they published a sketch of Rosina Whyatt (Figure 5.4).[82] She is an interesting case for this study because unlike the French communist women and Florence Saward, she does make use of her wartime activities in her post-war rhetoric, using her war service as proof of a form of patriotic sacrifice. Alongside the Workers' Record article, Whyatt herself also wrote a short memoir, part of which was published in 1974 in John Burnett's edited collection of working-class life-writing, Useful Toil, the remaining pages of which are held in

[79] The Workers' Union, 158 (January 1927): 142.
[80] Interview with Richard Hyman, 1965. Warwick Records Centre, MSS 51/3/1/6 Balaam, F.
[81] Essex Newsman, 2 January 1932; Chelmsford Chronicle, 7 July 1933.
[82] Rosina Whyatt used both spellings of her name in various documents throughout the interwar period. She adopted the name 'Rosina' in the 1930s, and added 'Jenny' as a second name, which is the name she used in her life-writing.

MISS WHYATT.

Figure 5.4 Rosina Whyatt, *The Workers' Union Record*, Modern Records Centre, University of Warwick.

Warwick Records Centre.[83] A comparison of the ways in which Whyatt's life story and achievements are presented in these different sources allows

---

[83] John Burnett, *Useful Toil: Autobiographies of Working People from the 1970s to the 1920s* (London: Allen Lane/Penguin, 1974). Burnett was first introduced to Whyatt's memoirs by Richard Hyman. See Warwick Records Office, MSS51/3/1/55 Miss R Whyatt.

us to see the extent to which an identity as 'female veteran' had currency for Whyatt at different points in the decades following the war.

In *The Workers' Record* biographical sketch, the author emphasised Whyatt's rural working-class roots, stating that 'she came in contact with the rough side of life at a very early age' and went to work as a domestic servant at the age of eleven. Her move into war work and subsequent initiation into union activism was described as an opportunity for social mobility and a new vision of her role as a worker:

After some years of this life spent under degrading and unhealthy conditions for excessive hours with very low wages, she obtained work at a munition[s] factory in 1915, where about 4,000 women and girls were employed, all of whom were unorganised. Within a very short time after entering the factory, and as a result of attending meetings organised by the Workers' Union, Miss Whyatt obtained a glimpse of the wider view of life offered by the Labour Movement.[84]

The article praised the leadership skills she showed during a strike at the munitions factory, and later mentioned that in 1918 she led a further successful strike of 700 workers at a blanket mill in Witney. In addition to her credentials as a strike leader, the writer equally underscored the fact that during the war she became very ill from TNT poisoning, making it clear she had physically suffered as a result of her war work. In this sense, she was presented in a manner reminiscent of potted biographies of male union organisers, in which their war service and sacrifices were frequently emphasised. However, equally important for the WU biography was Whyatt's positioning as a worker who had overcome what was presented as her exploitation by employers in order to find a new identity as a union organiser. Her credentials and usefulness to the WU in terms of the recruitment of new women members were summed up towards the end of the article: 'With her first hand knowledge and a practical experience of both domestic service and factory life, Miss Whyatt is able to fully understand and interpret the ideas and desires of working women.'

In his introduction to the 1974 extract from Whyatt's own memoirs, social historian John Burnett introduces her in similar terms to the WU biography, pointing to her humble rural origins: 'Rosina Whyatt was born in Somerset in 1888, the daughter of a farm worker who brought up a family of 6 on a wage of 16 shillings a week.' Further, and following 1970s approaches to the impact of the war on women's lives, Burnett goes on to position her as an example of a woman 'emancipated' by the war: 'She speaks, simply and naively, for the thousands of women for

---

[84] *The Workers' Record*, 114 (May 1923), p. 9.

whom the First World War brought a new involvement in society, greatly increased earnings, and a measure of independence and emancipation.'[85] However, in several respects her self-presentation in her memoirs was far from 'naïve'; nor did she present herself as a 'typical' female war worker. Writing in the third person, and using the name 'Jenny', Whyatt emphasised the extent to which the TNT poisoning, hard work, poor conditions and risk to life experienced by female munitions workers (in March 1918 four of her co-workers were killed in an explosion[86]) should be recognised as valuable war service: 'They were called the Chaul End Canaries. Even the bed linen became yellow. Jenny found that she had to pay her landlady more money for laundry, especially for the feather bed, and felt a little incensed by this; after all she was helping the war effort, to help the lads at the front.'[87] She noted with pleasure the fact that she was recommended by her employers for the OBE, 'in recognition of [her] great service during the war', and that 'songs were sung in her honour'. In terms of her initiation into the labour movement, she presented her experiences as a munitions worker as the opportunity for education and self-advancement that she had been seeking earlier in her life, and as one that she eagerly embraced:

[In the munitions factory] she already had a feeling of a new freedom and time to think. When Jenny had been in domestic service she had always felt a driving force of something unexplainable. . . . She attended lectures, bought books, and studied the questions of economics, and social life and welfare. [She] was learning fast and furiously.

She equally presented herself as learning the key skills of a successful union organiser, writing with pride of her successes in recruiting women and negotiating with owners and other unions in complicated episodes of industrial unrest. Wartime strikes such as the 1918 Witney Blanket Mill inter-union action, of which she claimed that it taught her 'enough to last [her] a lifetime', set her up as a trusted organiser and negotiator in later strikes, and also led to her appointment on several committees. While she showed an awareness of the extent to which her initiation into the labour movement, and into industrial relations, involved a degree of social mobility, she equally revealed an awareness of the limitations placed on women union organisers because of the patriarchal nature of

---

[85] Burnett, *Useful Toil*, p. 116.

[86] Whyatt worked in George Kent Ltd munitions factory, Biscot Rd, Luton. See www.worldwar1luton.com/object/george-kents-munition-works for further information, and for the names of the four women workers killed in the explosion on 1 March 1918.

[87] Unpublished typewritten memoirs by Rosina Whyatt, Warwick Records Centre, MSS51/3/1/55 Miss R Whyatt.

the WU, which while arguing for equal pay for women war workers continued to pay female union organisers at a lower rate than their male colleagues:

I found myself in a very different world and responsibilities. One thing I always felt was unfair: the women officers were never given an Area or District of their own to organise and develop, but all their work . . . was placed in branches controlled by male officers, and of course women had less wages.

She was lucid too about the demise of the WU because of financial mismanagement, stating that '[i]t wasn't until Charles Duncan had the brainwave of giving 4d for £1 that the General Fund was somewhat depleted.' In sum, her self-presentation in her memoirs is a dual one: she casts herself both as a female war veteran who served and who had sacrificed her health for her country as an industrial worker, and as a gifted and successful trade union organiser who understood political and economic realities, who had front-line experience and who could bring about change.

It is interesting that none of the versions of her life story mentioned that she was illegitimate, born in April 1886 to Mary Ann Wyatt, although as she kept her mother's maiden name this would have been evident to those who knew her.[88] It remained important for the women organisers to be seen as 'respectable', and illegitimacy was a social stigma that would not have been easy to acknowledge, even in the 1960s when Whyatt wrote her memoirs. Her mother married Charles Batt in 1890, and by the 1891 census Rose was living with them in Paulton, a small rural town in Somerset. Her Batt half-siblings had limited social mobility: her sister Elizabeth was an unmarried domestic servant all her life, her brother Charles a railway guard, and another brother, Frederick, a farm carter. Census records confirm that, as she claimed before the war, she had worked as a live-in domestic servant. In addition to being initiated into trade unionism through her war work, like many activists she became involved in the local Labour Party. In later life, she became a school governess and the Mayor of Camberwell. Her will after her death in 1971 reveals the extent to which her involvement in industrial action during the war had been a springboard for a different life, leading her to engage in different networks and have a political career in a way which clearly differentiates her from her siblings. The solicitor, John Silkin, was later MP for Lewisham and a prominent member of the Labour Party, and beneficiaries included the women's wards in a local hospital, the

---

[88] She was baptised as 'Sarah Wyatt' on 6 March 1887, alongside the youngest daughter of her grandparents, at Paulton Parish Church, Somerset.

'Mary McCarthy Holiday Home Fund', Peckham Labour Party and Florence Pilbrow, a fellow WU organiser.

Conclusions

Both the French communist women and the British WU organisers positioned themselves differently to the female veterans whose self-presentations I examine in my other chapters. Former war nurses and, to some extent, WAACs, could claim to have carried out a role that had proximity to the front; their war service could be mapped onto that of ex-servicemen. Strike leaders were often presented in direct opposition to veterans, and were attacked by both men and women for having 'betrayed' the men in the trenches. During a strike by male engineers working in a munitions factory in Leeds in 1916, for example, female munitions workers wrote angry letters to the local newspapers condemning their actions. Some wanted to make the striking male workers parade through the city wearing petticoats, in order to expose their lack of 'manliness' and their distance from the front-line fighters. The next day, one anonymous letter writer wrote in response:

I think it is an insult to us women workers to say that the strikers, so called skilled men, should be put in petticoats. I might say that some of us in petticoats also wear khaki overalls and caps, while those who should be wearing khaki are shielding themselves behind an enamel badge. I am a soldier's wife and also have two brothers out, one in Mesopotamia, and one in Salonica. Neither has had a leave for 18 months. If the strikers were sent out to relieve our lads they might have something to down tools for – and were they to do so they would be shot, and not given the chance they have had.[89]

Here, a woman war worker claimed her 'double sacrifice' as both war worker and wife of a combatant in the same way as the other female strikers I have highlighted in this chapter. However, rather than using this to justify industrial action, she used her claims to war service to condemn male strikers as anti-patriotic shirkers. Thus, as I have noted, the political debates over strike action made it very difficult for female strike leaders to claim 'veteran' status.

This is borne out by the case studies I have explored here. In their speeches, interviews, letters and memoirs the French communist women and British WU organisers presented themselves as working-class women who were able to speak to and for other working-class women in a way in which their male colleagues, or indeed other middle-class women activists, could not. The war had provided them with the planks to build

[89] *Yorkshire Post*, 26 March 1918.

platforms on which to stand as representatives of women workers, but only one of them, Rosina Whyatt, was able to refer to her war service as a key factor in their credentials. This is because of the differences in national contexts. Whyatt was able to claim status as a 'Canary girl', Alice Brisset as one of the 'singing midinettes'. However, when she was interviewed Brisset defined her relationship to the war as suffering from shortages and from news of men in the army rather than via her wartime work and strike activity. In contrast, Whyatt referred to her 'sacrifice' and 'service', and argued that she deserved respect and recognition for her high-risk work as a munitions worker. In Britain – or at least in the Britain of the 1960s – Whyatt was able to claim the identity of war veteran, whereas the more ambiguous legacy of wartime strike action in France meant that Brisset's claim to this status remained muted and shaky.

Conclusion

A feature of the events organised to commemorate the centenary of the First World War has been a concentration on the remembrance of the dead in both Britain and France. The most well-known and most-discussed artistic responses in Britain were Paul Cummins' *Blood Swept Lands and Seas of Red* (2014), in which ceramic poppies represented the dead of the British empire, and Jeremy Deller's haunting 'we're here because we're here' (2016), in which young male actors represented the dead of the Battle of the Somme in cities, towns and villages across the United Kingdom. In France, Philippe Prost's 'Anneau de la Mémoire' ('Ring of Remembrance') (2014) performed a similar function, honouring the 576,606 soldiers of forty different nationalities who died in the Nord-Pas-de-Calais region. One hundred years on, then, the hierarchy of war experience, at the top of which are the men who died, remains largely in place. It is often assumed in commemorative events, moreover, that the dead all died as a result of combat: less attention is paid to the thousands who died of influenza, malaria or tuberculosis, for example, whose names also appear on war memorials as having died on active service. One way of attempting to 'globalise' First World War commemoration, or to address questions of diversity, has been to highlight the contributions of men from former colonies of the British and French empires who were mobilised in the war, or Jewish members of the British and French armed services, on the basis that they, too, can be counted amongst the dead.[1] To some extent, this has also been the case in relation to women. In Britain, the Commonwealth War Graves Commission is currently running a project in collaboration with the Women's Institute that asks branch members to research the women killed in both world wars in their local areas.[2] A new British campaign has been launched to erect a memorial to nurses and

---

[1] See for example the 'we were there too' campaigns in Britain: https://twitter.com/wewerethere2?lang=en; www.jewsfww.london/ or the rhetoric of the French government's 'Mission Centenaire' project on the *tirailleurs sénégalais*: http://centenaire.org/fr/dans-le-monde/afrique/senegal/tirailleurs-senegalais-temoignages-epistolaires-1914–1919.

[2] www.cwgc.org/about-us/cwgc-projects/living-memory.aspx

VADs killed in the war.[3] In France, new memorials to the women who died in the occupied regions of France and Belgium have been erected.[4]

Examples of public commemoration that focus exclusively on the remembrance of those who died can result in a distorted view of the history and legacies of the war. Hew Strachan, interviewed in the *Daily Telegraph* in 2014, argued that it is important that First World War centenary activities should not be just about remembering the dead. For Strachan, the centenary should be 'an opportunity to review the First World War afresh, to shake out the clichés and tired preconceptions and to develop new understandings of a global conflict that had long-term repercussions for the entire world'.[5] However, a narrative of the war that primarily focuses on the experiences and losses of front-line soldiers on the Western Front largely continues to dominate, as it did in the interwar years. This serves to remind us what women who had been on active service during the First World War were up against when they attempted to present themselves as members of a war generation with a story that deserved to be heard, or as individuals with a political view on the war that was grounded in lived experience. Then, as now, the ultimate measure of war service and individual sacrifice was through 'blood tax'. This helps to explain the continuing focus on exceptional heroines, and especially on heroines who died 'for their country', in the discourse not only of nationalists keen to score political points in relation to either external or internal political enemies, but equally by women themselves who wished for a variety of reasons to present their own service as valuable war service.

During and in the immediate aftermath of the war, the deaths of women that occurred while the women carried out war work, or of female civilians who died as a result of enemy action, were generally also treated as 'war deaths' that deserved recognition and commemoration. This was true not only of the nurses and members of the British auxiliary services that I focused on in Chapter 1 but also of other kinds of female casualties. As I noted in Chapter 5, the deaths of French munitions workers were not reported, whereas in Britain, although there was government censorship in relation to the deaths of munitions workers who died of TNT poisoning or in explosions, the names of those who had died were nevertheless sometimes added to Rolls of Honour.[6] As Deborah Thom points out,

---

[3] www.nursingmemorialappeal.org.uk/the-nurses.html

[4] See for example the recent 'Monument aux femmes fusillées' in Saint-Amand-les-Eaux, www.monnuage.fr/point-d-interet/monument-femmes-fusillees-a106353#modal-36456.

[5] 'Interview with Hew Strachan', *The Daily Telegraph*, 18 July 2014.

[6] For instance, the Roll of Honour for the workers of the No. 1 National Filling Factory at Crossgates, Leeds, who died in an explosion on 5 December 1916, lists forty names, thirty-five of them women, above the inscription 'They Died Serving'. They are also listed on the Five Sisters' Window memorial in York Minster.

this meant in practice that a death from an industrial disease or accident was translated into a death 'on active service'.[7] In April 1918, for example, a memorial service to commemorate the deaths of civilian workers at St Paul's Cathedral ended with renditions of 'The Last Post' and 'Réveillé' as a 'tribute to the munition[s] workers and others engaged in war work who have laid down their lives for their country'.[8] After the war, as non-military deaths, both men's and women's deaths in munitions factories were excluded from the government's schemes for official recognition of the war dead, but these men and women were nevertheless publicly praised for their 'sacrifice', and families and communities tended to commemorate their deaths in ways that provided points of comparison with male combatants killed in action.[9]

A similar situation persisted in relation to civilian victims of bombing raids in France. Once again, despite the fact that censorship limited the publication of the numbers of civilian men, women and children who were killed, public sympathy for the victims was high. The press roundly condemned the bombing of civilians as evidence of the enemy's barbarity, and municipal authorities responded by offering funds for burials and memorials, and to help bereaved family members.[10] After the war, some politicians argued that civilian casualties should be considered as 'mort[s] pour la patrie' for the purpose of the repatriation of remains, and the names of civilian victims were listed side by side with military deaths on local war memorials.[11] Women's deaths during the war, then, were sometimes understood and presented as sacrifices for the nation that merited comparison, at least to some extent, to male military deaths.

[7] Thom, *Nice Girls and Rude Girls*, p. 136. On censorship see Woollacott, *On Her Their Lives Depend*, pp. 84–86; Thom, *Nice Girls*, p. 125.

[8] *The Times*, 22 April 1918.

[9] Woollacott highlights the newspaper report of the death by TNT poisoning of Florence Gleave in 1917, which uses her alleged final words, '[i]f I die, they can only say I have done my bit,' as its headline. *The Chronicle*, 8 May 1917, quoted in *On Her Their Lives Depend*, p. 82. Families of munitions workers who had died produced commemorative ephemera such as handkerchiefs, mourning cards and memorials, listed deaths in the military death section of local newspapers, and held funerals that combined peacetime mourning customs with military display, such as a uniformed presence and military band. Hughes, 'Death, Service and Citizenship', chapter 3.

[10] Grayzel, 'Souls of Soldiers'. A similar public response in Britain can be seen in relation to the bombing of Hartlepool and Scarborough in December 1914, the war memorial for which was inscribed '[t]hey died for us'. In this case, however, the emphasis in the press coverage at the time was on the necessity of British men to enlist in order to protect vulnerable female civilians.

[11] Grayzel, 'Souls of Soldiers', p. 619. See for example the war memorial in Bully-les-Mines (Pas de Calais), which lists 'victimes militaires' and 'victimes civiles' side by side, and has a sculpted family of a soldier, wife and child posed as mourners, reflecting the local families that had lost mothers and children as well as husbands and fathers.

However, while it was commonplace to elevate the deaths of women to the level of the dead male combatants' 'supreme sacrifice', both during and after the war women's wartime activities were not universally seen as worthy of praise and gratitude. While certain female war workers continued to maintain, and even accrue, considerable social and cultural capital after the war, sometimes being considered part of the wider 'war generation' or 'veteran community', others had a more ambiguous standing. To some extent, this was an extension of the dichotomous attitudes that existed during the war towards women engaged in war work. Gender historians have effectively argued that there was considerable antagonism towards wage-earning female war workers that was related to a class-based perception of working women as sexually promiscuous, profligate and potentially socially disruptive.[12] Deborah Thom, Angela Woollacott, Laura Lee Downs and Françoise Thébaud have chronicled, for example, contradictory attitudes towards female munitions workers on both sides of the Channel during the war, whether or not they engaged in industrial action. While to some extent their work was understood as patriotic service with an element of risk to life that made it possible to relate (if not equate) it to men's service at the front, female workers were also frequently criticised for their alleged frivolous spending habits, promiscuity and selfishness, which in the context of nationalist discourse functioned in direct opposition to patriotism.[13] Like many women war workers, the WAAC, particularly its working-class members, also faced criticism and attacks on the sexual morality of its members. In France, there was also widespread concern about the sexual behaviours of working women who came into contact with mobilised men, particularly with troops and workers conscripted from British and French colonies and stationed in France.[14] In the context of these publicly expressed anxieties and criticisms, the morality of women mobilised for the war effort, and particularly that of lower-middle-class and working-class

---

[12] See Lucy Bland, '"Khaki Fever" and Its Control: Gender, Class, Age and Sexual Morality on the British Homefront in the First World War', *Journal of Contemporary History* 29: 2 (1994): 325–47; Watson, 'Khaki Girls'.

[13] Thom, *Nice Girls*; Woollacott, *On Her Their Lives Depend*; Downs, *Manufacturing Inequality*; Thébaud, *La Femme*.

[14] See Tyler Stovall, 'Colour-Blind France: Colonial Workers during the First World War', *Race & Class* 35: 2 (1999): 35–55; Horne, 'Immigrant Workers in France during World War I', *French Historical Studies* 14: 1 (1985), 57–88; Richard S. Fogarty, 'Race, Sex, Fear and Loathing in France during the Great War', *Historical Reflections* 34: 1 (2008): 50–72; Jean-Yves Le Naour, *Misères et tourments de la chair durant la Grande Guerre* (Paris: Aubier, 2002), pp. 249–90.

women, became the topic of public debate and government scrutiny.[15]

Elite women who took on unpaid charity work, or, as in the case of VADs, operated with terms of pay and conditions (such as the purchase of their own uniform) that tended to limit recruitment to the middle and upper classes, were not immune from criticism during and after the war. The chief accusations were of a mere simulation of service and sacrifice for women's own selfish ends, which was contrasted with the 'true' service and sacrifice offered by other kinds of civilians, or more obviously by combatants. Uniforms were frequently instrumentalised in this discourse, with women facing attacks for simply 'dressing up' for war, their donning of the uniforms being regarded as play-acting or disguise rather than evidence of any lasting self-transformation.[16] In French popular journalism, middle-class volunteers and frivolous socialites (*mondaines*) were accused of becoming volunteer nurses for less-than-noble reasons, usually the glamour of the uniform and the lure of potential husbands amongst the doctors and patients.[17] Novelist Lucien Descaves claimed in 1916, for example, that '[l]adies played at being nurses at the bedsides of men who had never played at being soldiers.'[18] The khaki-wearing British women involved in early militarising initiatives such as the Women's Volunteer Reserve (WVR), which recruited mainly from the middle classes, were similarly attacked for 'playing at being soldiers'.[19] However, in general terms middle- and upper-class volunteers were deemed more 'patriotic' and 'altruistic' than working women, and were less likely to be attacked after the war.

Women therefore had to fulfil certain criteria if they were to succeed in their claims to veteran identity in the interwar years. They had to align themselves with broader public understandings of war service and sacrifice. But the case studies I have discussed in this book show that many women in both France and Britain were able to fulfil these criteria in their self-presentations. War service endowed a select cohort of French and

[15] The government became concerned about the effect on recruitment to the WAAC, and in response the War Office set up a Commission of Enquiry in March 1918, which concluded that 'not only are the rumours untrue, but ... the number of undesirable women who have found their way into the Corps has been very small.' Quoted in Noakes, *Women in the British Army*, pp. 80–82.

[16] See Joanna Shearer, 'Dressing Up for War: Women and Militarism in the Writings of French Women Journalists in the First World War', *Minerva: Journal of Women and War* 1: 2 (2007): 66–76.

[17] See Darrow, *French Women*, pp. 146–48.

[18] Lucien Descaves, *La Maison anxieuse* (Paris: Georges Crès & Cie, 1916), pp. 81–82. See Noakes, 'Demobilising the Military Woman', p. 147, for examples of similar attacks in the British press.

[19] Noakes, *Women in the British Army*, p. 62; Watson, *Fighting Different Wars*, p. 53.

British women with cultural capital in the post-war years, and they used it for many and varied ends. However, the women who most often had success in projecting themselves as war veterans remained those who could be cast as heroines of the war – especially heroines such as nurses who fitted in most comfortably with pre-existing models of femininity. Those who did not reach broader audiences and whose writings and activities had more mixed receptions in the interwar years were those whose war stories strayed the furthest from these models, such as female combatants, spies or strikers. My case studies have also revealed important differences between the cultural and political climates that existed in interwar France and Britain. As I have shown in my discussions of the commemoration of Louise de Bettignies and in the reception of the memoirs of Louise Thuliez, women who were active in resistance networks in occupied France and Belgium achieved respectability and public acclaim despite the fact that they had carried out roles that blurred the line between combatant and non-combatant. Flora Sandes had a more mixed reception than either Bettignies or Thuliez, and was not politically exploited in Britain as an example of 'patriotic womanhood' as was the case with resistance heroines in France. The fact that no auxiliary services were created in France (despite the existence of women working for the French armed services in a civilian capacity) meant that veterans were perhaps more welcoming of nurses as 'sisters in arms', as their relatively low numbers and association with saintly maternal virtues meant that they did not threaten the status quo. In Britain, however, while some former WAACs had positive relationships with members of the British Legion, others were frustrated at their ambiguous status within the British veteran community, in which the Women's Section of the British Legion, for example, was primarily created to cater for the wives and daughters of ex-servicemen rather than for ex-servicewomen.

Another feature of recent commemorations of the First World War has been a tendency to focus on courageous, morally virtuous women or on 'feminist' heroines.[20] This means that those whose stories have been retold in centenary narratives tend to be either the same war heroines who were lauded in the interwar years such as Edith Cavell, or those women whose lives appear in hindsight to be tales of feminist emancipation from the constraints of patriarchal power structures. But it is important to recognise that not all of the women whose stories I explore in this study evoked their war service for 'worthy' purposes. Some war memoirs written by former female spies or members of resistance networks that

---

[20] See for example 'How Female Tommies and Sexism Helped Save Britain', *The Daily Telegraph*, 4 August 2014.

I discuss in Chapter 4 were exaggerations, or in some cases, total fabrications, of their war service. Other women occasionally fraudulently claimed an imagined war service, as had some men, or used their war service for fraudulent purposes. In Britain, one case of fraud involved a young woman named Laura Beak, who was imprisoned in both 1919 and 1920 for 'masquerading in nurse's uniform', which included wearing the ribbon of the Military Medal, in order to fraudulently obtain money and clothes. She claimed in her defence she was 'driven to the thefts in order to keep her child'.[21] The pension records also reveal the sad case of one former VAD nurse who served for three years during the war. She had her pension for neurasthenia stopped after being accused of fraud by several landlords and guest house proprietors, having falsely claimed that the War Office would pay the cost of her lodgings on account of her veteran status. She wrote tens of letters to the War Office in the 1920s and 1930s stating that she remained 'totally incapacitated' by her war service, and died intestate on 7 January 1940, the costs of her funeral being paid for by the London County Council.[22]

Equally, not all women who saw themselves as war veterans espoused women's rights or held progressive political views in relation to gender roles. Some women who were politicised by the war turned to the far right in the interwar years, often motivated by a desire to oppose the rise of communism. Renée Guérin-Charvin, who as I noted in Chapter 3 founded the AIBMG in the 1920s, went on to set up a rural retreat and Christian education centre for women under the Vichy regime in the Second World War, which was very much in tune with the regime's policy of 'Travail, Famille, Patrie'. In an interview in 1942 Guérin-Charvet proudly stated that Pétain had visited her centre and praised her initiative.[23] The attraction of right-wing political movements for women who had been active in the war as well as for male veterans was equally in evidence in the 1920s and 1930s.[24] Laura Lee Downs discusses female social workers in the nationalist Croix-de-feu movement who placed at the heart of their social mission the claim that they carried with them 'the orders of the 1.5 million dead of 1914–1918' as they moved onto the hostile territory of the red suburbs, a rhetorical move that allowed them to position themselves as soldiers in the struggle to win

---

[21] *Yorkshire Post*, 21 October 1919; *Illustrated Police News*, 23 September 1920.
[22] TNA PIN26/20062.   [23] *Notre Province* 7 (October 1942): 242.
[24] Caroline Campbell, *Political Belief in France 1927–1945: Gender, Empire and Fascism in the Croix de Feu and Parti Social Français* (Baton Rouge: Louisiana State University Press, 2015).

working-class families away from the communist 'menace'.[25] Julie
Gottlieb highlights the important role of women in the British fascist
movement, several of whom had been on active service during the
war.[26] Founder of the British fascists Rotha Lintorn Orman, for
example, was in the WVR and then an ambulance driver for the
Scottish Women's Hospital Corps before becoming head of the
British Red Cross Motor School in 1918. On Sunday,
14 November 1926, Lintorn Orman led 2,000 British fascist men
and women on a march from Trafalgar Square to the Cenotaph to
a lay a wreath, before laying another wreath at the tomb of the
Unknown Warrior. Lintorn Orman's war service gave her credibility
in her leadership of this act of remembrance, which was accompanied by a call to the government to 'put an end to Soviet interference
with the affairs of the Empire'.[27] Popular histories of women in the
war tend not to focus on women who used their war service for
financial gain, or to endow themselves with credibility in far right
political groupings. Rather they remain largely focused on heroines
who complement the dominant cultural narratives of the war, and
resurrect stories of heroism that were first told in wartime and interwar accounts.[28]

In the countless books, articles, websites, films and television
dramas and documentaries that have been produced in response to
the centenary of the First World War it has become commonplace to
speak of these women as the 'forgotten' heroines of the war.
As I have argued, it is true that popular memories of the conflict
are dominated by a 'War Story' in which the central role is played by
a male combatant. However, the contributions and activities of
women who were on different forms of active service in the war
have consistently been more visible than these repeated claims suggest. Many women inserted themselves into national memories of the
war. Many women's stories have been subsequently 'rediscovered' by
journalists on repeated anniversaries. It was not the case that women

---

[25] Laura Lee Downs, '"Nous plantions les trois couleurs": Action sociale féminine et
recomposition des politiques de la droite française. Le mouvement Croix-de-feu et le
Parti social français, 1934–1947', *Revue d'histoire moderne et contemporaine* 58–3 (2011):
118–62; Laura Lee Downs, '"Each and Every One of You Must Become a *Chef*":
Towards a Social Politics of Working-Class Childhood on the Extreme Right in 1930s
France', *Journal of Modern History* (2009): 1–44.

[26] Julie Gottlieb, *Feminine Fascism: Women in Britain's Fascist Movements* (London:
I. B. Taurus, 2003).

[27] *The Scotsman*, Monday, 15 November 1926.

[28] See for example Binot, *Héroïnes*; Elisabeth Shipton, *Female Tommies: The Frontline
Women of the First World War* (Stroud: The History Press, 2014); Kate Adie, *Fighting
on the Home Front: The Legacy of Women in World War 1* (London: Hodder, 2014).

were denied a voice in relation to the war. What this book has shown, however, is that some women's stories counted more than others. And it was those who could claim veteran status who were the most likely to find a route into public life via their war service in the years following the war.

Bibliography

Primary Sources

Archives

Archives générales du Royaume, Belgium (AGR)
Archives nationales françaises (ANF)
Bibliothèque Marguerite Durand (BMD)
Bibliothèque Nationale Française (BNF)
Borthwick Institute, University of York
Imperial War Museum (IWM)
Liddle Collection, Brotherton Library, University of Leeds
National Army Museum (NAM)
National Library of Scotland
Rawtenstall Library
The National Archives (TNA)
Warwick Records Centre, University of Warwick
York Minster Archives

Newspapers and Journals

L'Action française
L'Africain: hebdomadaire illustré
Almanach de l'Action française
L'Almanach du Combattant
The Berwick Advertiser
British Journal of Nursing
Bulletin de l'Ordre de l'Etoile d'Orient
Bulletin mensuel de l'Union des Femmes de France
Bulletin Trimestriel de l'Association Mutuelle des Infirmières de la Société de Secours aux Blessés Militaires
Bury Free Press
Chelmsford Chronicle
The Chronicle
Le Combattant du Poitou: Organe du Groupe Poitevin de l'Union Nationale des Combattants et des Sociétés affiliées du département de la Vienne
Current History and Forum

The Daily Telegraph
The Darwen News
Des deutschen Volkes Kriegstagebuch
Dundee Courier
Dundee Evening Telegraph
Echo de Bougie, Organe d'union républicaine démocratique et sociale
L'Echo de Paris
L'Enchaîné
Essex Newsman
Femmes
Le Figaro
La France Héroïque: Revue mensuelle du courage civil et militaire
La Gazette de Liège
La Gazette de Mostaganem
Glasgow Herald
Hartlepool Northern Daily Mail
Hull Daily Mail
L'Humanité
L'Illustration
L'Intransigeant
Irish Times
Le Journal
Le Journal de Fourmies
Journal des mutilés, réformés et blessés de guerre
Journal Officiel de la République française
The Ladies' Garment Worker
Le Matin
Le Mutilé de l'Algérie
Northern Whig
Notre Province
Ouest-France
L'Ouvrière
Le Pays de France
Le Petit Echo de la mode
Le Petit Parisien
The Manchester Guardian
QMAAC Old Comrades Association Gazette
Reading Eagle
Regards
Revue Internationale de la Croix Rouge
Rossendale Free Press
The Scotsman
The Sphere
Sunderland Daily Echo
Le Temps
Thanet Advertiser
The Times

Times Literary Supplement
La Vie au patronage: Organe catholique des œuvres de jeunesse
La Voix du Combattant
The War Budget
Western Daily Press
The Workers' Union Record
York Herald
Yorkshire Gazette
Yorkshire Post

Printed Primary Sources

Abensour, Léon, *Les Vaillantes: Héroïnes, martyres et remplaçantes* (Paris: Librairie Chapelot, 1917).

Argoeuves, Hélène d', *Louise de Bettignies* (Paris: La Colombe, 1956).

Association des Dames Françaises, *Secours donnés aux victimes des inondations de Paris et des Départements (Janvier et Février 1910): Rapport Général du Comité Central* (Amiens: A. Grau, 1910).

Barton, Edith M. and Marguerite Cody, *Eve in Khaki: The Story of the Women's Army at Home and Abroad* (London: Nelson, 1918).

Bertier de Sauvigny, Albert de, *Pages d'histoire locale, 1914–1919* (Soissons: Association Soissonnais, 1934), pp. 14–18.

Bochkareva, Maria, *Yashka: My Life as Peasant, Exile, and Soldier* (New York: Frederick A. Stokes, 1919).

Bourcier, Claudine, *Nos Chers Blessés: Une infirmière dans la grande guerre* (Tours: Editions Alain Sutton, 2002).

Brittain, Vera, *Testament of Experience: An Autobiographical Story of the Years 1925–1950* (London: V. Gollancz, 1957).

Brittain, Vera, *Testament of Youth: An Autobiographical Study of the Years 1900–1925* (London: Virago, 1978).

Brittain, Vera, 'War Service in Perspective', in George A. Panichas (ed.), *Promise of Greatness: The War of 1914–1918* (New York: John Day Co., 1968), pp. 363–76.

Carrier-Belleuse, Charlotte, *Le Panthéon de la guerre* (Paris: Georges Michau, 1919).

Clemenceau Jacquemaire, Madeleine, *Les Hommes de bonne volonté* (Paris: Calmann Levy, 1919).

Congrès national ordinaire (3e congrès de la CGTU Paris 26 au 31 août 1925) (Paris: Confédération Générale du Travail Unitaire 1925).

Congrès national ordinaire (4e congrès de la CGTU Bordeaux 19 au 24 septembre 1927) (Paris: Confédération Générale du Travail Unitaire, 1927).

Croix, Rouge Française, *Assemblée générale du 23 nov 1919 de la Société de Secours aux Blessés Militaire: Rapport du Colonel de Witt-Guizot* (Paris: Au siège de la Société, 1920).

Croÿ, Marie de, *Souvenirs de la princesse Marie de Croÿ* (Plon: Paris, 1933).

Descaves, Lucien, *La Maison anxieuse* (Paris: Georges Crès & Cie, 1916).

Drake, Barbara, *Women in Trade Unions* (London: Virago, 1984).

Duhamelet, Geneviève, *Ces dames de l'hôpital 336* (Paris: Albin Michel, 1917).

Dyle, Juliette, *Au Fils de Mars: Journal d'une infirmière* (Paris: Editions 2 rue Guersant, 1926).

Eydoux-Démians, M., *Notes d'une infirmière 1914* (Paris: Plon, 1915).

Gleason, Arthur, *Young Hilda* (New York: Frederick A. Stokes: 1915).

Gwynne-Vaughan, Helen, *Service with the Army* (London: Hutchinson, 1942).

Hay, Ian, *Their Name Liveth: The Book of the Scottish War Memorial* (London: Bodley Head, 1931).

Little, Helen D., *The Restoration of the Five Sisters' Window, York Minster* (York: Yorkshire Herald Newspapers, 1925).

[Luard, Kate Evelyn] Anon, *Diary of a Nursing Sister on the Western Front* (London: William Blackwood and Sons, 1915).

Luard, Kate Evelyn, *Unknown Warriors: The Letters of Kate Luard, RRC and Bar, Nursing Sister in France 1914–1918*, edited by John Stevens and Caroline Stevens (Stroud: The History Press, 2014).

Mackenzie, Donald A., *From All the Fronts* (Glasgow: Blackie, 1917).

Mitton, Geraldine, *The Cellar House at Pervyse: A Tale of Uncommon Things* (Milton Keynes: Oakpast, 2011).

Moreau, Emilienne, *La Guerre buissonnière* (Paris: Solar Editeur, 1970).

Muzart, Georges, *Soissons pendant la guerre* (Amiens: Association Soissonnais, 1998), pp. 14–18.

Norton Cru, Jean, *Témoins: essai d'analyse et de critique des souvenirs de combattants édités en français de 1915 à 1928* (Nancy: Presses universitaires de Nancy, 2006).

Painlevé, Paul, 'Introduction' in Anon, *La Vie et la mort de Miss Edith Cavell* (Paris: Fontemoing et cie., 1915).

Pinney, Thomas (ed.), *The Letters of Rudyard Kipling, 1911–1919*, vol. 4 (London: Macmillan, 1999).

Poirier, Léon, *Soeurs d'armes. Photographies du film* (Paris: Mame, 1937).

Redier, Antoine, *La Guerre des femmes: Histoire de Louise de Bettignies et de ses compagnes* (Paris: Les Editions de la Vraie France, 1924).

Sandes, Flora, *Autobiography of a Woman Soldier: A Brief Record of Adventure with the Serbian Army, 1916–19* (London: H., F. and G. Witherby, 1927).

Thuliez, Louise, 'Condamnée à mort par les Allemands. Récit d'une compagne de Miss Cavell', *Revue des Deux Mondes*, 50 (1919): 648–81.

Thuliez, Louise, *Condemned to Death*, translated by Marie Poett-Veltichko (London: Methuen, 1934).

T'Serclaes, Elsie de, *Flanders and Other Fields* (London: Harrap, 1964).

Vic, Jean, *La Littérature de guerre: manuel méthodique et critique des publications de langue française*, 5 vols. (Paris: Payot, 1918–23).

Weiss, Louise, *Mémoires d'une Européenne: Vol 3, Combats pour les femmes* (Paris, Editions Albin Michel: 1980).

Secondary Sources

Adie, Kate, *Fighting on the Home Front: The Legacy of Women in World War 1* (London: Hodder, 2014).

Ambroselli, Catherine, *George Desvallières et le Salon d'Automne* (Paris: Somogy éditions d'art, 2003).

Amossy, Ruth, 'Argumentation, situation de discours et théorie des champs: l'exemple de *Les Hommes de bonne volonté* de Madeleine Clemenceau Jacquemaire', *Contextes* 1 (2006). Available online at: http://contextes.revues.org/index43.html.

Amossy, Ruth, 'L'image de l'infirmière de la Grande Guerre de 1914 à 2004. La construction de la mémoire', in Annamaria Laserra, Nicole Leclerq and Marc Quaghebeur (eds.), *Mémoires et anti-mémoires littéraires au XXe siècle. La première guerre mondiale. Colloque de Cerisy-la-Salle 2005*, 2 vols. (Bern: Peter Lang, 2008), pp. 273–96.

Anderson, Benedict, *Imagined Communities: Reflections on the Origin and Spread of Nationalism* (London: Verso, 1991).

Antier, Chantal, *Louise de Bettignies* (Paris: Tallandier, 2013).

Antier, Chantal, Marianne Walle and Olivier Lahaie, *Les Espionnes dans la Grande Guerre* (Rennes: Editions Ouest-France, 2008).

Atkinson, Diane, *Elsie & Mairi Go to War: Two Extraordinary Women on the Western Front* (London: Random House, 2009).

Bader-Zaar, Birgitta, 'Controversy: War-Related Changes in Gender Relations: The Issue of Women's Citizenship', in *1914–1918 online. International Encyclopedia of the First World War*. doi: http://dx.doi.org/10.15463/id1418.10036

Ball, Simon, *The Guardsmen: Harold Macmillan, Three Friends, and the World They Made* (London: HarperCollins, 2004).

Bard, Christine, *Les Filles de Marianne: Histoire des féminismes* (Paris: Fayard, 1995).

Bard, Christine and Jean-Louis Robert, 'The French Communist Party and Women 1920–1939: From "Feminism" to Familialism', in Helmut Gruber and Pamela Graves (eds.), *Women and Socialism. Socialism and Women. Europe between the Two World Wars* (Oxford: Berghahn, 1998), pp. 321–47.

Barr, Niall, *The Lion and the Poppy: British Veterans, Politics and Society, 1921–1939* (Westport, CT: Praeger, 2005).

Bass-Krueger, Maude, 'From the "union parfaite" to the "union brisée": The French Couture Industry and the Midinettes during the Great War', *Costume* 47: 1 (2013): 28–44.

Bayser, Catherine Ambroselli de, *George Desvallières, Catalogue raisonné de l'œuvre complet* (Paris, Somogy éditions d'art: 2015).

Bayser, Catherine Ambroselli de, *George Desvallières et la Grande Guerre* (Paris: Somogy éditions d'art, 2013).

Beaupré, Nicolas, *Écrire en guerre, écrire la guerre: France, Allemagne 1914–1920* (Paris: CNRS Editions, 2006).

Becker, Annette, 'From Death to Memory: The National Ossuaries in France after the Great War', *History and Memory* 5 (1993): 32–49.

Becker, Annette, *La Guerre et la foi: De la mort à la mémoire* (Paris: Armand Colin, 1994).

Berry, Paul and Mark Bostridge, *Vera Brittain: A Life* (London: Pimlico, 1995).

Bertin, Célia, *Louise Weiss* (Paris: Albin Michel, 1999).

Bingham, Adrian, 'An Era of Domesticity: Histories of Women and Gender in Interwar Britain', *Cultural and Social History* 1 (2004): 225–33.

Binot, Jean-Marc, *Héroïnes de la Grande Guerre* (Paris: Fayard, 2008).

Birebent, Christian, 'Militantes pro-SDN en France et au Royaume-Uni dans les années 1920: quelle influence?', in Yves Denéchère and Jean-Marc Delaunay (eds.), *Femmes et relations internationales au xxᵉsiècle* (Paris: Presses Sorbonne Nouvelle, 2007), pp. 255–66.

Bland, Lucy, '"Khaki Fever" and Its Control: Gender, Class, Age and Sexual Morality on the British Homefront in the First World War', *Journal of Contemporary History* 29: 2 (1994): 325–47.

Bock, Gisela and Pat Thane, *Maternity and Gender Policies: Women and the Rise of European Welfare States 1880s–1950s* (London: Routledge, 1991).

Bond, Brian, *The Unquiet Western Front: Britain's Role in Literature and History* (Cambridge: Cambridge University Press, 2002).

Boston, Sarah, *Women Workers and the Trade Union Movement* (London: Davis Poynter, 1980).

Bourdieu, Pierre, 'The Forms of Capital', in John G. Richardson (ed.), *Handbook of Theory and Research for the Sociology of Education* (New York: Greenwood Press, 1986), pp. 241–58.

Bourke, Joanna, *An Intimate History of Killing: Face to Face Killing in Twentieth Century Warfare* (London: Granta, 2000).

Bracco, Rosa, *Merchants of Hope: British Middlebrow Writers and the First World War* (Providence, RI: Berg, 1993).

Braybon, Gail, 'Winners or Losers: Women's Role in the War Story', in *Evidence, History and the Great War: Historians and the Impact of 1914–1918* (Oxford: Berghahn, 2003), pp. 86–113.

Braybon, Gail, *Women Workers in the First World War* (London: Croom Helm Ltd, 1981).

Bresc-Bautier, Geneviève and Anne Pingeot, *Sculptures des jardins du Louvre, du Carrousel et des Tuileries, tome 2* (Paris: Editions de la Réunion des musées nationaux, 1986).

Brosman, Catherine Savage, 'French Writing of the Great War', in Vincent Sherry (ed.), *The Cambridge Companion to the Literature of the Great War* (Cambridge: Cambridge University Press, 2005), pp. 166–90.

Bruce, Alex, 'The Oxford War Memorial: Thomas Rayson and the Chester Connection', *Oxoniensia* 56 (1991): 155–68.

Buck, Claire, 'British Women's Writing of the Great War', in Vincent Sherry (ed.), *The Cambridge Companion to the Literature of the First World War* (Cambridge: Cambridge University Press, 2004), pp. 85–112.

Burgess, Alan, *The Lovely Sergeant* (London: Heinemann, 1963).

Burnett, John, *Useful Toil: Autobiographies of Working People from the 1970s to the 1920s* (London: Allen Lane/Penguin, 1974).

Butler, Janet, *Kitty's War: The Remarkable Wartime Experiences of Kit McNaughton* (Brisbane: University of Queensland Press, 2013).

Butler, Judith, *Precarious Life: The Power of Mourning and Violence* (London: Verso, 2004).

Cabanes, Bruno, 'Génération du Feu: aux origines d'une notion', *Revue Historique*, 641 (2007): 139–50.

Calder, Angus, 'The Scottish National War Memorial', in William Kidd and Brian Murdoch (eds.), *Memory and Memorials: The Commemorative Century* (Aldershot: Ashgate, 2004), pp. 61–74.

Campbell, Caroline, *Political Belief in France 1927–1945: Gender, Empire and Fascism in the Croix de Feu and Parti Social Français* (Baton Rouge: Louisiana State University Press, 2015).

Campbell, James, 'Combat Gnosticism: The Ideology of First World War Poetry Criticism', *New Literary History* 30: 1 (1999): 203–15.

Casey, Frances, 'Gender and UK War Memorials', unpublished paper delivered at the 'War and Gender' conference, Newcastle University, 12 March 2011.

Chaperon, Sylvie, *Les Années Beauvoir 1945–1970* (Paris: Fayard, 2000).

Chrastil, Rachel, 'The French Red Cross, War Readiness and Civil Society 1866–1914', *French Historical Studies* 31 (2008): 445–76.

Clegg, H. A., *A History of British Trade Unionism since 1889, Volume 3, 1934–1951* (Oxford: Oxford University Press, 1994).

Cohen, Deborah, *The War Come Home: Disabled Veterans in Britain and Germany 1914–1939* (Berkeley: University of California Press, 2001).

Colin, Madeleine, *Ce n'est pas d'aujourd'hui: femmes, syndicats, luttes de classe* (Paris: Editions sociales, 1975).

Contamine, Philippe, 'Mourir pour la patrie', in Pierre Nora (ed.), *Lieux de mémoire, t. II* (Paris: Gallimard, 1986), pp. 11–43.

Cooke, Miriam, *Women and the War Story* (Berkeley: University of California Press, 1998).

Cordier, Marcel and Rosalie Maggio, *Marie Marvingt: La Femme d'un siècle* (Sarreguemines: Pierron, 1991).

Cowper, Julia Margaret, *A Short History of Queen Mary's Army Auxiliary Corps* (London: Women's Royal Army Corps Association, 1966).

Darrow, Margaret, 'French Volunteer Nursing and the Myth of War Experience in World War 1', *The American Historical Review* 101: 1 (1996): 80–106.

Darrow, Margaret, *French Women and the First World War* (Oxford: Berg, 2000).

Darrow, Margaret, 'In the Land of Joan of Arc: The Civic Education of Girls and the Prospect of War in France, 1871–1914', *French Historical Studies* 31 (2008): 263–91.

Debruyne, Emmanuel, *Le Réseau Edith Cavell: Des femmes et des hommes en résistance* (Brussels: Racine, 2015).

Debruyne, Emmanuel and Alison S. Fell, 'Model Martyrs: Remembering First World War Resistance Heroines in Belgium and France', in Peter Tame et al. (eds.), *Mnemosyne and Mars: Artistic and Cultural Representations of Twentieth-Century Europe at War* (Newcastle: Cambridge Scholars Press, 2013), pp. 145–65.

Diebolt, Evelyne, 'Utile, utilitaire, utilise … Naissance et expansion du secteur associatif sanitaire et social (1901–2001)', *Connexions* 2002 (77): 7–24.

Downs, Laura Lee, '"Each and Every One of You Must Become a *Chef*": Towards a Social Politics of Working-Class Childhood on the Extreme Right in 1930s France', *Journal of Modern History* (2009): 1–44.

Downs, Laura Lee, *Manufacturing Inequality: Gender Division in the French and British Metalworking Industries 1914–1939* (New York: Cornell University Press, 1995).

Downs, Laura Lee, 'Nous plantions les trois couleurs': Action sociale féminine et recomposition des politiques de la droite française. Le mouvement Croix-de-feu et le Parti social français, 1934–1947', *Revue d'histoire moderne et contemporaine* 58–3 (2011): 118–62.

Downs, Laura Lee, 'War Work', in Jay Winter (ed.), *The Cambridge History of the First World War*, vol. 3 (Cambridge: Cambridge University Press, 2014), pp. 72–95.

Eichenberg, Julia and John Paul Newman (eds.), *The Great War and Veterans' Internationalism* (Basingstoke: Palgrave Macmillan, 2013).

Englander, David, 'The National Union of Ex-Servicemen and the Labour Movement', *History* 76 (1991): 24–42.

Fell, Alison S., 'Germaine Malaterre-Sellier, la Grande Guerre et le féminisme pacifiste de l'entre-deux-guerres', in Christine Bard (ed.), *Les Féministes de la première vague* (Rennes: Presses universitaires de Rennes, 2015), pp. 207–16.

Fell, Alison S., 'Life after Léa: War and Trauma in Colette's *La Fin de Chéri*', *French Studies* 59: 4 (2005): 495–507.

Fell, Alison S., 'Myth, Countermyth and the Politics of Memory: Vera Brittain and Madeleine Clemenceau Jacquemaire's Interwar Nurse Memoirs', *Synergies Royaume Uni et Irlande*, 4 (2011): 11–24.

Fell, Alison S., 'Remembering the First World War Nurse', in Alison S. Fell and Christine Hallett (eds.), *First World War Nursing: New Perspectives* (New York: Routledge, 2013), pp. 173–92.

Fell, Alison S., 'Remembering French and British First World War Heroines', in Christa Hämmerle, Oswald Uberegger and Birgitta Bader Zaar (eds.), *Gender and the First World War* (Basingstoke: Palgrave, 2014), pp. 108–126.

Fell, Alison S., 'Witness or Participant', *Knjizenstvo* (2015). Available online at www.knjizenstvo.rs.

Fogarty, Richard S., 'Race, Sex, Fear and Loathing in France during the Great War', *Historical Reflections* 34: 1 (2008): 50–72.

Frader, Laura Levine, *Breadwinners and Citizens: Gender in the Making of the French Social Model* (Durham, NC: Duke University Press, 2008).

Frader, Laura, 'Social Citizens without Citizenship: Working-Class Women and Social Policy in Interwar France', *Social Politics: International Studies in Gender, State and Society* (1996): 111–35.

Gillis, John R. (ed.), *Commemorations: The Politics of National Identity* (Princeton, NJ: Princeton University Press, 1994).

Gilmore, Leigh, 'Policing Truth: Confession, Gender and Autobiographical Authority', in Kathleen Ashley, Leigh Gilmore and Gerald Peters (eds.), *Autobiography and Postmodernism* (Boston: University of Massachusetts Press, 1994), pp. 54–78.

Goebel, Stefan, 'Re-Membered and Re-Mobilized: The Sleeping Dead in Interwar Germany and Britain', *Journal of Contemporary History* 39 (2004): 487–501.

Goldman, Dorothy, *Women Writers and the Great War* (New York: Twayne, 1995).

Gottlieb, Julie, *Feminine Fascism: Women in Britain's Fascist Movements* (London: I. B. Taurus, 2003).

Graves, Pamela M., *Labour Women: Women in British Working-Class Politics, 1918–1939* (Cambridge: Cambridge University Press, 1994).

Grayzel, Susan R., '"The Souls of Soldiers": Civilians under Fire in First World War France', *The Journal of Modern History* 78: 3 (2006): 588–622.

Grayzel, Susan R., *Women's Identities at War: Gender, Motherhood and Politics during the First World War* (Chapel Hill: University of North Carolina Press, 1999).

Gregory, Adrian, *The Last Great War: British Society and the First World War* (Cambridge: Cambridge University Press, 2008).

Gubin, Eliane et al. (eds.), *Dictionnaire des femmes belges* (Brussels: Editions Racine, 2006).

Guillermand, Jean, 'Nelly Martyl Scott (1884–1953)', *Revue de l'Infirmière* 163 (2010): 45–50.

Gullace, Nicoletta, *'The Blood of Our Sons': Men, Women and the Renegotiation of British Citizenship during the Great War* (New York: Palgrave Macmillan, 2012).

Hallett, Christine E., *Containing Trauma: Nursing Work in the First World War* (Manchester: Manchester University Press, 2010).

Hallett, Christine E., *Nurse Writers of the Great War* (Manchester: Manchester University Press, 2016).

Hanna, Martha, 'Iconology and Ideology: Images of Joan of Arc in the Idiom of the Action Française, 1908–1931', *French Historical Studies* 14: 2 (1985): 215–39.

Hannam, June, 'Women as Paid Organisers and Propagandists for the British Labour Party between the Wars', *International Labour and Working Class History* 77: 1 (2010): 69–88.

Heathorn, Stephen, 'The Civil Servant and Public Remembrance: Sir Lionel Earle and the Shaping of London's Commemorative Landscape, 1918–1933', *Twentieth Century British History* 19: 3 (2008): 259–87.

Heathorn, Stephen, 'The Mnemonic Turn in the Cultural Historiography of Britain's Great War', *The Historical Journal* 48: 4 (2005): 1103–24.

Higonnet, Margaret R., 'Another Record: A Different War', *Women's Studies Quarterly* 23 (1999): 85–96.

Higonnet, Margaret et al. (eds.), *Behind the Lines: Gender and the Two World Wars* (New Haven, CT: Yale University Press, 1987).

Higonnet, Margaret R. and Patrice Higonnet, 'The Double Helix', in Margaret Higonnet et al. (eds.), *Behind the Lines: Gender and the Two World Wars* (New Haven, CT: Yale University Press, 1987), pp. 31–47.

Hogenhuis-Seliverstoff, Anne, *Juliette Adam* (Paris: L'Harmattan, 2001).

Holmes, Diana, *French Women's Writing 1848–1994* (London: Athlone, 1996).

Horne, John, 'Beyond Cultures of Victory and Cultures of Defeat? Inter-War Veterans' Internationalism', in Julia Eichenberg and John Paul Newman (eds.), *The Great War and Veterans' Internationalism* (Basingstoke: Palgrave Macmillan, 2013), pp. 207–22.

Horne, John, 'Immigrant workers in France during World War I', *French Historical Studies* 14: 1 (1985): 57–88.

Horne, John, 'L'impôt de sang: Republican Rhetoric and Industrial Warfare in France, 1914–1918', *Social History* 14: 2 (1989): 201–23.

Hughes, Anne Marie, 'Death, Service and Citizenship in Britain in the First World War', unpublished PhD thesis, University of Manchester, 2009.

Hughes, Anne Marie, 'War, Gender and Mourning: The Significance of the Death and Commemoration of Edith Cavell in Britain', *European Review of History* 12: 3 (2005): 425–44.

Hunt, Cathy, '"Her Heart and Soul Were with the Labour Movement": Using a Local Study to Highlight the Work of Women Organisers Employed by the Workers' Union in Britain from the First World War to 1931', *Labour History Review* 70: 2 (2005): 167–84.

Hunt, Cathy, *The National Federation of Women Workers 1906–1921* (Basingstoke: Palgrave Macmillan, 2014).

Hurcombe, Martin, 'Raising the Dead: Visual Representations of the Combatant's Body in Interwar France', *Journal of War and Culture Studies* 1: 2 (2008): 159–74.

Hyman, Richard, *The Workers' Union* (Oxford: Clarendon Press, 1971).

Isherwood, Ian, 'The British Publishing Industry and Commercial Memories of the First World War', *War in History* 23: 3 (2016): 323–40.

Jeannelle, Jean-Louis, 'Une guerre des Mémoires', in Annamaria Laserra, Nicole Leclercq and Marc Quaghebeur (eds.), *Mémoires et antimémoires littéraires au XXe siècle: La Première guerre mondiale*, second volume (New York: Peter Lang, 2008), pp. 107–28.

Jennings, Eric, 'Reinventing Jeanne: The Iconology of Joan of Arc in Vichy Schoolbooks, 1940–44', *Journal of Contemporary History* 29: 4 (1994): 711–34.

Kent, Susan, *Making Peace: The Reconstruction of Gender in Interwar Britain* (Princeton, NJ: Princeton University Press, 1993).

Kidd, William, '"To the Lads Who Came Back": Memorial Windows and Rolls of Honour in Scotland', in William Kidd and Brian Murdoch (eds.), *Memory and Memorials: The Commemorative Century* (Aldershot: Ashgate, 2004), pp. 70–127.

Kidd, William, 'The Lion, the Angel and the War Memorial: Some French Sites Revisited', in Nicholas J. Saunders (ed.), *Matters of Conflict: Material Culture, Memory and the First World War* (London: Routledge, 2004), pp. 149–65.

King, Alex, *Memorials of the Great War in Britain: The Symbolism and Politics of Remembrance* (Oxford: Berg, 1998).

Klejman, Laurence and Florence Rochefort, *L'Egalité en marche* (Paris: des femmes, 1989).

Knibiehler, Yvonne, *Cornettes et blouses blanches: Les infirmières dans la société française* (Paris: Hachette, 1984).

Knibiehler, Yvonne, *L'Histoire des infirmières* (Paris: Hachette, 2008).

Koos, Cheryl A., 'Fascism, Fatherhood and the Family in Interwar France: The Case of Antoine Redier and the Légion', *Journal of Family History* 24 (1999): 317–29.

Koos, Cheryl and Daniella Sarnoff, 'France', in Kevin Passmore (ed.), *Women, Gender and Fascism in Europe, 1919–45* (Manchester University Press: Manchester, 2003), pp. 168–89.

Kriegel, Annie, *The French Communists*, translated by Elaine P. Halperin (Chicago: University of Chicago Press, 1972).

Kuhlman, Erika, *Of Little Comfort: War Widows, Fallen Soldiers, and the Remaking of the Nation after the Great War* (New York: New York University Press, 2012).

Lam, David M., 'Marie Marvingt and the Development of Aeromedical Evacuation', *Aviation, Space and Environmental Medicine* 74: 8 (2003): 863–68.

Laqueur, Thomas, 'Memory and Naming in the Great War', in John Gillis (ed.), *Memory and Commemoration* (Princeton, NJ: Princeton University Press, 1993), pp. 150–67.

Le Naour, Jean-Yves, *Misères et tourments de la chair durant la Grande Guerre* (Paris: Aubier, 2002).

Levitch, Mark, *Panthéon de la Guerre: Reconfiguring a Panorama of the Great War* (Columbia: University of Missouri Press, 2006).

Levitch, Mark, 'The Great War Re-Remembered: The Fragmentation of the World's Largest Painting', in Nicholas J. Saunders (ed.), *Matters of Conflict: Material Culture, Memory and the First World War* (London: Routledge, 2004), pp. 90–109.

Lewenhak, Sheila, *Women and Trade Unions* (London: Ernest Benn Ltd, 1977).

Light, Alison, *Forever England: Femininity, Literature and Conservatism between the Wars* (London: Routledge, 1991).

Macleod, Jenny, '"By Scottish Hands, with Scottish Money, on Scottish Soil": The Scottish National War Memorial and National Identity', *The Journal of British Studies* 49: 1 (2010): 73–96.

Malvern, Sue, '"For King and Country": Frampton's Edith Cavell (1915–1920) and the Writing of Gender in Memorials to the Great War', in David Getsy (ed.), *Sculpture and the Pursuit of a Modern Ideal in Britain, 1880–1930* (Aldershot: Ashgate, 2004), pp. 219–84.

Mann, Keith, *Forging Political Identity: Silk and Metal Workers in Lyon, France 1900–1939* (Oxford: Berghahn, 2010).

Marbeau, Michel, 'Les Femmes et la Société des Nations (1919–1945): Genève, la clé de l'égalité?', in Yves Denéchère and Jean-Marc Delaunay (eds.), *Femmes et relations internationales au xx^{e}siècle* (Paris: Presses Sorbonne Nouvelle, 2007), pp. 163–76.

Marcus, Jane, 'The Asylums of Antaeus: Women, War and Madness. Is There a Feminist Fetishism?', in Elizabeth Meese and Alice Parker (eds.), *The Difference Within* (Amsterdam: John Benjamins, 1989), pp. 49–83.

Marwick, Arthur, *Women at War 1914–1918* (London: Fontana, 1977).

McMillan, James F., *Housewife or Harlot? The Place of Women in French Society 1870–1940* (Brighton: Harvester Press, 1981).

McPhail, Helen, *The Long Silence: Civilian Life under the German Occupation of Northern France 1914–1918* (London: I. B. Tauris, 2001).

McPherson, Kathryn, 'Carving Out a Past: The Canadian Nurses' Association War Memorial', *Histoire sociale/Social History* 29 (1996): 417–29.

Meyer, Jessica, 'The Tuition of Manhood: 'Sapper's War Stories and the Literature of War', in Mary Hammond and Shafquat Towheed (eds.), *Publishing in the First World War: Essays in Book History* (London: Palgrave Macmillan, 2007), pp. 113–28.

Milligan, Jennifer E., *The Forgotten Generation: French Women Writers of the Inter-War Period* (Oxford: Berg, 1996).

Millington, Chris, *From Victory to Vichy: Veterans in Interwar France* (Manchester: Manchester University Press, 2012).

Mitchell, David, *Women on the War Path: The Story of the Women of the First World War* (London: Cape, 1966).

Monte, Jean-François, 'L'Office National des anciens combattants et victimes de guerre: Créations et actions durant l'entre-deux-guerres', *Guerres mondiales et conflits contemporains* 205 (2002): 71–83.

Moriarty, Catherine, 'Private Grief and Public Remembrance: British First World War Memorials', in Martin Evans and Ken Lunn (eds.), *War and Memory in the Twentieth Century* (Oxford: Berg, 1997), pp. 125–42.

Morin-Rotureau, Evelyne, *1914–18: Combats de femmes* (Paris: Editions Autrement, 2004).

Mosse, George, *Fallen Soldiers: Reshaping the Memory of the World Wars* (Oxford: Oxford University Press, 1990).

Murphy, Libby, 'Trespassing on the Trench-Fighter's Story: Re-Imagining the Female Combatant of the First World War', in Ana Carden-Coyle (ed.), *Gender and Conflict since 1914* (Basingstoke: Palgrave, 2012), pp. 55–68.

Nivet, Philippe, *La France occupée 1914–1918* (Paris: Armand Colin, 2014).

Noakes, Lucy, 'Demobilising the Military Woman: Constructions of Class and Gender after the First World War', *Gender and History* 19 (2007): 143–72.

Noakes, Lucy, '"A Disgrace to the Country They Belong To": The Sexualisation of Female Soldiers in First World War Britain', *Revue LISA* 4 (2008). Available online at http://lisa.revues.org/951.

Noakes, Lucy, 'Gender, War and Memory: Discourse and Experience in History', *Journal of Contemporary History* 36: 4 (2001): 663–72.

Noakes, Lucy, *Women in the British Army: War and the Gentle Sex 1907–1948* (London: Routledge, 2006).

O'Brien, Catherine M., *Women's Fictional Responses to the First World War: A Comparative Study of Selected Texts by French and German Writers* (New York: Peter Lang, 1997).

Orr, Andrew, *Women and the French Army during the World Wars* (Bloomington: Indiana University Press, 2017).

Ouditt, Sharon, *Fighting Forces, Writing Women: Identity and Ideology in the First World War* (London: Routledge, 1993).

Outteryck, Pierre, *Martha Desrumaux: Une femme du nord. Ouvrière, syndicaliste, déportée, Féministe* (Paris: Comité Régional CGT Nord-Pas-de-Calais, 2006).

Pederson, Susan, *Family, Dependence and the Origins of the Welfare State, Britain and France 1914–1945* (Cambridge: Cambridge University Press, 1993).

Perrot, Michelle, 'Préface', in Françoise Thébaud (ed.), *Les Femmes au temps de la guerre de 1914* (Paris: Stock, 1986), pp. 7–13.

Pickles, Katie, *Transnational Outrage: The Death and Commemoration of Edith Cavell* (Basingstoke: Palgrave, 2007).

Pineau, Frédéric, *Les Femmes au service de la France: Vol 1, La Croix-Rouge Française 1914–1940* (Paris: Histoire et collections, 2006).

Potter, Jane, *Boys in Khaki, Girls in Print: Women's Literary Responses to the Great War 1914–1918* (Oxford: Clarendon Press, 2005).

Potter, Jane, 'For Country, Conscience and Commerce: Publishers and Publishing, 1914–1918', in Mary Hammond and Shafquat Towheed (eds.), *Publishing in the First World War: Essays in Book History* (London: Palgrave Macmillan, 2007), pp. 11–26.

Poynter, Denise, '"The Report on the Transfer Was Shell-Shock": A Study of the Psychological Disorders of Nurses and Female VADs Who Served Alongside the British and Allied Expeditionary Forces during the First World War, 1914–1918', Unpublished doctoral thesis, University of Northampton, 2008. Available online at http://nectar.northampton.ac.uk/2682/1/Poynter20082682 .pdf.

Proctor, Tammy, *Female Intelligence: Women and Espionage in the First World War* (New York: New York University Press, 2006).

Prost, Antoine, *Les Anciens Combattants et la société française 1914–1939*, 3 vols. (Paris: Presses de la fondation nationale des sciences politiques, 1977).

Prost, Antoine, 'Les Monuments aux morts', in Pierre Nora (ed.), *Lieux de mémoire*, vol. 1 (Paris: Gallimard, 1984), pp. 195–225.

Quaghebeur, Roger, *Ik was een spionne. Het mysterieuze spionageverhaal van Martha Cnockaert uit Westrozebeke* (De Klaproos: Coxyde, 2000).

Rabaut, Jean, *Histoire des féminismes* (Paris: Stock, 1978).

Read, Geoff, *The Republic of Men: Gender and Political Parties in Interwar France* (Baton Rouge: Louisiana State University Press, 2014).

Read, Philippa, 'Female Heroism in First World War France: Representations and Lived Experiences', unpublished PhD thesis, University of Leeds, 2017.

Rey, Jean-Philippe, 'Desvallières et la guerre de 1914–1918', *Société de l'histoire de l'art français* (1988): 197–211.

Reynolds, Siân, *France between the Wars: Gender and Politics* (London: Routledge, 1996).

Ridel, Charles, *Les Embusqués* (Paris: Armand Colin, 2007).

Robert, Jean-Louis, *Les Ouvriers, la patrie et la Révolution. Paris 1914–1919* (Besançon: Annales littéraires de l'université de Besançon, 1995).

Roberts, Mary Louise, *Civilization without Sexes: Reconstructing Gender in Post-War France, 1917–27* (Chicago: University of Chicago Press, 1994).

Rousseau, Frédéric, *Le Procès des témoins de la Grande Guerre: L'affaire Norton Cru* (Paris: Seuil, 2003).

Schaepdrijver, Sophie de, *Gabrielle Petit: The Death and Life of a Female Spy in the First World War* (London: Bloomsbury, 2015).

Schoentjes, Pierre, *Fictions de la Grande Guerre: Variations littéraires sur 14–18* (Paris: Classiques Garnier, 2009).

Schoentjes, Pierre, 'Les véritables écrivains de guerre ont-ils "rarement dépeint ce qu'ils avaient vu"', in Pierre Schoentjes (ed.), *La Grande Guerre: Un siècle de fictions romanesques* (Geneva: Droz, 2008), pp. 17–43.

Schultheiss, Katrin, *Bodies and Souls: Politics and the Professionalization of Nursing in France, 1880–1922* (Oxford: Harvard University Press, 2001).

Shearer, Joanna, 'Dressing Up for War: Women and Militarism in the Writings of French Women Journalists in the First World War', *Minerva: Journal of Women and War* 1: 2 (2007): 66–76.

Sherman, Daniel, *The Construction of Memory in Interwar France* (Chicago: University of Chicago Press, 1999).

Sherman, Daniel, 'Monuments, Mourning and Masculinity in France after World War I', *Gender and History* 8 (1996): 82–107.

Shipton, Elisabeth, *Female Tommies: The Frontline Women of the First World War* (Stroud: The History Press, 2014).

Siim, Birte, *Gender and Citizenship: Politics and Agency in France, Britain and Denmark* (Cambridge: Cambridge University Press, 2000).

Sloan Goldberg, Nancy, *'Woman Your Hour Is Sounding!' Continuity and Change in French Women's Great War Fiction 1914–19* (New York: St Martin's Press, 1999).

Smith, Angela K., 'How to Remember: War, Armistice and Memory in post-1918 British Fiction', *Journal of European Studies* 45: 4 (2015): 301–15.

Smith, Angela K., *The Second Battlefield: Women, Modernism and the First World War* (Manchester: Manchester University Press, 2000).

Smith, Leonard V., *The Embattled Self: French Soldiers' Testimony of the Great War* (Ithaca, NY: Cornell University Press, 2007).

Sniter, Christel, 'La gloire des femmes célèbres: Métamorphoses et disparité de la statuaire publique parisienne de 1870 à nos jours', *Sociétés et Représentations* 26 (2008): 153–70.

Søland, Birgitte, *Becoming Modern: Young Women and the Reconstruction of Womanhood in the 1920s* (Princeton, NJ: Princeton University Press, 2000).

Soldon, Norbert C., *Women in British Trade Unions 1874–1976* (Dublin: Gill and Macmillan, 1978).

Souhami, Diana, *Edith Cavell* (London: Quercus, 2010).

Stovall, Tyler, 'Colour-Blind France: Colonial Workers during the First World War', *Race & Class* 35: 2 (1999): 35–55.

Tate, Trudi, *Modernism, History and the First World War* (Manchester: Manchester University Press, 1998).

Taylor, David, 'Fiction and Memoir of Britain's Great War: Some Further Thoughts', *European Review of History* 22: 5 (2015): 814–18.

Thébaud, Françoise, *Les Femmes au temps de la guerre de 1914* (Paris: Stock, 1986).

Thébaud, Françoise, 'Femmes et genre dans la guerre', in Stéphane Audoin-Rouzeau and Jean-Jacques Becker (eds.), *Encyclopédie de la Grande Guerre 1914–1918* (Paris: Bayard, 2004), pp. 613–25.

Thom, Deborah, *Nice Girls and Rude Girls: Women Workers in World War I* (London: I. B. Tauris, 1998).

Tilly, Charles, *Stories, Identities and Political Change* (Oxford: Oxford University Press, 2002).

Todman, Dan, *The Great War: Myth and Memory* (London: Hambledon Continuum, 2005).

Tonnet-Lacroix, Eliane, *La Littérature française de l'entre-deux-guerres 1919–1939* (Paris: Nathan, 1993).

Tristan, Anne and Annie de Pisan, *Histoires du MLF* (Paris: Calmann Lévy, 1977).

van Ypersele, Laurence and Emmanuel Debruyne, *De la guerre de l'ombre aux ombres de la guerre: L'espionnage en Belgique durant la guerre 1914–1918* (Editions Labor: Bruxelles, 2004).

Wall, Richard and Jay Winter (eds.), *The Upheaval of War: Family, Work and Welfare in Europe, 1914–1918* (Cambridge: Cambridge University Press, 1988).

Warner, Marina, *Joan of Arc: The Image of Female Heroism* (Berkeley: University of California Press, 1981).

Watson, Janet S. K., *Fighting Different Wars: Experience, Memory and the First World War in Britain* (Cambridge: Cambridge University Press, 2004).

Watson, Janet, 'Khaki Girls, VADs, and Tommy's Sisters: Gender and Class in First World War Britain', *The International History Review* 13: 1 (1997): 32–51.

Wierbicki, Sandrine, 'Germaine Malaterre-Sellier: Un destin aux croisées du féminisme et du pacifisme (1889–1967)', unpublished mémoire de maîtrise, Université de Paris 1, 2001.

Winter, Jay, *The Great War and the British People* (London: Macmillan, 1986).

Winter, Jay, 'The "Moral Witness" and the Two World Wars', *Ethnologie française* 37: 3 (2007). doi:10.3917/ethn.073.0467

Winter, Jay, *Sites of Memory, Sites of Mourning: The Great War in European Cultural History* (Cambridge: Cambridge University Press, 1995).

Wohl, Robert, *The Generation of 1914* (Cambridge, MA: Harvard University Press, 1979).

Woollacott, Angela, *On Her Their Lives Depend: Munitions Workers in the Great War* (Berkeley: University of California Press, 1994).

Wootton, Graham, *The Politics of Influence: British Ex-Servicemen, Cabinet Decisions and Cultural Change* (London: Routledge, 1963).

Wyke, Terry and Harry Cocks, *Public Sculpture of Greater Manchester* (Liverpool: Liverpool University Press, 2004).

Zancarini-Fournel, Michelle, 'Femmes, genre et syndicalisme pendant la grande guerre', in Evelyne Morin Routureau (ed.), *1914–1918: combats de femme* (Paris: Autrement, 2004), pp. 98–114.

Index